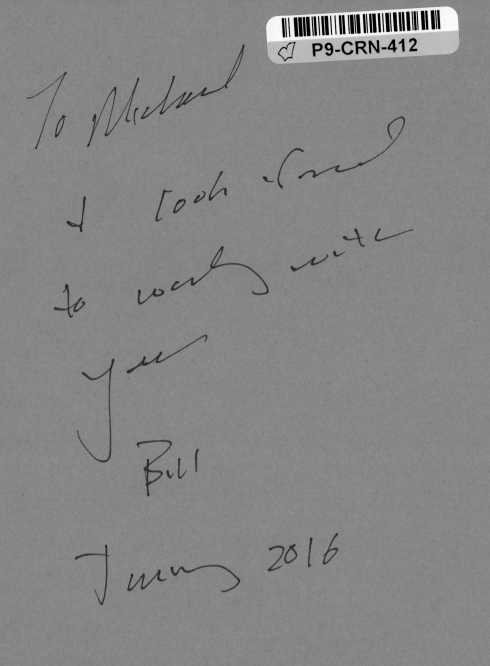

To Michael

I look forward
to working with
you

Bill

January 2016

Praise for World Class

"This story gives management and leadership in any industry the template by which to ensure their businesses thrive, even in the most dire circumstances. Few organizational transformations tell a story as inspiring and instructive as the one that took place, over the past decade, at NYU Langone Health. It is a story of a leadership team of rare passion and vision, led by Dr. Bob Grossman, whose medical expertise and zest for innovation are second to none, and Ken Langone, whose love of people, renowned business acumen, and philanthropic enthusiasm are an unstoppable force of nature. Together, and supported by an ever more stellar team of medical and management professionals, they have changed one institution—and healthcare—forever for the better."

—Jack Welch, former Chairman and CEO, General Electric, and author of *Jack: Straight from the Gut* and *Winning*

"The spectacular transformation of NYU Langone Health is a vivid example of what can be accomplished when leaders blend vision, courage, conviction and an uninterrupted quest to achieve unprecedented objectives. NYU Leadership revitalized a staid culture and the collaborative efforts that followed blazed the way to new frontiers of excellence. William Haseltine, scientist and healthcare expert, has written eloquently about how NYU Langone executed a path to world class status, overcame many obstacles, and provided employees the confidence needed to perform beyond what was previously thought impossible. *World Class* is a compelling read, particularly for leaders of other healthcare facilities with a need to replicate this extraordinary story."

—Larry Bossidy, former Chairman and CEO Honeywell International and author of *Execution: The Discipline of Getting Things Done* and *Confronting Reality: Master the New Model for Success*

"William Haseltine's comprehensive analysis of the critical steps that NYU Langone Health took to achieve success—establishing a vision, actionable strategies, effective communication and data-driven decision-making—is consistent with WellPoint's experience. *World Class* adds to the evidence that a road map for transformation exists that can help organizations respond to the challenges of a changing external environment."

—Leonard D. Schaeffer, founding Chairman and CEO, WellPoint and former Administrator of the Health Care Finance Administration

"*World Class* tells a remarkable story: how a gifted group of individuals turned a medical school with a poor record into one of the top academic medical centers in the United States. It took vision, leadership, trust, and continuous measurement. This book transcends the healthcare field and should be read by all those interested in institutional innovation. In writing it, William Haseltine has mobilized his vast repertoire of talents as a Renaissance man with wide-ranging interests, vast culture, and boundless creative force."

—Julio Frenk, MD, PhD, President of the University of Miami, former Dean of the Harvard Chen School of Public Health, and former Minister of Health, Mexico

"The swift and all encompassing transformation of NYU's Langone Health stands as a case study for academic medical centers worldwide. The relentless commitment to putting the patient first invariably enhances employee pride and financial success. William Haseltine captures the nuances as well as the lessons."

—John A. Quelch, Vice Provost, University of Miami, Dean of the School of Business Administration at the University of Miami; Charles Edward Wilson Professor of Business Administration Emeritus at Harvard Business School; coauthor, *Choice Matters: How Healthcare Consumers Make Decisions*

"William Haseltine has written a remarkable story about how the transformation of NYU happened over a ten-year period. It is indeed a story of a system moving from good to great, from a relatively low point in 2007 to its becoming one of the leading healthcare institutions by 2017. This is a remarkable journey replete with a number of steps and decisions that led to the systematic transformation and one that Dr. Haseltine has brought out with clarity and readability. *World Class* could be very useful for other institutions that are starting their own journey and act as a guide to future leaders in medicine."

—K. Ranga Rama Krishnan, Dean Rush Medical College, Senior Vice President Rush University Medical Center

"The message of this book is that positive change in healthcare or other human institutions is not about money or technology—though they matter—but about inspired teams of normal people working together in extraordinary ways."

—Esther Dyson, Executive Founder, Way to Wellville

"Getting more for our healthcare dollars will not come from magic or simple solutions. Instead, it requires the gritty, often unappreciated work of improving the performance of our delivery system—including our nation's leading medical centers. That is precisely the focus of *World Class*, in which William A. Haseltine chronicles and assesses the recent history of NYU Langone. Both healthcare leaders and policymakers will learn from the struggles, and, in Haseltine's telling, the ultimate success of one of our nation's leading academic medical centers."

—Peter Orszag, 37th Director of the Office of Management and Budget and former Director of the Congressional Budget Office

WILLIAM A. HASELTINE

WORLD CLASS

A Story of Adversity, Transformation, and Success at NYU Langone Health

FAST COMPANY PRESS

Fast Company Press
New York, New York
www.fastcompanypress.com

Distributed by Greenleaf Book Group

For ordering information or special discounts for bulk purchases, please contact Greenleaf Book Group at PO Box 91869, Austin, TX 78709, 512.891.6100.

Design and composition by Greenleaf Book Group
Cover design by Greenleaf Book Group
Cover credits: digital stream ©iStockphoto.com/johnason; Caduceus Hermes ©Olexander Zahozhyy. Used under license from Shutterstock.com.

Permission to reprint copyrighted material granted by NYU Langone Health, unless otherwise noted. Grateful acknowledgment is given on the Image Credits page (page numbers therein reflect placement in book).

Publisher's Cataloging-in-Publication data is available.

Print ISBN: 978-1-7324391-0-8

eBook ISBN: 978-1-7324391-1-5

Part of the Tree Neutral® program, which offsets the number of trees consumed in the production and printing of this book by taking proactive steps, such as planting trees in direct proportion to the number of trees used: www.treeneutral.com

Printed in the United States of America on acid-free paper

18 19 20 21 22 23 24   10 9 8 7 6 5 4 3 2 1

First Edition

Contents

PART IV: BUILDING ON SUCCESS

Why Read This Book?

On August 16, 2018 NYU Langone Health captured the attention of the world with the surprise announcement that all medical school students will receive full tuition scholarships. What is special about NYU Langone that allowed such a bold move? In *World Class* internationally renowned scientist, business leader, author, and philanthropist William A. Haseltine answers this question and far more.

Free medical education is only one step in a decade of stunning transformations that led a once faded and money losing institution to world class prominence in patient care, education, and research—one that can afford billions of dollars of investment in the future.

The story of NYU Langone Health offers lessons for enterprise transformation that transcend healthcare. If you are in a retail business, the story will help you improve customer service and satisfaction. If you are in manufacturing, the NYU story will help achieve zero fault. If you are in the service business, the NYU Langone approach to information systems and dashboards will help you improve performance and accountability. If you are a university, this story will help you achieve excellence in teaching and improve your rankings. Finally, there are profound lessons for how to manage a research enterprise to improve productivity and profit.

NUMBERS TELL THE STORY

To summarize briefly, the numbers show that:

NYU Langone Health moved from the bottom third in national quality and safety rankings to number one or two in the country.

NYU Langone Health is now ranked as the number three medical school in the United States, just behind Harvard and Johns Hopkins, up from a ranking of thirty-fourth.

NYU Langone transformed a safety net hospital in Brooklyn from loss making to profit, from low to high quality, in two years.

Funding for research has more than doubled.

The top line of NYU Langone Health grew from $2 billion to $7 billion a year.

A deficit of $150 million a year was transformed into a surplus of $240 million.

Total charitable donations over the past ten years average more than $240 million a year.

NUMBERS TELL A CRYSTAL-CLEAR STORY OF SUCCESS

FINANCIAL

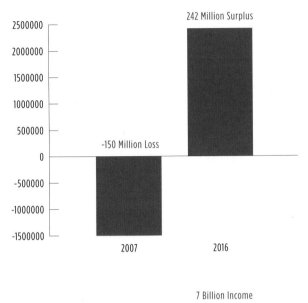

242 Million Surplus

-150 Million Loss

2007   2016

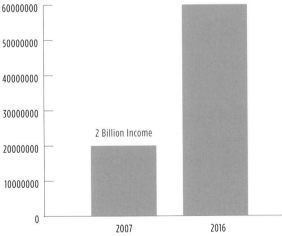

7 Billion Income

2 Billion Income

2007   2016

QUALITY AND SAFETY RANKING

2007: Ranked 60th of 90 Academic Medical Center Hospitals for Quality and Safety

2013 to 2015: Ranked 1st of 112 Academic Medical Center Hospitals (Vizient rankings)

2015 to 2016: Ranked 1st in Ambulatory Care in the United States for three consecutive years (Rankings initiated in 2015)

2017: Ranked number one among Academic Medical Centers in "Overall Performance and Improvement" over the period 2011 to 2015 in a report by Truven Health Analytics, an IBM Company

2017: Received five-star Overall Hospital Quality Star Rating from the Centers for Medicare and Medicaid Services

2017: Ranked number one in 2015 performance and five-year rate of improvement for New York Acute Care Hospitals in a report by Truven Health Analytics

AWARDS 2016 TO 2017

Ranked by *U.S. News & World Report* as one of the top hospitals nationwide

Modern Healthcare's "Top 100 Hospitals" annual survey placed NYU Langone number seven among the top fifteen major teaching hospitals (the only New York hospital in the list of top one hundred).

U.S. MEDICAL SCHOOL RANKING

2007: 34th

2017: 3rd (*U.S. News & World Report* 2017 Best Graduate Schools rankings)

INDEPENDENT RESEARCH SUPPORT

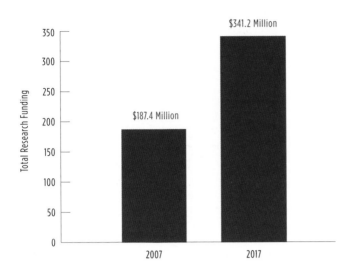

INCREASE IN NATIONAL INSTITUTES OF HEALTH AWARDS

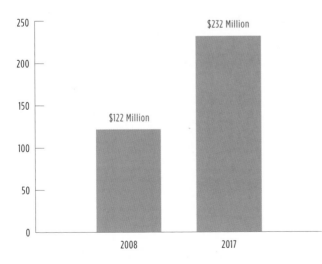

AMBULATORY CARE FACILITIES

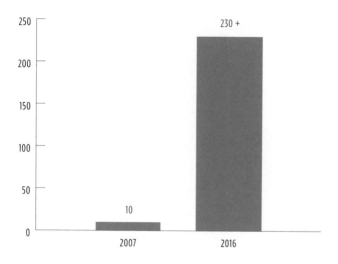

TOTAL EMPLOYEES

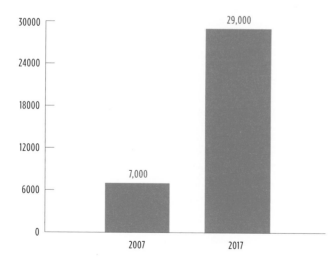

PHYSICIANS ON STAFF

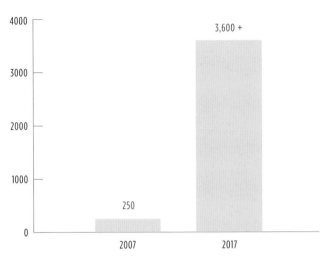

FACILITIES

2007 to 2017: Added more than 1.2 million square feet of hospital and research facilities

INNOVATIONS IN EDUCATION

Launched three-year MD Program in 2013

Launched C21, Curriculum for the 21st Century

CHARITABLE CONTRIBUTIONS

2007 to 2018: Total gifts and donations: $2.68 billion

NYU Langone Health is now ranked as the number three medical school in the United States, just behind Harvard and Johns Hopkins, up from a ranking of thirty-fourth.

Research funding has more than doubled.

Total charitable donations over the past ten years average more than $240 million a year.

What NYU Langone Health Achieved and Why It Matters

I believe that the 2007 to 2017 transformation of NYU Langone Health is one of the most hopeful and positive healthcare stories of our time. In less than a decade NYU Langone transformed from being mediocre to becoming a world class institution. Ten years ago the Medical Center was losing tens of millions of dollars. NYU Langone Health now generates a substantial surplus and delivers world class patient care in hospitals as well as ambulatory and family medicine practices. NYU Langone is now also a national leader in medical education and research. How did all this happen? How did a healthcare institution turn itself around to become one of the greatest healthcare centers in the world? These are the questions that drive *World Class*.

I am pleased to be the one to tell this story in its entirety for the very first time. New York City is blessed with several excellent hospitals and academic medical institutions. I chose NYU Langone Health for this study as none other has experienced such rapid and radical transformation to achieve excellence in patient care, research, and teaching, as is needed for so many hospitals and universities in the United States and elsewhere. My method was to interview the change makers: members of the board of trustees of New York University and the board of NYU Langone Health; Robert I. Grossman, the CEO and dean who led the transformation; many of his current and former direct reports; and others throughout the institution who played important roles in bringing about the dramatic improvements that occurred in patient care, teaching, research, and finance. From the many threads of these conversations I have been able to weave a tapestry that tells the whole story.

This book is about the transformation of one institution. It is not a survey of health system change in America. It is not a comparison of one New York City hospital versus another, let alone a comparison of hospitals and medical schools throughout the United States or indeed the world. However, the transformation that occurred at NYU Langone is, in my experience, exceptional by any standard anywhere in the world, and I have had the opportunity to view such change around the globe. I recount this story not to extol NYU Langone but in the hope that the lessons they learned and practices they developed will assist others to improve patient care, research, and teaching in the United States and abroad. I have no connection to NYU or to NYU Langone Health other than becoming a patient while researching the book.

Let me say from the outset that there is no magic to the NYU Langone Health story. Americans have always believed that given the freedom to act, we can find solutions to pressing problems and adapt to changing circumstances. The transformation of NYU Langone was not the result of changes in federal, state, or local health policies. Nor were there significant changes in the demographic or economic profile of the community. NYU Langone works within its complex environment of rules and regulations. If NYU Langone can do it, so can other institutions around our country and internationally. This book is a call to action for hospitals and medical systems throughout the United States, and indeed the world, to up their game.

LEVERS OF CHANGE

To my readers seeking to improve their own hospitals or academic medical schools, or for you who are looking to improve your retail, manufacturing, or service business, I ask you to look within this story for what I call "levers of change." My understanding of the levers that drove the transformation of NYU Langone derives from my many hours of conversation with Bob Grossman, who led the transformation. These are the levers that were used to pry the organization from its past behaviors and put it on the path to a productive future.

CULTURAL TRANSFORMATION

Cultural transformation is the most important of these levers. Under the leadership of Bob Grossman and the chair of the NYU Langone Health Board of Trustees, Ken Langone, the culture changed from one of complacency to what Grossman calls an *aspirational culture*, the desire to be the very best. It changed from a culture that was content with the status quo to *a culture of continuous improvement*. There are several crucial elements comprising this culture.

Agility

This describes the ability to respond rapidly and positively to change.

A lean management system

This system allows rapid responses to new opportunities and challenges as they arise.

Access to transparent, real time, actionable data

Data should be transparent vertically, from a manager to their reports, and horizontally, from peer to peer.

Accountability

At NYU Langone everyone involved in patient care, teaching research, and administration is evaluated on objective data based upon performance standards.

Horizontal data transparency

This encourages each professional to improve by comparing their own performance to that of the best.

Crystal-clear communication

It's important to ensure that everyone knows the long-term goals and short-term objectives of the entire organization. People need to understand how their individual efforts contribute to a shared collective goal.

Breaking silos

Silos are the inevitable consequence of multidimensional organizations. Breaking the barriers between the silos is key to improving collective performance. Silo busting is accomplished by creating shared goals and rewards for previously siloed activities. Transparent information also breaks silos.

Silos are the inevitable consequence of multidimensional organizations. Breaking the barriers between the silos is key to improving collective performance.

Focus

Relentless *focus* is a critical lever of transformation. The NYU Langone mantra over the past ten years has been focus, focus, focus on the clearly stated goal to become a world class, patient centered, integrated academic medical center.

These levers of change, when applied in unison to the problem of transformation, create the momentum behind a flywheel of change, one that can transform any institution.

The NYU Langone story is not simply about inspired management. Effective and vibrant new medical and information technologies were critical to its success. Progress in minimally invasive surgery and medical imaging enables the creation of an ambulatory care network. Advances in information technology allow for real time data collection and display. Vertical and horizontal data transparency allows both the leadership and those who care for patients to know and continually improve outcomes. Sharing the success of these methods is one of the primary reasons I wrote this book.

In our nation's continuing debate on how to pay for healthcare, we seem to forget a fundamental lesson: We must focus on what we get for our money as well as how much money we spend. All too often the focus is on cost, not quality. We should only buy excellence. The NYU Langone story shows that excellent quality is also cost effective, a lesson many manufacturing companies have learned. High-quality patient care saves money.

MY BACKGROUND

My experience in academia, business, and philanthropy allowed me to appreciate the full dimension of NYU Langone's achievements. For almost twenty years I was a professor at Harvard Medical School and the Harvard School of Public Health. There I directed cancer and HIV/AIDS research and chaired two research departments. Over the past thirty years, I founded more than a dozen biotechnology companies, which have brought to market more than eight products, including the first immune-cell cancer therapy, the first protease inhibitor for HIV treatment, and the first new drug for the autoimmune disease lupus. I am now chair and president of ACCESS Health International, a foundation I created ten years ago that works across the globe to improve access to high-quality affordable healthcare. In that context I wrote this book and several others, including *Affordable Excellence* and *Every Second Counts*. Each is a story of healthcare transformation. My own experience tells me that achieving world class excellence in patient care, teaching, and research while dramatically improving the bottom line is unprecedented.

While writing this book, the NYU Langone Health story became my own personal story. After I had finished most of the interviews, I was diagnosed with head and neck cancer. I was treated at the Perlmutter Cancer Center, part of NYU Langone. This book is now informed not only by my professional background but also by my perspective as an NYU Langone patient. Although I have successfully completed my treatment, I know that I will be a patient at NYU Langone for many years to come, for monitoring if for nothing else.

I can personally attest to the high quality of patient centered care that I received. My judgment of my own medical care comes both as a professional working in a cancer hospital for many years and now as a patient. In a sense we are all professional patients—if not for ourselves, then for our families. I can say with utter conviction that my experience as a patient at NYU Langone has been qualitatively better than care I have received elsewhere, even in the most renowned hospitals in New York City and Boston.

The benefits of patient centered care were tangible to me as a patient. Within five minutes of my biopsy I had a clear diagnosis. The treatment plan selected was one that required the insight of a deeply knowledgeable and experienced team. That plan was assembled and executed rapidly. I was a partner in the discussions of the possible options. The coordination of different team members, and there were many, was seamless and flawless.

I can say with utter conviction that my experience as a patient at NYU Langone has been qualitatively better than care I have received elsewhere, even in the most renowned hospitals in New York City and Boston.

Detailed information about my case was readily available to all my doctors and nurse practitioners at the touch of a button. Only once, when I initially registered for a minor issue a year earlier, did I fill out any paperwork. For every other appointment, I needed only a palm scan. Blood test results were online for my doctors within minutes of the blood draw. Within a few hours of my appointment, the results were posted for me to see on the patient portal. Perhaps even more remarkable in the busy, sometimes surly city that is New York, everyone I met was meticulously polite, friendly, and helpful.

I do not believe my experience is unique. I saw others treated as I was. Being a patient with a serious disease is not pleasant, but my experience was as good as this sort of thing can be. Being a patient at NYU

Langone Health did not start me on the journey that is recounted in this book, but it showed me in the most personal way how important it is to get the system right. All of us in America and elsewhere are entitled to the excellent care I received. My hope is that this book draws us closer to that day.

PART I

Vision and Strategy

CHAPTER 1

From Adversity to Hope

This is a story of how in a few short years the NYU Medical Center, recently renamed NYU Langone Health, went from a low-ranked medical school to the number three medical school in the country, just behind Harvard and Johns Hopkins; from a stagnant research enterprise to a research powerhouse; and from losing money to producing substantial, sustainable operating surpluses. The NYU Langone trifecta—excellence in patient care, teaching, and research—is one of the great turnaround stories in business, let alone medicine. New additions to the NYU Langone portfolio in this story show that the NYU Langone transformation from loss to profit and from low to high quality can be replicated for very different kinds of hospitals, whether they be a safety net hospital serving low income households or a suburban hospital situated amid affluence.

The NYU Langone story is all the more remarkable, as the transformation occurred between 2007 and 2017, a tumultuous period in healthcare in the United States. These years were the setting for a prolonged debate over the Affordable Care Act, rapid changes in payment for medical services, and a revolution in health technologies. The transformation at NYU Langone occurred in the most highly regulated medical environment in the United States and possibly the world, namely

New York City. To top off the years of tumult and change, Hurricane Sandy destroyed much of the infrastructure, resulting in a forced closure of the hospital and medical school, delaying most of the research, while inflicting more than a billion dollars' worth of damage.

Core to the transformation is the leadership of Bob Grossman. His understanding of medicine, biomedical research, information technology, and the business of academic medicine have been the defining elements of success. To many who work with him he is a "pathological optimist." Key to the transformation is also the close working partnership between Bob Grossman as CEO and Ken Langone, chair of the board of trustees of NYU Langone Health. The support of then–New York University president John Sexton and NYU board chair Martin Lipton set the stage and cleared the way for the changes to follow; then they wisely left Grossman almost alone to work his magic.

NYU Langone Health CEO and dean Robert I. Grossman (left)
and chair Kenneth G. Langone (right) in 2017

ADVERSITY

The stories of most transformations, those that succeed and those that fail, in business and academia, begin with adversity. The story of NYU Langone Health is no exception. What was then called the NYU Medical Center slid from excellence in the 1960s and '70s to near disaster by the end of the century. The financial situation was so dire that many thought the Medical Center would bankrupt the entire university unless they took drastic action. Something clearly had to be done and fortunately was. In this chapter we outline the proud history of the NYU Medical Center, its decline, and the first steps toward transformation and rebirth.

> The stories of most transformations, those that succeed and those that fail, in business and academia, begin with adversity. The story of NYU Langone Health is no exception.

HISTORY

The institutions that would become NYU Langone Health were the New York University School of Medicine, founded in 1841, and New York University Hospital, founded in 1960. Throughout most of their history, both the NYU School of Medicine and the NYU Hospital, later named after the Tisch Family and known as Tisch Hospital, enjoyed excellent reputations. The hospital was known for high-quality care and for outstanding work in cardiology, cardiac surgery, and neurosurgery. It was there that Dr. Frank C. Spencer developed new open-heart surgical techniques. The medical school nurtured great physician scientists who made groundbreaking discoveries that led to the eradication of polio and effective treatments for serious mental disorders.

In the 1970s the hospital and medical school were among the top ten in the nation in research funding. By the 1990s they were falling behind. Medicine was changing rapidly, but the NYU Medical Center was not. By 2007, the hospital was in the bottom third in academic medical school rankings for quality and safety and had dropped to 34th in the country in medical school rankings. It ranked 39th in receipt of funds from the National Institutes of Health.

Richard Woodrow, formerly the executive director of the Organizational Development and Learning Department at NYU Langone Health, told me that the NYU Medical Center as a whole "was a complacent, isolated institution, content to rest on past accomplishments." By the 1990s it had become

"a lovely place to work. People were genuinely nice, civil, content, and disconnected from harsh realities. If you did not want to work hard, you could find a way to appear busy. There was little concern for the external-funding environment. Very few, if any, internal measures for accountability existed, except the budget, which was always in decline. The prevailing belief was that they could ignore the external realities, because the consulting doctors who were part of their network would always refer their private patients to the hospital. There was a belief that great scientists would always be attracted to the historical reputation of the NYU School of Medicine and that excellent students would continue to apply because of its reputation. This was a cordial and polite culture, which valued treating people with kindness, competence, collegiality, and compassion. Yet, this was unwittingly an individualistic, self-congratulatory, inward-looking, top-down, elitist, risk-averse, conflict-averse model of care."

EXTERNAL CHANGES

As so often happens in any enterprise, external changes precipitated the crisis. The economic structure of medicine was changing. The hospital had traditionally relied on reimbursements for specific services from private paying patients and individual insurance. By the late 1990s the university board believed that the number of private payers would decline sharply and that hospitals would be reimbursed by insurance companies not for individual services they performed but for the number of people they cared for. This was the era of managed care.

The steps to recovery began with the board of trustees of the university. They recognized that the business model of the Medical Center was no longer sustainable. In my interview with William Constantine, a trustee, he noted, "Every aspect of funding a medical center was bleak. There was no money to do anything. You cannot magically bring a fifty-year-old hospital building up to code. It was hard to recruit anyone."

From left to right: Martin Lipton, John Sexton, Kenneth G. Langone, and Dr. Robert Berne in 2012 at the Dean's Honor's Day

Cost recovery was inefficient and bookkeeping was below par for an institution of its size. Bob Berne, former executive vice president for Health at NYU and the person who first introduced me to the changes that had occurred at NYU Langone, told me, "If healthcare reimbursement was going to be capitated, then healthcare providers would be responsible for covered lives, and we would move away from payment for diagnostic-related groups and cost-based procedures. Our trustees believed we were not prepared for such a shift."

The trustees also knew that NYU was about to lose one of its major sources of income, royalties from the drug Remicade, which compensated for the losses that were piling up at the Medical Center. The research that led to the development of Remicade was conducted by a professor at the NYU School of Medicine. When the patent expired, so too would the substantial royalty-based income. Steven Abramson, senior vice president and vice dean for Education, Faculty, and Academic Affairs at NYU Langone Health, said in our interview, "Our budget deficit was about $150 million a year. Royalties from the sale of Remicade had been covering our deficit, and we knew these would expire soon."

Saul Farber served as chairman of the NYU Department of Medicine from 1966 to 2000. He was acting dean of the School of Medicine from 1963 to 1966 and again from 1982 to 1987. He then served as dean and provost of the school until 1997. During that time, the school and the hospital were both administrative units of NYU and were together known as the NYU Medical Center. Farber was a great doctor and a mentor to other great doctors. Under his guidance, NYU became known for having a culture of caring and a sense of dedication to patients. While Abramson expressed great admiration for Farber, he said, "Resources declined in the latter period of Saul Farber's administration. Change became difficult, and most often funds for innovation were not available. As brilliant as he was, the reality of the Medical

Center was that the status quo lingered, and leadership in various departments stagnated."

In our interview on the eve of his retirement as president of NYU, John Sexton recalled, "Saul Farber was a great doctor and a great human being, but dramatic changes were occurring in medicine. New technologies were being introduced. There were significant changes in the economics of medicine." He added, "When I was named president in May 2001, I began to look at the university from a strategic perspective. It was very clear that the Medical Center was in trouble. It was in such trouble that it had the potential to bring down the entire university, because it was such a huge part of the enterprise."

Martin Lipton, my friend and former attorney, who was then nearing the end of his long tenure as chair of the board of trustees of New York University, agreed that there was apprehension "for the university as a whole, if we began to have deficits at the Medical Center." The board of the university had good reason to feel that the losses being experienced by the hospital could threaten the entire university. NYU had suffered a financial crisis in the 1970s. The school was forced to sell its Bronx campus to the City University of New York and to essentially give away its engineering school by merging it with the Polytechnic Institute of Brooklyn. As a result of the board's concerns, Lipton said, "We began a series of discussions led in large part by Larry Tisch, then chairman of the university board of trustees, and by George Heyman, a trustee of the university. We considered separately incorporating the hospital to shield the rest of the university. We also began to think about whether or not we should merge the hospital with another hospital."

The board at NYU held a broader vision for the institution than did its chief executives. The board knew change was necessary, and they were prepared to undertake major changes. This was in contrast to the senior staff members, who appeared inclined to keep doing what they were doing.

> The board at NYU held a broader vision for the
> institution than did its chief executives. The board
> knew change was necessary, and they were
> prepared to undertake major changes.

A FAILED MERGER

In times of trouble, businesses often turn to mergers. Some mergers work to revitalize failing companies. Most do not. Some end up worsening an already bad situation. A common cause of failure is the inability to adapt to changes in external conditions that led to the crises in the first place. Such was the case for the mergers planned for the Medical Center.

As NYU struggled to right its medical school and hospital, one of the first initiatives was to attempt to merge with another institution. The eventual choice was Mount Sinai, a New York hospital with its own medical school. A plan was negotiated under which the two medical schools would merge into the NYU School of Medicine and the two hospitals would merge into the Mount Sinai Hospital. Bob Berne explained the plans to me: "Mount Sinai would manage the hospitals, and New York University would manage the medical schools."

The NYU medical faculty opposed the merger of the medical schools. They sued New York University. Though the suit was later dismissed, the School of Medicine faculty remained rebellious. Bob Berne said: "Saul Farber resigned his administrative positions in 1997 as the merger talks progressed." As a result of faculty opposition, the merger plan was modified so that the medical schools continued as separate institutions, though both maintained the School of New York

University aegis for degree purposes. The trustees still decided to merge the two hospitals. Berne said the trustees "thought this would avoid agitation of our faculty. They would find out they were wrong."

The merger of the hospitals took place in 1998. Andrew Brotman, senior vice president, vice dean for Clinical Affairs and Strategy, and chief clinical officer at NYU Langone Health, arrived at New York University hospital just after the merger. During our lengthy interview he recalled, "I had experienced five hospital mergers during my time in Boston. Within five minutes of my first meeting with the NYU-Sinai merged hospitals, I knew the merger was going to fall apart."

William Constantine said, "It was a complete disaster. The more inside you were, the more you realized that everything was being held together by Scotch tape."

John Sexton recalled, "What looked on paper like an easy blending of complementary or even supplementary strengths between Mount Sinai and New York University did not work out in practice."

NYU quickly sought to end the association with Mount Sinai. William Berkley, who later became the NYU board chair, recalled, "Marty Lipton did a fabulous job in managing the de-merger. Only a person with his background and skills could unwind that transaction." Lipton had a background as one of the nation's leading mergers and acquisitions lawyers. The merger discussions that began in 1997 were consummated in 1998, and in 2001 the trustees agreed to separate. They could not immediately seek a complete divorce, however, because they were both responsible for a substantial amount of debt.

The first attempt to solve the problems at the Medical Center failed. The merger was more of an attempt to get rid of a problem that threatened the entire university, not an attempt to solve the fundamental problems behind the decline. In the end, the board decided to end the merger. The NYU hospitals returned to the university with all the same issues and with $500 million of additional debt.

FIRST STEPS TO RECOVERY

A failed merger will cause both a board and management to reevaluate the fundamentals of their business and operations. The failure of the merger prompted NYU leaders to begin serious thinking about how to survive, recover, and grow stronger. In discussing the process of transformation with me, Robert Press, formerly the senior vice president and vice dean, and former chief of Hospital Operations of NYU Langone Health, remarked, "As sometimes happens even with personal setbacks, the problems that arose from the failed merger with Mount Sinai made us stronger. It wasn't that the failure itself made us stronger, but that we began to think seriously about how to survive and recover."

"The problems that arose from the failed merger with Mount Sinai made us stronger. It wasn't that the failure itself made us stronger, but that we began to think seriously about how to survive and recover."

John Sexton met with the NYU board soon after the de-merger was agreed, and he told them, "I promise you that by September we will come to you with a plan. Everything has to be on the table. It may well be that the plan is to offer our medical school to another university that can afford to have a medical center." Sexton added: "I do not think it is likely we will get to that point. I know that if we do not have a first-class medical center, then we cannot be a first-class research university. But we must ask if we can risk having a medical school at all."

Bob Berne said, "The period following the dissolution of the merger was difficult for NYU. We had to rebuild emotionally, financially, organizationally, and structurally. The first years were traumatic. People were nervous about the future. We were still excellent in teaching and research, but we took a hit from the merger. We knew that we had to do a lot of repair work."

The NYU board took a deep look at what led to the problems in the first place. To begin with, they recognized the need for the hospital and the medical school to operate as a single entity, not two organizations that were often at serious odds with one another. Richard Woodrow said, "The hospitals and the medical school were two very different and separate institutions. They had great individuals, but it was not a great institution. In fact, I would not even call it an organization. It was more a conglomerate of individuals who created a hospital so that their patients could have a place to go other than Bellevue," which had served as a teaching hospital for NYU.

As the board explored new opportunities, they made several strategic decisions. One was to consolidate leadership of the Medical Center by having one person run both the hospital and the medical school. Aligning leadership was seen as a way to ensure that the entire institution would work together toward shared goals.

Robert M. Glickman was named dean in the summer of 1998. He was hired to oversee the reintegration. Glickman had been physician-in-chief and chair of the department of medicine at Beth Israel Deaconess Medical Center in Boston, a Harvard-affiliated hospital. During the summer of 2001, Bob Glickman, Bob Berne, Jack Lew, John Sexton, and NYU's chief financial officer developed their ideas. "Finally, we presented the plan at a trustee meeting on September 10, 2001," Sexton said, "and the trustees quickly approved the plan, which had two parts—'untangling the merger' and determining how to 'establish clear reporting lines.'"

Going forward, Sexton decided that Bob Berne would be the link between the university and the medical school. As the de-merger unfolded and NYU thought about the organizational structure of its medical activities, Berne said, "We realized that there was an advantage to integration of the hospital and the medical school. I realized that any serious initiative—for example, creating new programs in radiology, cardiology, or rehabilitation—always involves the school and the hospital. In many academic medical centers, the heads of the hospital and the medical school continually negotiate over programs, personnel, and resources. The negotiations are frequent and sometimes difficult. We decided that it was to our advantage to run the school and hospital as an integrated academic medical center."

Aligning leadership was seen as a way to
ensure that the entire institution would
work together toward shared goals.

Recovery from a crisis often requires fundamental restructuring of the relationships between business units. The decision to place the medical school and the hospitals under a single leader was one such decision. So too was the decision to insulate the finances of the university from those of the medical school and the hospital.

Bob Berne emphasized, "It is important to understand the evolution of the organizational structure for the hospital and the medical school." Before the merger with Mount Sinai, he explained, "the hospital was fully a part of the university, like the English department. We had a School of Medicine, a College of Arts and Sciences, and we had a hospital. As part of the merger, the hospital left the university structure and became part of Mount Sinai. When the hospital came back, the trustees thought there was an advantage to bringing it back with the university as the sole member of the hospital, but with its own board, appointed by the [NYU] board, devoted only to the Medical Center."

As a result, the hospital gained a board of trustees appointed by the university. However, the university board would be obliged to review certain decisions taken by the hospital board, including decisions involving additional debt or acquisitions of major assets. The budget and finances of the hospital were to be approved by the hospital board; and while they would be reviewed by the university board, they would not require university board approval. Moreover, this hospital board would also serve as the advisory board of the School of Medicine. This board would, in effect, oversee the Medical Center.

In creating the new board for the Medical Center, nine people who were also on the university board were named as trustees of the hospital. "In effect, we made the advisory board of the medical school identical to the board of the Medical Center," Berne said.

One goal of this structure, Berne said, was that the university wanted the Medical Center board "to act in the interests of the integrated whole, not just the hospital, but rather in the combined interests of the school and the hospital." Berne added that today "the university board spends a lot of time on Medical Center matters. I cannot recall an issue that came before the university board without a full vetting and recommendation from the Medical Center board. The university appoints the members of the Medical Center board, usually with recommendations from the Medical Center board. The two boards share eight or nine members."

The net result of all these changes is that a financial wall was erected to separate the finances of the university from those of the Medical Center. Financial failure of the Medical Center would no longer threaten the survival of the university. Conversely, should the Medical Center recover and thrive, the university would not benefit financially, a consequence I suspect they must now regret.

Merging the administration of the hospital and the medical school was a direct result of the failed merger with Mount Sinai. In the future, one person would be the dean of the medical school and CEO of the hospital. This would be a very powerful job, a job that offered the capability of making major changes in the Medical Center. The person in this role could align all of the chairs of the clinical and academic departments toward meeting shared goals. Agility, the ability of a complex organization to respond quickly and appropriately to rapidly changing circumstances, is a significant advantage of the combined leadership structure.

Academic medical centers typically split the jobs of hospital CEO and dean. Department chairs in academic medical centers are often very independent. They have agendas for their own departments. The NYU trustees perceived that when there is a single person holding both jobs, there is no confusion regarding goals. That person has the power to define how each department will contribute to the three main missions of the Medical Center: education, research, and patient care. Each of the department chairs can be held accountable for executing the plan to fulfill all three missions.

Given the obvious success of the new management structure, it is my strong recommendation that the two positions be fused whenever possible. Countries planning new medical schools should unify management rather than follow the traditional model where the jobs of dean and CEO are separate.

The decision to integrate the administrations of the school and the hospital and to put one person in charge of the new organization turned out to be inspired. It set the stage for the eventual rise to excellence of the entire institution, though not at first.

Bob Glickman, who had been hired in 1998 as dean of the medical school, became the first person to hold the new joint position beginning in 2001. Despite the changes made by the trustees, Glickman was unable to take advantage of the new opportunity the structure provided. It would take a more visionary leader. Structural and administrative changes in organizations are usually not sufficient to transform an enterprise without having dynamic and visionary leadership. Such changes are, however, needed to set the conditions for eventual success, as we shall see.

Structural and administrative changes in organizations
are usually not sufficient to transform an enterprise
without having dynamic and visionary leadership.

For the next five years both the hospital and the medical school languished. The hoped-for recovery and return to excellence did not occur. During Glickman's years, there was little money available for growth or improvement. Facilities were falling into disrepair. The staff was demoralized, and a sense of gloom pervaded the institution.

Ken Langone, the former chair of Home Depot, agreed to join the board of both the university and the Medical Center in response to an invitation from his friend and lawyer, Martin Lipton. Langone quickly became a major supporter. In 2000, he donated $100 million to the NYU Medical Center, and in 2008 he and his wife, Elaine, gave another $100 million. The institution was renamed the NYU Langone Medical Center in honor of their contributions.

The Medical Center did make some progress during the Langone-Glickman years. Glickman had secured a donation of $25 million from the Smilow family for a new building, which was helpful but still far below the initial goal of $150 million. Glickman hired a number of department chairs and increased the full-time physician staff from eighty to about three hundred and fifty.

In recalling the early days, Langone told me in a series of fascinating discussions, "I talked to a lot of people, and the thing that came through loud and clear is how depressed, how disappointed these people were." Glickman's leadership style did not improve matters. He was essentially an interim leader, but not the transformational leader the hospital and medical school needed. He was resistant to criticism or disagreement. In 2006, Glickman announced that he was going to step down the following year, several years short of his ten-year contract.

FINDING A NEW LEADER

A search for new leadership began. Prior to determining who the best candidates might be, the university board needed to decide whether to search for one person who would lead the medical school and the hospital, or two people—one to lead the hospital and another to lead the medical school. The board was split as to which path to follow. Berne said: "Many of the trustees felt that the hospital part of the Medical Center should be run as a business and should be headed by someone with business experience, and the medical school should be headed by someone with strong academic credentials. Their initial idea was to recruit a strong academic to be dean of medicine and a strong health business person to run the hospital."

Bob Berne made what was probably the determining argument. He explained, "If we split the job, we would give up a unique advantage. We would re-create a situation where the top leaders would have to negotiate with one another again, unnecessarily complicating and slowing decisions." As he saw it, "very few of the major decisions made in an academic medical center are purely clinical or purely research. Major decisions require close cooperation of both the hospital staff and the medical school faculty. I said if we search for two people, we will find two. If we search for one, we may find one with the skills to do both."

An executive search firm was engaged to find one person who would be the dean and chief executive officer. "The committee had about seven or eight faculty members," Berne said. Two trustees played an active role: Martin Lipton, as chair of the university, and Ken Langone, as chair of the Medical Center. Langone felt very strongly that the Medical Center needed to find a person who would serve as both CEO and dean, as Berne suggested.

Martin Lipton said of the search, "Our fundamental criterion was to find the best person we could find, but hopefully that person would combine both medical distinction and what I call business acumen." He added, "We received many resumes. We invited sixteen people in for a one-hour interview. We then narrowed the field to six. All came back for a day and a half of interviews. Then we had a couple of people who we looked at seriously. Bob Grossman emerged as the consensus choice." The process began in the summer of 2006. "Then we met in earnest in the fall," Berne said. "We selected Bob Grossman in March 2007."

ROBERT I. GROSSMAN

At the time of his appointment, Bob Grossman was fifty-nine years old and in his sixth year at NYU Langone, where he served as chairman of the department of radiology and professor of neurology, neurosurgery, and neuroscience and physiology. Grossman was educated at Tulane University and the University of Pennsylvania. He had a reputation as an excellent physician and scientist, someone who understood how to translate fundamental science into practical advances in patient treatment.

When Grossman was being interviewed by the search team for the position of CEO and dean, Langone said, "I knew Bob well and thought he would be an excellent leader, one that combined excellence in medicine, excellence in science, and excellence in management." Langone had seen Grossman in action as chair of the radiology department, and he had a sense that Grossman had the skills to lead on a much larger scale.

As chair of the radiology department, Grossman had proven himself to be an effective manager who revitalized the department and turned it into a profit center. Moreover, Grossman had pulled off an interesting coup in acquiring equipment for his department. Grossman explained, "When I arrived, the radiology department was a third-class place. They had lousy equipment. Somebody said to me, 'We are a showplace for Siemens for magnetic resonance imaging.' I asked, 'What do we get in exchange?' They replied, 'We get some pulse sequences.' I said, 'That seems like an asymmetric relationship. Let's see how much we are really worth to them as a show site.'"

Grossman issued a request for a proposal for a single vendor to supply all of the radiology department's needs. It was a winner-take-all proposal pitting Siemens against General Electric. Siemens won by offering a package valued at $100 million.

Grossman's handling of this deal got Langone's attention. Grossman clearly had a vision for the radiology department. Langone acknowledged he was impressed by the deal, as well as by his efficient management of the radiology department. "When I saw how well he managed his department, I really got excited. I thought, 'This guy has got a lot of bandwidth; this guy has got a lot of runway.' It became clear that Bob has an incredible, very rare combination of skills, incredible scientific capacity, and the ability to manage. Most scientists work seven days in a row and then pass out from exhaustion. They do not think about management." By contrast, Langone said, "Bob Grossman's managerial skills and visionary capabilities came as wonderful surprises."

John Sexton recalled, "I had long talks with Ken as we moved to choosing Bob Grossman. In the end, I made the independent judgment to hire Bob; but Ken was enthusiastically in support also."

Focusing on an insider to lead the transformation was a key decision. Langone wanted an insider to take over. In his view, there were clear advantages in choosing an insider such as Bob Grossman, who had been successfully leading an important department in the hospital. He believed that a smart and successful insider already knows the organization in detail. An insider knows the strengths and weaknesses of the institution, including which managers are good at their jobs and which are not.

Despite all the positives, Bob Grossman was a risky choice. He did not have most of the credentials expected of one who would lead an academic medical center. He did not have prior business experience. He had never been trained or mentored as a manager or as an executive. He did not sit on any outside boards of directors. He had never managed anything larger than the radiology department.

Grossman acknowledges that he did not fit the mold. As he put it frankly, "I had not come up the normal way. I had never been to business school. I did not know what a board was. I had never worked with a board of directors. There is a book about unfiltered leaders entitled *Indispensable: When Leaders Really Matter* by Gautam Mukunda. By Mukunda's definition, I was a very unfiltered leader. Winston Churchill and Franklin D. Roosevelt are examples of unfiltered leaders. There is a chance that an unfiltered leader can achieve more than one who is carefully filtered, but the risk is much higher." Grossman said, "I felt pretty confident, and probably delusional, that I could turn it around. There was no question in my mind that I could turn it around. That stems probably from never having been to business school and never taking a business course." But, he added, "I did have a good idea what was wrong."

According to Richard Woodrow, Bob Grossman "was the shock to the system that was needed." Grossman would turn out to be the perfect person to head NYU Langone and provide it with a powerful and effective leader. The stellar results he has achieved during his tenure are proof of his effectiveness. He has been described as "a visionary who sees the details."

I believe the skills and experience Bob Grossman brings to the job can be a model for organizations anywhere as they search for new leaders. Academic medical centers in particular should look for outstanding academic achievement as well as excellent physician credentials. Just as important are the candidate's leadership credentials and skills as a manager of people. Grossman's success would also serve as a tribute to a unified, integrated command structure, thus ensuring that actions taken would be in the interests of the integrated whole.

The skills and experience Bob Grossman brings to the job can be a model for organizations anywhere as they search for new leaders. Academic medical centers in particular should look for outstanding academic achievement as well as excellent physician credentials. Just as important are the candidate's leadership credentials and skills as a manager of people.

In the next few chapters we will examine the strategy and the leadership underpinning the transformation of NYU Langone, and then we will turn to the specific steps taken to turn this institution around. We will see the management tactics initiated by Bob Grossman and supported by his board of trustees that propelled NYU Langone from mediocre to world class.

CHAPTER 2

The Vision

Enterprise transformation requires a vision and a road map. The vision is an inspirational view of the future and lets everyone know toward what goal they are working. The road map provides specific directions for how to transition from a bleak present to a bright future; it outlines specific tasks, milestones, and markers of the path ahead. The road map also allows everyone to understand their specific roles in realizing an ideal future.

When Bob Grossman took over the NYU School of Medicine and hospitals, there was no such vision and no such road map. The institution was divided and seemed paralyzed. No clear goals were articulated. No pathways for change were evident.

Grossman believed conditions were even worse than that. The Medical Center had in many ways become a dysfunctional, demoralized set of separate fiefdoms. The hospitals often fought with the medical school for scarce resources. The university had tried but failed to divest the hospitals. Many at the medical school were dispirited. To make the point, Bob Grossman often tells the woeful tale of his early days at NYU. Soon after he arrived, a pipe burst in his office, doing considerable damage to a wall and causing plaster to come down. At the time, he was recruiting for the radiology department, and the condition of the office did not leave a good impression. Yet he found it almost impossible to get the necessary repairs made. He said to me that finally, a month after the pipe burst, "the dean comes up and looks at it and says, 'Yeah, it looks terrible.' Then the school and the hospital had to negotiate who owned the wall and who owned the pipes for the $5,000 to fix it. The school and the hospital were constantly finessing each other so that they did not have to spend anything. As a result, little got done, and necessary improvements were not made."

CREATING A VISION STATEMENT

Despite this state of affairs, Grossman saw a great opportunity. He knew that the NYU Medical Center could become great. He had a vision of how a team of talented and dedicated people, combined with the full power of modern medical technology, could transform NYU Langone into a world class institution for patient care, teaching, and research. He set about crafting an inspirational vision statement.

> *NYU Langone was to be "a world class, patient centered, integrated academic medical center."*

Bob Grossman's vision of what NYU Langone should be, and could be, was not formulated in a vacuum. He had spent the previous six years as chairman of the department of radiology. He modernized the department and led it to new levels of effectiveness and profitability. As department chairman, he observed and participated in the life of the Medical Center. He formed clear ideas about what needed to be done. He knew where many of the problems lay. Creating a vision statement that reflected his views became a collective process, involving all elements of the NYU Medical Center community.

To obtain institutional buy in for the vision, Grossman hired a consulting firm to work with a broad group of senior leaders across the entire institution, including doctors, scientists, nurses, and senior level administrators. They conducted in-depth interviews and workshops with each of these groups, soliciting opinions and feedback from more than one hundred members of the staff. Grossman and his direct reports listened carefully to the feedback. In the months that followed, Grossman and his leadership met with members of the entire NYU Langone community, in groups large and small, to make sure they understood and were enthusiastic about the vision behind the changes ahead. Bob Grossman told me, as he told the entire staff of NYU Langone, "Every one of the words in the vision statement means something." Let's now examine the meaning of each of those words.

Grossman and his leadership met with members of the entire NYU Langone community, in groups large and small, to make sure they understood and were enthusiastic about the vision.

WORLD CLASS

World class means to be among the best in the world at everything you do. Institutions must find the right mix between future hope and current reality. To aspire to be best in New York City is significant. To be best in the United States is a stretch. To be world class in everything you do is a reach beyond. The vision declares that NYU Langone will become one of the best institutions in the world in patient care, teaching, and research.

Bob Grossman first began thinking about a vision of the Medical Center as he was preparing for the competitive bid for the new radiology equipment, well before becoming CEO. He was surprised to discover that no such vision statement existed, so he began to formulate his own while the senior leadership team assembled to retrofit a vision. Richard Woodrow, who was working on organizational development with Grossman at the time, told me, "I remember the word 'good' coming up in the discussions. Bob immediately said, 'No, not good, great. We need to be not only the best in New York but the best in the world.' It was the first time I had ever heard the concept. Up to then, conversations with senior leadership were often modest tactical attempts to manage within the declining revenue—how to cut or contain."

Proposing to become world class was, as Grossman acknowledged, an "audacious idea, but it struck a chord for a lot of people here who thought we could be better." Building consensus among the NYU Langone leadership and staff around the concept of world class was not difficult. Most people endorsed the aspiration enthusiastically. He said, "The physicians and scientists at NYU Langone were tired of being considered to be second to other academic medical schools and hospitals in New York City and the country. The idea of becoming 'world class' resonated with many here—not everybody, but many."

PATIENT CENTERED

The words *patient centered* are key to the vision and to the operations of NYU Langone. In Grossman's view everything that NYU Langone does must be for the benefit of patients. To Grossman, being patient centered includes the delivery of care but extends well beyond healing. Patient centered also means excellence in teaching new generations of doctors to provide the highest quality of compassionate care. Patient centered means conducting cutting-edge research so that future generations of patients receive the best care science and medicine can provide. Nader Mherabi, NYU Langone's senior vice president, vice dean, and chief information officer, takes this to mean, "We are here for the patients to find novel cures and to educate and train excellent doctors. Everything we do is all about the patient. We do not do research just for the sake of research. We do research hoping to find cures for diseases. That is Bob's vision. It was about connecting all the parts for better results for our patients."

Patient centered means that everyone who is part of NYU Langone, including those who greet patients at the door, escort them through the buildings, maintain the equipment, or clean the facilities, will treat everyone with the utmost care and respect. It means that doctors and patients will have readily available, detailed, transparent information about the health of each patient so they need not fill out innumerable reports and repetitive paperwork. It means that everyone in the institution, no matter what their role, understands that they play a vital part in delivering the highest quality of patient care. Ken Langone insists that patient centered also means that every employee of NYU Langone is treated with an equal measure of respect. The principles of individual respect for customers and employees that Ken Langone applied to building Home Depot are integral to the patient centered concept of the revitalized NYU Langone that he worked passionately to build.

The words *patient centered* emerged from the early discussions of the vision statement by the top leadership team. According to Richard Woodrow, inclusion of *patient centered* in the vision statement emerged from a retreat Grossman organized for senior staff members to discuss development of a vision statement. Initially, according to Richard Woodrow, "Many of the doctors felt insulted by the term *patient centered*. They argued that doctors do not need standards imposed by a bureaucracy. The physicians maintained that they had their own professional standards. They did not want to be told how to relate to patients. There was real pushback on the term 'patient centered.'"

I found in the dozens of interviews I conducted in research for this book that there is now universal and enthusiastic support of the concept of patient centered care throughout the entire organization, including the physicians. There is widespread acceptance of the idea that patient satisfaction is a key measure of the quality of service.

In the eyes of patients, many medical institutions seem to be run for the convenience of the doctors and the staff, and patients are there only as test cases for research projects. Grossman saw the purpose of a medical facility differently. To Grossman "exceptional patient care would be the only reason for their existence." The patient was to be at the center of everything the Medical Center was going to be doing as it was revitalized. His mantra became "It is all about the patient."

The recollections of Kimberly Glassman, chief nursing officer and associate dean for Partnership Innovation, illustrate how the full meaning of Grossman's vision was expounded and what it meant to the staff. She recalled that there was substantial debate about the concept of *patient centered*. She said Grossman "was very specific and deliberate in imparting the message that NYU Langone was about serving patients in everything we do, patients in our care, and others that we can touch through our research. Advances in medicine and science that NYU Langone might achieve could benefit people everywhere."

INTEGRATED ACADEMIC MEDICAL CENTER

The words *integrated academic medical center* reflect the new structure the trustees and Bob Grossman envisioned for the future of NYU Langone. Grossman knew that NYU Langone would have to change dramatically to become fully integrated. He was determined that all NYU operations, including patient care, teaching, research, and support services, would be integrated into a single management and financial structure. All of the operations would report to a single management team. The creation of a single comprehensive, transparent information system that included all patient and medical operations, all research, all teaching, and all administrative functions would be central to the concept of an *integrated academic medical center*.

According to Grossman, NYU Langone would not be a medical school *and* a hospital, or a hospital *with* a medical school. All activities were to be part of an inextricable whole. In a truly patient centered institution, all parts of the organization must work together for the ultimate benefit of the patient. That meant there would be no separation between the School of Medicine and the Hospitals Center. They would have to function as a single integrated organization, with one administration and one unified approach to healthcare. All would contribute to the well-being of patients.

In a truly patient centered institution,
all parts of the organization must work
together for the ultimate benefit of the patient.

As Grossman formulated his vision statement, Woodrow recalled, "he began trying out his vision statement for the Medical Center with the new leadership team he was building. Those people who had worked with him before understood it right away. He had a much harder time with people who had been in the Medical Center for a long time. He needed to find ways to influence them." Woodrow added, "Bob is brilliant one on one. He is very good with small groups." Over time he learned to communicate his vision effectively with large groups as well. Today everyone from top to bottom at NYU Langone knows, understands, and is proud of the vision they share.

THE ROAD MAP

A year and a half into the job as CEO and dean of NYU Langone, Bob Grossman sat down to draft, on a single handwritten page, a road map for translating the vision of creating a world class, patient centered, integrated academic medical center into reality. This single page both summarizes what happened in the first eighteen months of his tenure and formulates a precise guide for all the actions needed to transform the institution from what it had been to what it would become. The map was necessarily complex. All the parts of this diverse institution would integrate into a coherent whole. The road map was an effort to organize Grossman's own thoughts and to formulate a plan of action. Sharing the road map would guide others along the same route.

Bob Grossman sat down to draft, on a single handwritten page, a road map for translating the vision of creating a world class, patient centered, integrated academic medical center into reality.

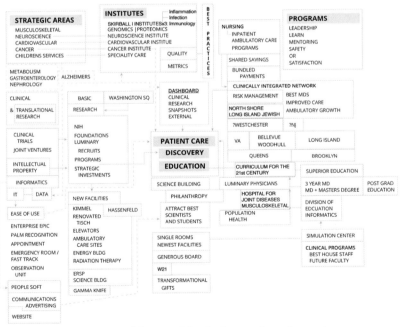

Grossman's handwritten road map for creating a world class,
patient centered, integrated academic medical center

A typed version of Grossman's handwritten road map for creating a
world class, patient centered, integrated academic medical center

READING THE MAP
The Core Mission

At the center of the map, Grossman lists the three interrelated missions of NYU Langone: *Patient Care*, *Discovery*, and *Education*. All three support care that is patient centered. Performance that is world class in all three areas is the bedrock of the transformation. Every other effort summarized on Grossman's road map connects to the core mission.

Best Practices

At the top center of the road map are the words *best practices*. These words are a reminder that NYU Langone intends to be world class in all they do. They will either adopt or create the best practices in patient care, research, and teaching.

Strategic Areas

Grossman realized that focus is essential to success. Given available resources, Grossman knew that the Medical Center could not be excellent in all areas of medicine, at least initially. His decision was to focus on five strategic areas of greatest need in the community and those in which the Medical Center was already strong. These areas shown in the upper right of the map are *musculoskeletal*, *neuroscience*, *cardiovascular*, *cancer*, and *children's services*. Grossman also outlined areas of future focus. These include *metabolism*, *Alzheimer's*, *gastroenterology*, and *nephrology*.

Institutes

Supporting and closely related to these five areas of clinical medicine are research institutes. The institutes draw faculty from the academic departments. The research of each institute is mission focused. For example, the research of the neuroscience institute both advances fundamental knowledge of the nervous system, including brain science, and supports research on new treatments for brain and peripheral nerve disorders. Some of the institutes existed prior to Grossman's tenure; others were created later. The lines between these two boxes show the connection between the research institutes and the corresponding departments that treat patients. Here, too, a future institute is imagined that focuses on the "I³": inflammation, infection, and immunology.

Quality

The word *quality*, in its own box at the top of the page, reflects Grossman's relentless drive to ensure that every aspect of patient care, research, and teaching be of the highest quality. It is this drive that has led the hospitals of NYU Langone Health to receive recognition for the highest standards of quality and safety in the country year after year.

Metrics

The word *metrics* also occupies its own box at the top of the page. Metrics reflects Grossman's determination that all aspects of performance at NYU Langone are measured in real time to assess performance and ensure accountability. Grossman imagined a comprehensive, real time, transparent, integrated, unified database. The data would be transparent both vertically and horizontally. The data would be real time and actionable. The data would be summarized in dashboards that were easy to use and tailored to the needs of each user.

Metrics means that progress toward every objective would be measured quantitatively. This was a central feature of Grossman's execution plan. Metrics provide objective measurement of all activities. Subjective measures would not color evaluations of performance. In Grossman's view of management, staff members must be held to agreed standards. Metrics would provide a clear picture of whether they were meeting the standards.

A key element of the quality metrics is the *dashboard*. Dashboards are easily legible, graphical summaries of actual versus expected performance. Dashboards provide a clear view of the vast array of measurements of all activities of the hospitals and the medical school. The dashboards Grossman envisioned provide a view in real time of everything that was happening at NYU Langone as it was happening. The dashboards would provide both vertical and horizontal views of all activities. All doctors, scientists, and administrators would review all activities under their supervision. The entire staff of the Medical Center could also look across at their own performance and compare their performance with that of others doing similar jobs. Everyone in the hospital and medical school could benchmark their own performance against that of their peers. Managers would have a clear view of their own performance and that of their team.

A key element of the quality metrics is the *dashboard*. Dashboards are easily legible, graphical summaries of actual versus expected performance. Dashboards provide a clear view of the vast array of measurements of all activities of the hospitals and the medical school.

Improving Patient Experience

The lower left quadrant of the road map summarizes initiatives that Grossman believed would improve the experience of individual patients.

At the very top of the list are the words *ease of use*, *informatics*, and *information technology (IT)*. Just below that are the words *Enterprise Epic*.

This section touches the very heart of patient centered healthcare. Epic is an information management system for health. Enterprise Epic would include the electronic health record that stores in one place the entire medical history of each patient. The information in the record will be instantly shared among all doctors and support staff with whom the patient interacts.

The Enterprise Epic system would allow identification and accurate accounting of all services provided to the patient and enable sufficient cost recovery from payers. As we shall see, Grossman made an early decision to rip out the existing electronic medical record system and replace it with Enterprise Epic, a bold decision that has played a critical role in enabling the transformation from mediocre to world class.

Grossman also planned to implement other changes to improve the patient experience. These include installation of a *palm recognition* system to eliminate the need for repetitive paperwork. Patients will register for each appointment simply by placing their palm over a reading device. NYU Langone implemented MyChart, a user-friendly online system that allows patients to view their medical records. MyChart tracks appointments, summarizes test results, communicates doctor recommendations, and allows patients the ability to chat with their caregivers online.

Programs

Execution requires people who are skilled in their specialty and dedicated to improvement. Grossman recognized the need to enhance the skills of all those charged with execution. He planned to create programs to assist his team in acquiring leadership skills and education in specialized management skills. The words *learn* and *mentoring* summarize this thought. He planned to establish programs to improve the *safety* of all processes and procedures related to patient care and to focus on improving *patient satisfaction.*

Nursing

A box devoted to *nursing* has pride of place at the top of the page. To achieve excellence in delivering medical care, Grossman's road map placed an emphasis on nursing. Grossman saw nursing as an independent force in dealing with patients. Nurses were not to be subservient to doctors. He envisioned organizing nursing staffs floor by floor rather than department by department. This structure would give nurses a powerful voice in the structure of medical care. The change would represent a major policy decision.

NYU Langone would become recognized as a workplace friendly to nurses. Grossman's thoughts on the organization of nursing care would inform his ideas about ambulatory care. From the very beginning, his idea was to treat people away from the hospital and move them to outpatient services. Nurses would be critical to this approach. As will be noted, this approach turned out to be one of his great successes. Nursing connects to the box containing the words *clinically integrated network,* reflecting the importance Grossman places on integration of nursing with all aspects of patient care, whether in or outside the hospital.

Nurses were not to be subservient to doctors. Grossman envisioned organizing nursing staffs floor by floor rather than department by department. This structure would give nurses a powerful voice in the structure of medical care.

Clinically Integrated Network

The box labeled *clinically integrated network* represents one of Grossman's key insights that has driven transformation over the past ten years. Grossman was one of the first to recognize that new technologies were transforming the way medicine was delivered. For the past one hundred years medicine in the United States and elsewhere has been hospital based. Almost all surgeries and major medical interventions were performed in hospitals that are open twenty-four hours a day, seven days a week. Following surgeries, people stayed in hospitals for days or weeks.

Grossman understood that new surgical methods, combined with advances in imaging and endoscopic surgery, allowed the majority of procedures that had been hospital based to be performed in ambulatory care centers. Patients could come in the morning and leave at night. Grossman was determined to lead the way in the transition from hospital-based care to ambulatory care. He reasoned that not only is ambulatory care cost effective, it is better for the patient. Patients who are not hospitalized have a much lower risk of contracting hospital-borne infections. Ambulatory care centers can be located in the communities where patients live. In the road map, the words *ambulatory growth* capture this concept.

Building an integrated care network would also need a dramatic change in staffing. Physicians that are part of the network would all be full-time employees of NYU Langone, not consulting physicians with their own practices. The transition would not occur overnight but would drive who would be brought on staff and where new physicians practiced. The concept also meant investing in a broad network of outpatient facilities throughout Manhattan and Brooklyn, which was the patient base at the time. The network of ambulatory care centers might extend to Westchester County and to Long Island, the commuter base for many who work in New York City. The words *best MDs* encapsulate the planned staff change.

As the network of ambulatory care centers grew to a certain size, it might require its own local hospital to serve as a hub for more routine care that required hospitalization. Having a local hospital would be far more convenient for patients in these communities, as the facilities are located closer to where they live. Very complex cases would still be referred to the Manhattan hospitals.

Building an integrated care network would not mean that hospitals would disappear. Hospitals would continue to serve as centers for complex patient care, for teaching of medical students, and for postgraduate medical training. Building such a network, however, does mean that the majority of patients are treated as outpatients. Grossman realized that the network concept of care meant that the hospitals themselves will be restricted to adapt to new ways of caring for patients. At NYU Langone Health the vast majority of hospital rooms would be converted to *single-patient facilities*. The words *VA* for Veterans Administration and *Bellevue* represent teaching hospitals for NYU Langone. Woodhull, Long Island, Queens, and Brooklyn would be potential sites for new ambulatory care networks and local hub hospitals.

As mentioned previously, a new, robust, comprehensive information system common to all the hospitals and ambulatory care centers would be essential to building the network. All data would be transparent across all locations.

What Bob Grossman envisioned for the future of NYU Langone Health was a transformative vision, not just for the NYU system but also for health systems everywhere in the United States and in every country.

What Bob Grossman envisioned for the future of NYU Langone Health was a transformative vision, not just for the NYU system but also for health systems everywhere in the United States and in every country. Grossman was among the first to realize and to implement a fundamental change in medicine that is friendly to the patient, provides a higher quality of care, is safer than what came before, and is cost effective. I suggest that the NYU Langone vision and road map be implemented countrywide and, indeed, worldwide.

Discovery

The lower middle left quadrant of the map summarizes the plans ahead for *discovery* and *research*. Discovery and research are divided into two broad categories: *Clinical* and *Basic research*.

Clinical research is patient based. In a clinical trial new methods and procedures are tested on patients under carefully regulated and defined conditions. Favorable results of clinical trials are required to assure adoption of new drugs and procedures that are both safe and effective. Bob Grossman foresaw significant expansion of the role of NYU Langone in *clinical trials,* in partnership with other institutions in the form of *joint ventures.*

Grossman wanted to make NYU Langone a favored site for clinical trials for the National Institutes of Health, as well as the entire industry. This would not be just a source of revenue. He envisioned NYU Langone being involved in the development and testing of new drugs. This would keep the Medical Center on the cutting edge of new developments. It would create *intellectual property* that could translate into the creation of new companies. NYU Langone might have a financial stake in these developments. Patenting inventions to capture the intellectual property rights would be an important area of growth. He would build a strong office of technology transfer and make *strategic investments* of NYU

Langone resources in companies in the early stages of developments that were based on NYU Langone research. He knew that Remicade, a drug recently created and based on the research of an NYU Medical Center scientist, yielded close to $1 billion in royalties for the university.

Grossman knew that to be a world leader in basic research, he would need to attract what he calls *luminary recruits*, scientists with stellar reputations and the charisma to attract other great scientists.

Basic research pushes back the boundaries of the unknown. Basic research focuses on understanding the deep, underlying functions of our bodies and the causes of our diseases. Most advances in basic research are driven by brilliant, innovative scientists. Grossman knew that to be a world leader in basic research, he would need to attract what he calls *luminary recruits*, scientists with stellar reputations and the charisma to attract other great scientists. Luminary scientists could also attract funding from the *National Institutes of Health (NIH)* and *foundations* that support disease-specific research and the careers of great scientists. Grossman also would encourage scientists and teach clinicians to submit joint grants called *program project grants*. These grants are typically much larger than individual grants and encourage the translation of ideas from bench to bedside.

New Facilities

The road map also outlines the plan for extensive renovation of existing facilities and the construction of vast new buildings to house a greatly expanded research enterprise. The existing Tisch Hospital would be entirely renovated. The Kimmel Pavilion would include all private inpatient beds and the Hassenfeld Children's Hospital.

NYU Langone would launch an ambitious program to acquire and build new ambulatory care sites throughout Manhattan, Brooklyn, and Long Island and to build new facilities to house a modern energy plant, *the energy building*, and a *radiation therapy* facility. Replacing the outdated Tisch Hospital elevators was a seemingly trivial, but in fact very important, early change to boost morale and improve efficiency.

Education

Education is a core mission of an academic medical center. Grossman devoted the bottom right quadrant of the map to his thoughts on the future of medical education at NYU. The words *superior education* right at the top and *attract the best scientists and students* capture what would be needed to become a world leader in medical education. At the time, the NYU School of Medicine was ranked thirty-fourth in the country. Under Grossman's leadership that would change. By 2017 the School of Medicine was ranked third in the country, just behind Harvard and Johns Hopkins.

Grossman also proposed major changes in the curriculum, summarized here as *curriculum for the 21st century*. Grossman and his team planned to revise medical education to integrate classroom knowledge with clinical experience that would prepare students for all career options in medicine. There were to be much more than words, as we shall see in the chapters to follow.

The road map proposes a transformative idea in medical education, including shortening medical education to three years from the traditional four. This was to be the first such program for a leading medical school in the country. The shortened eighteen-month preclinical curriculum opened the opportunity to combine a medical degree with a one-year master's degree program in any one of a number of areas, including a master's in business administration or public health. The master's program would draw upon the strength of the NYU graduate schools. In addition, the three-year pathway to a medical degree, linked with an NYU residency in one of twenty specialties, is the first such program in the country.

The road map proposes a transformative idea in medical education, including shortening medical education to three years from the traditional four. This was to be the first such program for a leading medical school in the country.

The road map includes the words *Division of Education Informatics* and *Simulation Center*. Grossman understood that medical education could be improved and enhanced by systematic incorporation of new education methods that rely on information technology. NYU would become a world leader in medical education technologies.

Financing

The execution of the plans outlined in the road map would require substantial investments. The bottom center of the map outlines Grossman's thoughts on financing change. At the top of this list is the word *Philanthropy*. In the middle are the words *Generous Board*, and at the bottom, the words *Transformational Gifts*. Although he anticipated a significant improvement in the financial performance of the hospitals, Grossman knew that would not be enough to finance all the changes he had in mind. Together with Ken Langone and the rest of the board he embraced a very active fundraising effort, one that has brought NYU Langone Health on average more than $240 million a year in philanthropic commitments. These gifts, together with a healthy flow of surplus from hospital revenues, have been the fuel to power the transformation to come.

Success

Both the vision statement and the road map highlight Bob Grossman's extraordinary clarity of thought and insight into the detailed nature of the task ahead. Even more impressive than creating the vision and the road map is the fact that everything outlined in the plan drafted in 2009 was a reality by 2017, thanks to superb execution by Grossman and his team. The ability to capture the complexity of the component parts and to summarize their relationships on a single piece of paper is the characteristic of a great leader, one that holds important lessons for CEOs in many other businesses.

> Even more impressive than creating the vision and the road map is the fact that everything outlined in the plan drafted in 2009 was a reality by 2017.

In the chapters to follow, I will expand on each element of the transformational vision and road map. It's my hope that the description will be clear enough to serve as a guide for others, both in the United States and worldwide, to create their own route to a healthier future for all people.

CHAPTER 3

Leadership, Culture, Communication, Metrics

Leadership and execution convert a vision to a reality. NYU Langone was blessed with three levels of strong and effective leaders: Bob Grossman and the senior executive team he assembled; Ken Langone, Martin Lipton, and the NYU Langone Board of Trustees; and Bob Berne, representing the central administration of New York University. The key element in transforming NYU Langone was leadership.

BOB GROSSMAN TAKES CHARGE

When Bob Grossman assumed the position of CEO and dean, he knew that it was not enough to tinker with the organizational structure to ensure that the NYU hospitals and the School of Medicine would operate as an integrated whole. To create a truly integrated institution, he needed new people to join him in leading the institution.

CLEANING HOUSE

In speaking about his first days on the job, Grossman told me he knew that most of the executive leadership team at the hospital and School of Medicine must go if he was going to create a new culture and seamlessly integrated medical center. He said, "That conviction led me to fire five people on the first day I assumed office." Those he removed included the president and senior vice president of the hospital, the senior vice president of the School of Medicine, the senior vice president of human resources, and the chief medical officer. The chief financial officer was spared only because he was about to take retirement.

"Change is a really difficult thing. In this case, people's livelihoods were suddenly shattered," said Joyce Long, an NYU Langone administrator who has worked under the governance of four deans, including Grossman. She said, "This was truly traumatic. A lot of employees were shaken to their core because the comfort of the culture they had nestled into over the years seemed to be unraveling. But while the leadership firings were abrupt and swift, the organization had indeed grown stale and complacent under their administration; change was inevitable in order for the organization to survive and thrive." Indeed, in Long's view, "sometimes what initially feels like the worst things to happen are really the best things; I'd say that this is true in this case."

Most of those who were walked out of the building on Grossman's first day on the job did not have ready replacements. Steven Galetta is a professor in the Departments of Neurology and Ophthalmology and chair of the Department of Neurology at NYU Langone Health. He said, "Let me tell you a story about my first visit here in 2007 to 2008. I walked up to Grossman's office on the fifteenth floor. His office is at the back of the floor, down a long hallway. Every office on the floor was empty. It was like a ghost town. I thought, 'How is this going to go down?' There he was, alone in the back office." Although a major shake-up was underway, Galetta said of Grossman, "He was his usual happy self, his pathologically optimistic, happy self."

The breadth of Grossman's removals was striking. Chandrika Tandon, a prominent management consultant and NYU Langone trustee, said, "Bob was probably the only chief executive officer I have ever worked with that I thought was proceeding too quickly, and I have worked with more than forty CEOs. I said, 'Bob, this is too fast. What are you thinking about? You cannot change so many things at the same time.'"

"The people Grossman removed should have been fired two, three, four years earlier. Whether they were capable or not, they were not doing their jobs."

This was not a case of a new CEO removing existing managers so that he could install a new team that had already been identified. He was simply removing people that he thought were not doing their jobs well, a view shared by a number of trustees.

In recalling these early traumatic days, William Constantine, a member of the NYU Langone board, said, "The people Grossman removed should have been fired two, three, four years earlier." In Constantine's view, "Whether they were capable or not, they were not doing their jobs." There were issues with everything from the operation of the pharmacy, to the health and safety of operating rooms, to the skills of the finance department. "Every single aspect of running the business of the hospital was struggling," Constantine said. "We did not have an administration even capable of organizing their thoughts on how to attack the broad issues."

Another NYU Langone trustee, Thomas Murphy, said simply, "He cleaned out all of the deadwood." Not until Grossman assumed control were those changes made.

Grossman had discussed his plans for shaking up the ranks of senior management with Ken Langone. At that point, Langone said he told Grossman, "Do whatever you have to do as quickly as you can. Announce you have made the necessary changes and that from now on we will look forward. No one will need to wait for the next shoe to drop."

While Grossman acted quickly, Constantine said, "I thought it was exactly what we needed." He added, "I think if we had brought in a chief executive from the outside, they would have spent a year trying to figure out what Grossman knew coming to work in the morning."

Once the old regime had been dismissed, Grossman began creating a new organizational structure designed to integrate the hospital and medical school staffs. At the same time, he would begin seeking people to fill the new roles. Brotman said the first thing Grossman told him was, "I am not going to have a hospital president. You will be responsible for programs, doctors, and centers. Someone else will be responsible for operations of the hospital." Brotman went on to say, "The two of us would be equal and split the responsibilities."

Dr. Steve Abramson with residents during weekly rounds

Brotman added, "When Bob told me what he was doing and showed me the organizational table, I said to him, 'You are out of your mind. This is a free for all.' He replied, 'Well, we are all clouds, and clouds have a certain overlap.' Bob hates organizational tables. Long story short, I was wrong, he was right. With the people he chose, it works."

Instead of hiring a president for the hospital, Grossman personally took charge of the hospital as well as the medical school so there would no longer be any hierarchy between himself and the department heads. Everyone in the administration would wear two hats, one for the school and one for the hospital. Grossman explained, "When we changed the system, we eliminated a whole level of management." As a result, he said, "We have an open system with no management layers. All the layers are on this floor, in my office. We are a flat organization. We are very agile."

"I said to him, 'You are out of your mind. This is a free for all.' Grossman replied, 'Well, we are all clouds, and clouds have a certain overlap.'"

The structure Grossman was putting in place both flattened the organization and broadened it; silos were being replaced with clouds.

RESHUFFLING DEPARTMENT CHAIRS

After firing most of the incumbent top management and setting out to replace them while restructuring the highest reaches of the NYU Langone organization, Grossman turned his attention to the next level of management. As he explained, "Early on, I visited all the departments for question and answer sessions. I said, 'This is where we want to be. This is the problem.' I pointed out that the researchers were not very productive. I told them we needed to set goals. We created what I call the snapshot process."

The new management team was going to be rigorously measured and reviewed on the basis of objective criteria, Grossman said. He would go on to create a high-tech management information system offering measures of various attributes in real time. Once this was up and running, he said, "We had all of their metrics. We knew what they were doing and where they were going. We knew what was working and what was not working. That gave us a clear view of the performance of each department. I wanted to eliminate what I call the 'ether of ambiguity,' the data free atmosphere wherein people are not accountable for their performance."

Over the next few years, he would replace thirty of the thirty-three department chairs. All of the removals were based on falling short of established performance standards. As he explained, "We worked together to set the performance measurement standards. We did not make a final decision based on one year only. Over time, we got rid of all the underperformers and brought in energetic people."

Changing thirty out of thirty-three department chairs was revolutionary; but in addition, Grossman said, "We cut the salary of tenured people. We took away the lab space of those who did not have independent grant support. We had very little dissent in implementing the new standards." How did he get buy in? "We were looking at the data," Grossman said. "The decisions were apolitical. We were asking each person, 'Do you meet our definition of world class?'"

HIRING THE NEW TEAM

As Grossman was removing so many NYU Langone executives and department chairs, he was also deeply involved in hiring their successors. Grossman sought to bring the same kind of objective measurement to this process, but he would readily admit it was combined with a substantial dose of intuition.

William Constantine said, "The time-honored tradition of selecting the oldest member of the department as chair was long gone." Grossman had developed skills over the years that helped him in choosing the next generation of leaders.

Grossman said, "I did a lot of research. I had a lot of National Institutes of Health funding. I was chair of the study sections. I was also on a National Institutes of Health Council. I understood science. I developed a management style for science."

According to Grossman, "The traditional way academics choose leaders is to review curriculum vitae by saying, 'The person has published X number of papers, received Y numbers of grants, and raised Z amount of money.' Then they interview the candidates one by one." By contrast, Grossman said, "I think I am pretty good at detecting who is good and who has what it takes to transform a department. It is just intuition." He was deeply involved in the selection of department chairs. "I have a search committee that analyzes and presents the candidates," he said, but he added, "I make the decision. It is very important to get the right person. If you get the wrong person, it sets everything back. I made one mistake in hiring thirty new chairs. I corrected that mistake."

Number of papers published by
NYU Langone researchers from 2007 to 2017

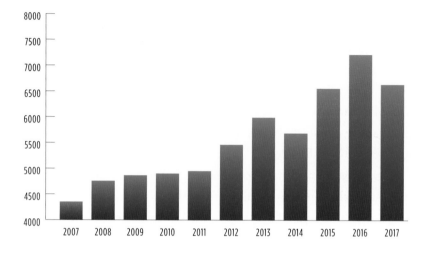

Once he identified a good candidate for a position, he could be decidedly persistent in his recruiting efforts. Steven Galetta said, "Bob tried to recruit me as chair of neurology when he first became CEO and dean. Over the years he would call up and say, 'I want you to be chair of neurology.' I said, 'Bob, I love you, but I do not want to be a chair of neurology. That was not my aspiration.'"

Galetta received twelve recruiting calls from Grossman over four years. Galetta said, "I remember that last call well. I was sitting in my car. It was 6pm, at the end of an April afternoon. He called and said, 'I want you to be chairman.' I said, 'I want you to know that I would not be good at this job.' He says, 'Why is that?' I said, 'I do not really like talking about money with people.' He said, 'You do not have to worry about that. We have that all centralized.' They really did." According to Galetta, "I think one really important thing about NYU Langone is that processes are very centralized. It operates very differently from most academic medical centers. In most schools, a new department chair is given a budget. I call it the dowry. The chair is then let loose to spend the money without having the complete mission of the institution in mind. I think a key element of our current success is centralization. The programs of each department must be consistent with and support the vision and mission of the entire Medical Center. Each chair understands the broader institutional perspectives in which we do our work. We work toward collective, shared goals."

"In most schools, a new department chair is given a budget. I call it the dowry. The chair is then let loose to spend the money without having the complete mission of the institution in mind. I think a key element of our current success is centralization."

Galetta added, "My deal with Bob Grossman was unique. I said to Bob when we were negotiating, 'Bob, I need X.' He said, 'You will get what you need. I might want to spend more money than that. I will not want to limit you to that number.' This was our conversation. He never said he would give me a predetermined budget or number of people to hire. I would have never, ever taken the job if it was not for Bob. I had to trust that he would do what he said he would. And he did. He absolutely did. In Bob Grossman I trust. If he had not lived up to his promise, we would be in a terrible, terrible mess. The department was really in tough shape when I arrived. There were some great people here, but the department needed to be reorganized." By the middle of 2017, Galetta had hired an unprecedented 114 new neurologists to his department with Grossman's support.

COMMUNICATING THE VISION

As Grossman set about installing a new senior staff, Richard Woodrow explained, the next major task was "aligning the vision within the institution" and "communicating the vision to the entire NYU Langone community." Woodrow, NYU Langone's former head of Organizational Development and Learning, argued that the challenges facing Grossman in implementing his vision were "astronomical" for several reasons.

For starters, Grossman "had to create a shared vision that built on and gave respect to the past but was clearly transformative," Woodrow said. He also noted that "many people at NYU Langone thought it was already a world class institution," and therefore "many viewed the vision as an insult." As a result, Woodrow added, "There was very little appetite for tearing down the wall of tradition."

To "facilitate the uptake of the vision," Woodrow said, NYU Langone hired TruePoint, a boutique consulting company that was supposed to "partner with the internal Organizational and Learning Development department and with the emerging senior leadership team." Woodrow said his department, together with TruePoint, "introduced the concept of a listening organization, in which the people at the top were listening to those below and really paying attention." They selected a hundred people throughout the hospital and medical school staff to be interviewed. "We were looking for people that were trusted by everyone in the school and in the hospital. We sought the widest representation possible," Woodrow explained.

Kimberly Glassman, associate dean for Partnership Innovation and chief nursing officer, was one of the eight key leaders tapped to fan out through the Medical Center and interview the one hundred key leaders. "We called ourselves the gang of eight," she said. "Most reported to the senior leaders who reported directly to Bob."

The interviews were scheduled for two hours each, according to Glassman. "The idea was to interview people who did not know me and who worked in areas different from mine. I was assigned to interview the basic science chairs and our top researchers, and the chairs of several clinical departments."

Glassman explained, "We would ask each person about their thoughts on the draft vision statement. We had a specific template to follow for the interview, and we took notes. Nobody wanted to book the full two hours. As it happened, most of the meetings went over time because once people started talking about their ideas, they would not stop."

At the end of the process, Glassman said, "The eight of us sat in a circle in the middle of a conference room. The senior leaders sat behind us and listened to what we had to say to one another. When we finished our discussion, only then were they allowed to ask clarifying questions, to which we could only answer yes or no. They were not allowed to express their opinions. We discussed what we each learned about what people thought about the vision statement based on our one hundred interviews."

"We all know what the mission of the Medical Center is . . . to serve patients, to educate future caregivers, and to advance medical science."

The interviewers had focused on several questions: Was there a clear understanding of what each part of the vision statement meant? Was there clear alignment among the different groups interviewed? Did people think this vision was hokey? Where did people think there were issues?

There was not much debate about the concept of world class, Glassman said, but "many of the basic scientists had concerns over the terms 'patient centered' and 'integrated academic medical center.' They live in a culture where their research is supported by grants. They wondered what the implications of the vision were for them practically. Many felt that the vision meant they would be forced to work closely with clinicians and that might take time away from their research. Never mind the fact that many complained that they had trouble finding clinical collaborators. Many were very clear that they thought that vision statements might be great for some people but had nothing to do with them."

Glassman said, "We arrived at a consensus for the vision statement, which I believe has been very helpful for everyone who works here. We all know what the mission of the Medical Center is as well: to serve patients, to educate future caregivers, and to advance medical science."

FROM CONSENSUS TO ALIGNMENT

Reaching a consensus was, of course, one of the fundamental objectives of this process, Woodrow said. "This exercise began the alignment process . . . Equally important was the discussion of where each group thought the institution was in relationship to the vision. Those discussions brought out critical assessments. We heard comments like 'We love the culture; we hate the lack of resources.' 'We hate the way that people at the top do not seem to really understand what is really going on here in the institution.' Long-buried issues began to come out." Thus, this interviewing process broadened staff members' horizons beyond their silos. Woodrow said, "We began to create a narrative about the identity of NYU Langone—not what we say we are but who we really are."

Glassman and the rest of the gang of eight were charged with developing a Statement of Strategic and Organizational Direction and sharing it with the entire staff. The staff in turn was invited to add ideas to this statement. Grossman's view was that "building belief in the vision" was critical. He said that he "wanted to show the institution that it was much better" than what its critics said, even while pointing out what could and should be improved.

Grossman also held a series of town hall meetings in which he would report on developments and take questions from the audience. . . . He said that people could and should offer their views and suggestions, whether positive or critical, and senior management would listen.

Woodrow added, "One outcome I remember was the need to change the discussions from 'I' to 'we.' We needed to go from the highly individualist culture to one of a shared identity and a shared culture. A consensus also emerged that 'we are good, but we are not excellent.' We have to raise the bar. We have pride in our organization, but we are ashamed of some of the things that were going on, like the sad state of our equipment, the lack of financial resources, and the silencing of people with good ideas."

As these interviews and discussions were being held with staff members, Grossman also held a series of town hall meetings in which he would report on developments and take questions from the audience. Initially, Grossman would deliver prepared speeches. One key message he communicated was that people could and should offer their views and suggestions, whether positive or critical, and senior management would listen.

Woodrow said, "The idea that people should be accountable for their performance emerged from these discussions. Bob very quickly grabbed hold of the idea of accountability."

In order to pursue this idea, Steve Abramson said, "The next step was to work with every leader to create a clear set of objectives. They were asked to describe what they thought needed to be done over the following year. We worked to make sure that each objective aligned with the overall vision. We created benchmarks for performance along the way. We awarded year-end bonuses for those who met objectives or exceeded them."

While this was going on, Grossman and his vice deans began to meet weekly to exchange information on what was going on throughout the organization. For Grossman, this was a means of improving communications and of enhancing collaboration. These meetings would help break down silos and focus on opportunities for integration. In contrast to earlier years, where dissent did not seem to be appreciated, Joyce Long said the message everyone heard from Grossman was, "Even if it is negative, I want to hear it—the good, the bad, the ugly. I want to know what's going on."

TRUST WITH ACCOUNTABILITY

As Grossman's management team set about implementing the new vision and developing a set of processes and procedures, it became clear that Grossman was bringing a unique management style to NYU Langone. He would give his reports broad authority, without micromanaging but remaining involved. He would observe progress and step in when needed to discuss ideas or solve problems.

By way of example, Press said, "At one meeting I mentioned that we needed to reduce our inpatient loss for Medicare patients by eliminating waste. Grossman said, 'You are right. Why don't you lead a program to reduce the loss? I think our goal should be to reduce our inpatient Medicare loss by fifty percent over three years.' I said, 'I do not really think I can do that.' He said, 'No, no. You are going to do it. I will give you some help. You can work with the head of decision support.' It became clear to me early on that we needed to focus on value—quality divided by cost, not just cost control—and to engage all of our staff. When I told Bob that was the focus I thought was best, he said, 'That's great. Do it that way.'"

Grossman was bringing a unique management style to
NYU Langone. He would give his reports broad authority,
without micromanaging but remaining involved.
He would observe progress and step in when needed
to discuss ideas or solve problems.

Senior vice president and vice dean for Real Estate Development and Facilities Vicki Match Suna has been with NYU Langone since 1994. She remembers sitting down and talking with Grossman shortly after he took on his new role. "One of the things that he said from the very beginning was, 'I want to create an environment of excellence and quality, and you need to define what that will require in your world.' When I laid out the path I thought we would need to take to transform our campus in a manner that was consistent with his vision, he immediately said, 'Done. Not a problem. That makes total sense to me and we are going to do it.' For me, as a leader, that was incredibly enabling."

Many others at NYU Langone shared similar experiences with me. Grossman gives his staff the freedom to plan and to execute. He does not micromanage. He works with staff to define a goal and then supports staff members as they develop their own path to achieve the goal. While Grossman does not second-guess his staff, everyone is held accountable. Staff members have goals and objectives, and they are expected to achieve them, or to explain why they didn't.

Robert Press emphasized that the way Grossman went about instilling accountability is by relying on careful, thorough, objective measurement. According to Press, "Bob is incredibly focused on measurement and performance metrics. He carries this focus to a level that allows us to be very successful. One of the first things he did was build an enterprise wide dashboard. The dashboard will never be finished because we keep adding new features."

Grossman agrees with that assessment, arguing that accountability is critical to improvement. "We continually reinforce a commitment to quality and safety. We get rid of people who are not performing." He added, "I work on improving quality and safety every day. Every Tuesday morning, I have all the hospital administrators around the table. We review everything that is going on. We are constantly refining our approach."

In the case of research, for example, Steve Abramson said, "Before Bob Grossman arrived, NYU Langone lacked articulated expectations for research funding and performance for faculty. Many department chairs and faculty were unfunded and beyond the prime of their academic careers. Nothing had changed for a long time. There were serious consequences of that stasis. Up to twenty percent of the research faculty had no grants, nor any expectation of future funding. The salaries of these unfunded faculty members exceeded $20 million a year. The culture was such that unfunded faculty felt entitled to collect their full salary until their retirement, and since there is no longer a fixed age of retirement, the majority stayed in place year after year. The attitude of many other faculty was protective of this culture of entitlement, not in small part due to their concern that in the future they too would be unfunded."

As Andrew Brotman, the medical school's vice dean for Clinical Affairs and Strategy and chief clinical officer, had said, Grossman "turned around the research culture at the School of Medicine. He took the whole research enterprise by the horns and basically said, 'You folks think you are good and productive. Let me show you the data and demonstrate to you that you are not as good or productive as the people we want to be compared to.'" Brotman added, "Grossman and Steve Abramson did the heavy lifting. They completely changed the culture of the research enterprise. They moved it toward big science. They encouraged the professors to work together to obtain cooperative research grants, rather than individually sponsored research grants. They made sure people were accountable for their research performance as measured by grants received and papers published."

Grossman's efforts to change the paradigm ultimately took five to seven years to achieve, according to Abramson. He explained, "One of the first things we did when Bob took over was to create a faculty committee to set performance standards, looking at other leading institutions to be consistent with current best practices. The work took about a year, both to establish standards and to achieve a faculty agreement for the changes. We developed a set of standards and implemented them over the next several years. Key features included the requirement that sixty percent of each faculty research salary be covered by grants. We decided to implement this provision gradually, fifty percent the first year, fifty-five percent the second year, and sixty percent thereafter. We rolled out the recommendation in 2007. The policy became effective in 2008. By 2009 we had implemented the sixty percent requirement. We gave the faculty some time to adjust to the change. In 2010 we announced that we would begin to lower the salary of faculty members whose extramural funding fell below twenty percent. That was a significant challenge to the system of academic tenure, not only at NYU Langone, but nationally."

CULTURE

Among students of management science, there is an ongoing debate as to whether process or culture is more critical in driving quality improvement. Is it more important to carefully design and implement specific methods and procedures in order to achieve desired results? Or is it more effective to establish a collection of attitudes and aspirations that will lead people to pursue the right means and achieve the designated ends? Again and again, Grossman made it clear that he is a firm believer in the importance of culture. In his view, culture has several components.

"In many hospitals, there are surgeons who think they are God. . . . We have people who work for us who are great surgeons, but they are not gods. We have none of the politicized behavioral problems that other institutions experience. We do not tolerate it."

One element of the patient centered culture Grossman sought to instill was an aversion to prima donnas. He said, "We do not have any individuals who are what I would call 'bad actors,' who build a cult of personality around themselves. In many hospitals, there are surgeons who think they are God. Then they think they get away with things. We have people who work for us who are great surgeons, but they are not gods. We have none of the politicized behavioral problems that other institutions experience. We do not tolerate it. We do not have acting out in the operating room. If someone acts out, they are gone. We have decorum in our operating rooms. We treat everybody professionally. It is part of our culture." Grossman emphasized that in the NYU Langone patient centered culture, "Any bad actors that we had soon realized they would not be able to exist here. I think that is really important, that the culture is about the patient. Everyone understands the culture today."

TACKLING TENURE

Another element of the NYU Langone culture is an aversion to permitting staff members to do just enough to get by, to exist in the "ether of ambiguity." Abramson said the process of weeding out underperformers was an arduous one. He explained, "The faculty council at the time was composed of many who felt that tenure protected a faculty member's current and usually peak salary, regardless of funding, publications, or performance." He added, "The intense battles with these influential members of the faculty council lasted at least two years and, frankly, continue though at a lower pitch to this day. There were town hall meetings where some of the faculty disparaged the school and the deans. Fortunately, we had the support of key faculty members and the board. In 2012, after a two-year grace period, we began to lower salaries gradually for faculty who did not meet funding standards for sustained periods."

Meanwhile, Abramson said, "we also established a generous retirement plan." The initial plan offered up to three years of salary and up to a total of $500,000 if faculty members gave up their tenure and retired. About forty faculty members retired with this plan. This was quickly followed by a revised plan, Abramson said, which featured "a program of phased retirement that in my opinion is even more significant. The plan allows for a gradual transition to retirement over three years. Being a faculty member at a medical school can be highly fulfilling as a researcher and teacher among a rich community of physicians and scientists. It is difficult to transition out of that community, often after decades of commitment. Many tenured professors are not willing or prepared for retirement. Since tenure also makes it possible to earn substantial income, retirement can be an even less attractive option. Therefore, we needed a culture change, by establishing fair and enforceable productivity metrics, and offering a respectful path to retirement."

The new retirement plan featured a three-step transition period. A faculty member who opts for this program declares a retirement date.

In the subsequent year, responsibilities and salary are set at seventy-five percent of the baseline rate, and are then reduced to fifty percent in year two. In year three, the faculty member reverts to part time, but receives a payment of one to two times their full-time salary at baseline. "It is a way for people to close their labs down slowly," Abramson said. "They maintain their full-time tenured status during the phase down. The phased plan has changed attitudes toward retirement. The retirement program led to fifty-eight signed agreements that generated a total savings of nearly $15 million over the course of eleven years."

Implementing this was not easy. Abramson said, "In 2013, we were sued by two faculty members. They were supported by the American Association of University Professors (AAUP). The Association has a history of defending tenured faculty when universities attempt to lower salaries." The case went to judgment in the Supreme Court of the State of New York, New York County, and the judge dismissed the lawsuit, finding for NYU and supporting the school's right to establish performance guidelines as well as the right to lower salaries as implemented. It was consistent with terms of tenure as described in the faculty handbook. This ruling was reversed at the appellate level, which ordered the lawsuit to be reinstated and to proceed with discovery.

But in Abramson's view, the results of these legal proceedings "may well turn out to be a landmark nationally, establishing a legal precedent for salary reduction of unproductive tenured faculty, a hotly debated and contentious issue nationwide."

"Mediocrity is not accepted here. There is a little bit of pressure, a little bit of heat to perform, to be your best. I think it filters right down all the way from the top. It is a special environment and you have to bring your 'A' game."

Gradually, Grossman's new template took hold. Jan Vilcek, the faculty member and trustee whose research led to the development of Remicade, said, "In the first couple of years Grossman ruffled some feathers. Over the last few years I have not heard anything negative about his leadership."

Abramson said, "When Bob Grossman took over, the culture changed—expectations consistent with those at other major academic medical centers were established. It took us seven years to fully change the culture. The change in the culture, the raising of expectations for academic productivity, has been one of the contributing factors that has brought NYU School of Medicine from a *U.S. News & World Report* rank of number thirty-four in 2007 to number three today."

Steven Galetta emphasized the importance of accountability. He said, "Mediocrity is not accepted here. There is a little bit of pressure, a little bit of heat to perform, to be your best. I think it filters right down all the way from the top. It is a special environment and you have to bring your 'A' game. We are lucky that we have a group of people we can hire who are all dedicated to our mission."

Galetta noted, "No one here, from top to bottom, wants to settle for being second best. Everybody wants to be the best. Everybody pulls in the same direction here. I really think that is the desire to be the best and that your work is not done until you get to that level. Our work is not yet done. There is a feeling of tremendous momentum. All our oars are in the water and everybody is rowing together. That is how I think it is different."

"Everybody wants to be the best. . . .
There is a feeling of tremendous momentum.
All our oars are in the water and everybody
is rowing together. That is how I think it is different."

Continuing communications is an important part of maintaining quality control and achieving accountability, in Grossman's view. Early on he instituted weekly meetings with the chairs of all thirty-three departments.

"It is a big, highly structured meeting. We discuss what we are doing so everyone understands," Grossman said. "I try to meet with the individual departments once a year, or at least once every other year. I have a one-on-one meeting with each department chair at least once every year. Every month, I write and circulate an article that speaks about the culture. It is called 'In Touch.' It is popular."

Because of the emphasis on open lines of communications, Grossman said, "People here know that if they have an idea of a better way to do things, we are willing to try to see if it works."

ETHICS

An organizational culture is not designed and implemented by fiat. It has to be planted and nourished, and a major part of that process is the tone at the top. This is the view that the way the most senior management conducts itself, what it does as well as what it says, generates messages that are absorbed and assimilated by the rest of the organization. If management cuts corners or dissembles, then it must be okay for others throughout the organization to do the same. If top management displays high ethical standards, disseminates information quickly and widely, or criticizes underlings in front of others, then others in the organization believe they can do the same.

Abramson said Grossman has established a particular tone that blends optimism and metrics. "I know that there are not many people who are as optimistic as Bob Grossman," Abramson said.

Press agreed. "Bob is not easily discouraged. If others tell him that one of the goals he sets is unattainable, he will say, 'No, we can do it.' We have met most of the goals Bob set that others thought were unrealistic."

For example, increased faculty research funding was one of Grossman's goals. He said he would make it a requirement that all researchers have at least one investigator-initiated grant from the National Institutes of Health, and preferably two. At the time, few of the research faculty were supported by NIH grants. Many doubted that they could achieve this goal. But Grossman offered help with writing grants for researchers and providing other support they need to submit grants.

"Needless to say, we met the goal," Press said. "Bob had a similar goal when it came to the quality and safety of our patient care. When he became CEO and dean, we were rated around number sixty in the country in terms of quality and safety according to our benchmarking organization, UHC (University HealthSystem Consortium), well below the middle of the pack." Bob worked closely with Bernard Birnbaum, former senior vice president and vice dean, chief of Hospital Operations, to launch the initiative. Since 2013, NYU Langone has been ranked either number one or number two in the country for quality and safety.

Grossman's optimism was interwoven with aspiration. He frequently made it clear he had high expectations. For example, Burke said, "I remember saying to our team, 'We have to get used to a paradigm shift in how you perform. It is no longer okay to have a one or two percent margin. You have to aspire toward ten percent.'" Press, the former chief of Hospital Operations, said that Grossman was very driven and that he loved working for him. "He is never satisfied with the status quo. No matter how well we do, he wants us to do better still. Bob will celebrate our successes, but he does not want us to rest on our laurels. Excellence is a moving target. If you sit on the status quo, you will fall behind. Bob's goal is for our Medical Center to be world class and to be as good, or better than, any other institution in the world. That aspiration is incorporated into our mission statement."

"Excellence is a moving target. If you sit
on the status quo, you will fall behind."

METRICS

While such themes as optimism and aspiration are important in the NYU Langone Health culture, the most critical element of the tone Grossman established is the emphasis on measurement. Grossman insisted that he and others should not be driven by opinions but by data. He built a comprehensive, real time information system, and his decisions would be guided by it. In every corner of the organization, in every activity undertaken, input and output would be measured closely. How much money was spent? How many hours were involved? What was the mortality rate for that procedure? On average, how many days was the patient in the hospital for that procedure this year as opposed to last year?

In his efforts to deploy new practices and measure them closely, Grossman was prepared to spend money, even though early in his tenure money was tight. Abramson said, "Bob Grossman's arrival changed the entire dynamic. Instead of looking at the annual $150 million deficit and saying, 'Cut budgets, you cannot do this, you cannot do that,' he said, 'We are going to strategically spend our way out of this.' Bold initiatives were taken at a time when the lack of revenue was a serious and potentially existential problem."

Most notably, as will be reported later in the book, when Grossman took office, he invested $200 million on a new information system called Enterprise Epic. Abramson insisted decisions like this one were transformative. He said, "Our information system now accounts for much of our success. There is no doubt. I cannot think of anyone I have ever worked with who would have taken that risk."

Grossman required a highly sophisticated and comprehensive management information system because of his emphasis on objective measurement and accountability. As Ken Langone put it, "Bob prays at only one altar, competence and ability. He is data driven." Langone added, "It is a mistake to think that because Bob hires you, you need not perform at your very best. Bob is objective about the decisions he makes, even his own decisions. If the data shows he hired the wrong person, he makes a change. We have replaced several of the department heads he hired. The toughest thing in the world to do is to correct one of your own faulty decisions."

EARLY WINS

While Grossman went to great lengths to ground decisions in data and focus on improving major components of NYU Langone's activities, he also understood the importance of symbolic gestures and actions. He understood that people need early wins to build enthusiasm and gather momentum.

The re-imagining of the much maligned elevators in the Tisch Hospital was one of those early wins. For many years, New York University board chairman William Berkley said that it was very clear that "we needed new elevators for the hospital. Everybody hated the elevators. They were detrimental to the quality of life for everyone who worked here." The elevators were notoriously slow; they often required passengers to go down before they could go up; there were often lengthy delays in getting an elevator; and they seemed perpetually crowded.

"Bob told us, 'While the money we spend on the elevators will not help make a patient better tomorrow, it changes how people feel about what we do.'"

"Before Bob, everyone explained why it was a problem and why we could not fix it," Berkley said. Grossman didn't believe that. He turned the elevator breakdown into a breakthrough community moment. A large anonymous gift from a longstanding benefactor family was dedicated to creating the Tisch Hospital Elevator Tower, which was a free-standing structure connected to the hospital and providing access to its eighteen-story bed tower. By doubling the number of elevators that serve patient floors, the new tower transformed daily life at the hospital for staff and visitors alike. The gift also helped expand and renovate the main lobby, adding new amenities for patients and visitors. NYU Langone also used the gift to renovate entrances on the first floor of the building and on all patient floors. When the new entrances were unveiled and the elevator tower was opened, the outpouring of gratitude and appreciation from the community was dramatic.

"It totally transformed people's image of what could be done," said Berkley. In Berkley's view, Grossman "understood how important it was for the employees to know that we were willing to spend money to fix what needed fixing. Bob told us, 'While the money we spend on the elevators will not help make a patient better tomorrow, it changes how people feel about what we do.'" Berkley said the elevator story is telling because it illustrates that Grossman "had a sense of how to have people understand that an institution is moving in the right direction."

In addition to expediting the improvement in the Tisch Hospital elevators, Berkley pointed out that "another small but significant early change was that Bob greatly improved cafeteria food." Both staff members and those visiting patients have had positive things to say about the high quality and low cost of the upmarket offerings in the hospital cafeteria. The cafeteria offers the usual pizzas and tuna sandwiches, but there are also daily specials like rack of lamb for eight dollars. The cafeteria, like the elevators, was a highly visible symbol of institutional change.

FOLLOW THE ROAD MAP

The steps Grossman took as CEO were replicating what he did as head of the radiology department. "He totally transformed the department," Sheilah Rosen, manager of the office of the dean and CEO, recalled. "His goal was to become the best department of radiology in the world. He asked each of the section chiefs to prepare a report in which they compared their respective sections to what they considered the best counterparts in other institutions. Based on their reports, the department created a strategic initiative." Rosen noted, "He met with the vice chairs of radiology every Tuesday, and there was a very open discussion. He encouraged them to speak their mind. Sometimes they would disagree with him. Then he would say 'I agree with you,' or explain why he didn't." She added, "When he became the dean and chief executive officer, he held similar meetings with the vice deans with the same open atmosphere." In other ways as well, Grossman worked off the same playbook he had used as a department chair.

As he made and implemented his continuing series of difficult and often controversial decisions, his standing was bolstered by three attributes. One was his willingness, indeed eagerness, to hear the views of others. He encouraged open expression as a means of obtaining information and guidance. Another important attribute was his reliance on objective data. He did not play favorites or hold grudges; he pushed hard for the development of data measuring every corner of NYU Langone, and he went where the data led him. His authority was also enhanced by his standing as a highly regarded radiologist. "Bob was not only a good scientist; he was also incredibly good clinically," Galetta said.

While Grossman was spearheading this revolution, there were two other important sources of leadership and power: his board of trustees and the university's hierarchy.

CHAPTER 4

The Board

Many stories of organizational transformation in business focus only on the CEO. In many stories of business transformation, the role of the board is confined to choosing a new CEO. As founder and chair of many companies, I have a different view. Yes, the choice of a CEO is critical to success. But that is not the beginning or the end of their responsibility.

While Grossman was spearheading this revolution, there were two other important sources of leadership and power: his board of trustees and the university's hierarchy.

CREATE THE CONDITIONS FOR SUCCESS

An effective board creates the conditions for success. The boards must agree to the need for fundamental change. The board must enthusiastically endorse the vision and the road map of the new leader. The board must then enable the new leader to do his or her job. The board must help wherever it can, especially financially. Boards must also run interference for the new leader. A board may delegate decision making day to day and week to week to a small internal executive group.

Very often powerful players within the existing enterprise will seek to use their connections with board members to undermine and derail changes they may view as personally threatening to their own positions of power. Boards must protect a leader of transformational change from such backstabbing.

What a board must not do is equally important. A board must not interfere or meddle with the daily execution. As a group the board must do what Bob Grossman did as an individual: agree to a broad outline of change, empower the changemaker, and leave the changemaker free to execute the plan, but measure and hold the changemaker accountable for the results. NYU Langone has been and continues to be blessed with a board that meets these criteria.

At many institutions, boards of directors or trustees show up monthly or quarterly to vote yes on whatever management asks with little direct interaction. Not so at NYU Langone. While Grossman formulated NYU Langone's strategy and direction, the board was actively involved in helping him shape his ideas and implement his aspirations.

The New York University and NYU Langone boards of trustees, particularly Ken Langone and Martin Lipton, played a critical role in driving the transformation of NYU Langone, as did Bob Berne acting on behalf of the university president, John Sexton. The university board created the framework for the integrated medical center central to Grossman's plans for transformation. The trustees of the Medical Center provided guidance on strategy and execution as well as leadership in fundraising, enabling Grossman to execute his strategy. The university administration was also involved in creating the initial conditions that allowed Grossman to transform NYU Langone into an integrated and successful medical center. Thereafter they maintained solidarity with Grossman as he pursued policies that his critics thought were inappropriate for universities or medical centers. Again and again, the administration refused to offer comfort to those who sought to undermine Grossman's policies.

AN ACTIVE BOARD

At many institutions, boards of directors or trustees show up monthly or quarterly to vote yes on whatever management asks with little direct interaction. Not so at NYU Langone. While Grossman formulated NYU Langone's strategy and direction, the board was actively involved in helping him shape his ideas and implement his aspirations. They not only contributed and raised money but also offered advice and ideas, and they worked with other members of the broader business and national community.

In explaining the role of the NYU Langone board, former NYU president John Sexton said, "When a vacuum in leadership exists, such as might have existed at the Medical Center in the late nineties, good folks who ordinarily would not get involved in daily operations often rush into the void. So, the trustees, notably Ken Langone and Marty Lipton, became much more involved in direct management of the university, and especially the Medical Center, than is customary."

Several other board members besides Langone and Lipton also played significant roles in driving the transformation of NYU Langone, including two members of the Tisch family. They were continuing their family's deep involvement with the university. Laurence Tisch became chairman of the university board in 1978, and Lipton noted Tisch "worked closely with former NYU president John Sawhill." After Larry Tisch died in 2003, his son, Tom, and Tom's wife, Alice Tisch, would serve on the NYU Langone board.

Other board members could be counted on to use their influence when asked to do so. The board of trustees comprised a number of influential, decisive business leaders. Recent trustees include

Kenneth G. Langone, Chair - President & CEO - Invemed Associates

Fiona B. Druckenmiller, Co-Chair - Founder - FD Gallery

Laurence D. Fink, Co-Chair - Chairman & CEO - BlackRock

William R. Berkley - Executive Chairman - W.R. Berkley Corporation

Casey Box - Executive Director - Land Is Life

Edgar Bronfman, Jr. - Managing Partner - Accretive

Walter W. Buckley, Jr. - Founder & President - Buckley Muething Capital Management Co.

Susan Block Casdin

Kenneth I. Chenault - Chairman & Managing Director - General Catalyst

Melanie J. Clark

William J. Constantine - Managing Director - 1919 Investment Counsel

Jamie Dimon - CEO & Chairman of the Board - JPMorgan Chase & Co.

Lori Fink

Luiz Fraga - Co-Founder & Co-CIO of Private Equity - Gavea Investimentos

Paolo Fresco

Trudy E. Gottesman

Mel Karmazin

Sidney Lapidus - Retired Partner - Warburg Pincus, LLC

Thomas H. Lee - President - Thomas H. Lee Capital, LLC

Laurence C. Leeds, Jr. - Chairman - Buckingham Capital Management

Martin Lipton, Esq. - Partner - Wachtell, Lipton, Rosen & Katz

Stephen F. Mack - Principal - Mack Real Estate Group

Roberto A. Mignone - President - Bridger Management

Edward J. Minskoff - President - Edward J. Minskoff Equities, Inc.

Thomas K. Montag - Chief Operating Officer - Bank of America

Thomas S. Murphy, Sr. - Chairman & CEO (Retired) - Capital Cities/ABC, Inc.

Thomas S. Murphy, Jr. - Co-Founder - Crestview Partners, LLC

Frank T. Nickell - Chairman & CEO - Kelso & Company

Debra Perelman - President & CEO - Revlon, Inc.

Ronald O. Perelman - Chairman & CEO - MacAndrews & Forbes Holdings, Inc.

Isaac Perlmutter - CEO - Marvel Enterprises

Laura Perlmutter

Douglas A. Phillips - CEO - GYST Advisors, LLC

Richard P. Richman - Founder & Chairman - The Richman Group

Linda Gosden Robinson - Senior Advisor - BlackRock

E. John Rosenwald, Jr. - Vice Chairman - JPMorgan

Alan D. Schwartz - Executive Chairman - Guggenheim Partners, LLC

Barry F. Schwartz - Executive Vice Chair & Chief Administrative Officer - MacAndrews & Forbes Holdings, Inc.

Bernard L. Schwartz - Chairman & CEO - BLS Investments, LLC

Larry A. Silverstein - Chairman - Silverstein Properties, Inc.

Carla Solomon, PhD

William C. Steere, Jr. - Chair Emeritus - Pfizer, Inc.

Charles M. Strain - Partner - Farrell Fritz

Daniel Sundheim - CEO - D1 Capital Partners

Chandrika Tandon - Chair - Tandon Capital Associates

Allen R. Thorpe - Managing Director - Hellman & Friedman

Alice M. Tisch

Thomas J. Tisch - Managing Partner - Four Partners - Chancellor, Brown University

Robert M. Valletta

Jan T. Vilcek, MD, PhD - Professor of Microbiology - NYU School of Medicine

Bradley J. Wechsler - Chairman of the Board - IMAX Corporation

Anthony Welters, Esq. - Executive Chairman - Black Ivy Group, LLC

Collectively, the roster of board members, which turns over very slowly, has included the elite from New York's powerful financial community and philanthropists. Despite the impressive board, not all were involved in the operations of the Medical Center. Martin Lipton, former chair of the university, pointed out, "Large boards do not work as a board on many issues. Most of the work is done by the board committees."

Two board members were deeply involved in guiding developments at NYU Langone: Ken Langone and Martin Lipton. They provided daily assistance, guidance, advice, and support—as well as protective cover—to Bob Grossman. From Grossman's first day, he was on the phone with Langone several times a day. Similarly, Martin Lipton was also on the phone to Grossman daily until his retirement as board chair in 2015.

KEN LANGONE

Ken Langone has played an important, multifaceted, and highly visible role at the Medical Center from the day he joined, both as chair of the board of the Medical Center and on the board of NYU. He has been a regular advisor to Bob Grossman. He has also been a visible figure at the hospitals. He drops by the hospital several times a week and often attends employee gatherings. He has been highly effective in connecting with political leaders and potential donors on behalf of NYU Langone.

Grossman said, "Ken Langone is an amazing board chair. If there is one person who made a key difference, it is Ken Langone. He did everything. He was totally aligned with me. He is a fantastic, phenomenal fundraiser. He bought into everything. He has given us more than $300 million in total and has worked tirelessly with our board and key donors to achieve our $3 billion dollar philanthropic goal. To this day, he remains fully engaged."

"Ken is a guy that backs his guy. When Ken backs somebody, he does not let go. In a way, the success of the Medical Center is the fruit of the marriage between Bob Grossman and Ken Langone."

The university and the Medical Center have overlapping boards, and Ken Langone is on both. In explaining the close relationship between Langone and Grossman, NYU board chair William Berkley said, "In many ways the New York University Medical Center board is much more like an entrepreneurial founder board than it is like a large corporate board. You do see that kind of involvement in entrepreneurial companies. I will say it is unusual for a university board." He added, "There is really a symbiotic relationship."

Anthony Welters, a vice chair and officer of the board, agreed. As he put it, "Ken Langone's engagement cannot be underestimated. It is hard to push change as a chief executive officer if the board of trustees and the leadership are not in sync."

One trustee said, "Ken is a guy that backs his guy. When Ken backs somebody, he does not let go. In a way, the success of the Medical Center is the fruit of the marriage between Bob Grossman and Ken Langone."

Langone is always in constant contact with Grossman, offering advice and counsel on almost every aspect of the institution's operations. But Langone was also deeply involved in interacting with NYU Langone employees at all levels, as well as with any and all other stakeholders.

In Langone's view, to motivate people, "the three most powerful things in the world are a kind word, a thoughtful gesture, and passion for what you do." He said, "If you can show people that something is critical to you and you really want to do it, they will understand what you want and do their very best to help you, or they will leave."

Chair of the NYU Langone board of trustees Ken Langone at a staff appreciation lunch

The aspirations to improve everything, to move forward, to be the best, were constantly reinforced by Langone's management style. Langone said, "We let the people at the Medical Center know that we were in the trenches with them. As long as they did their very best, we would do our very best to reward them."

In Langone's view, to motivate people, "the three most powerful things in the world are a kind word, a thoughtful gesture, and passion for what you do."

Nancy Sanchez, senior vice president and vice dean, human resources and organizational development and learning, credits Langone with instilling a new spirit in the employees and helping to raise their morale as they worked to make the new vision of the Medical Center a reality. Sanchez believes Langone brought a page of his Home Depot playbook to the Medical Center as he sought to develop a highly engaged workforce. "I know that he truly believes what he says about the importance of each employee," she said. "He also demonstrates his philosophy. His office is not that far from here. He will come in at any time. He will stop and speak to people. He will say hello to the guards. He remembers them and their families. He holds town hall meetings with the faculty and the nurses. He is very engaged with the support staff. Everyone loves talking with him. He comes to our employee recognition events."

Langone agrees that he brought the same focus on customer service to NYU Langone that he had emphasized at Home Depot. He sought to ensure that "patient centered" was not merely a slogan but a guiding force in decision making. Langone said this high touch and friendly approach is his trademark

"That is my style. For example, Bernie Marcus and Arthur Blank ran Home Depot on a day-to-day basis. About three years on we had a meeting of the outside directors of Home Depot. None of them had any retail experience. I started making some comments about the details of the operation. The other board members asked, 'Where did you learn that?' 'In the store.' They said, 'What do you mean?' I replied, 'I go to the store and I talk to the kids. They tell me.' I said, 'You know what? How about if we make it a policy that every director must visit three stores unannounced every ninety days. Walk through the store, talk to a customer, talk to an associate. Then go to the store manager, introduce yourself to the store manager, and say, 'Do me a favor, send me a dozen kids into the break room. I want to talk to them.' And you get there and you say, 'I am one of the directors of the company. What is on your mind? What bothers you? What are we doing wrong that needs to be fixed?' We set that policy then and there."

Langone has been doing much the same at the Medical Center. In describing his personal approach, he told me, "It may seem theatrical, but I hope you believe that it is more than theatrical for me. When I walk into the hospital, I dearly hope there is something on the floor so I can bend down and pick it up. I want everyone to say to themselves, 'If he's not above doing it, then I'm not above doing likewise.' I make it a point to make a fuss over the guards. I shake their hands. I ask, 'How are you doing? Is everything okay?' I tell them, 'You guys are doing a great job. Is this place not wonderful?'"

A number of NYU Langone executives have said that Langone's interactions with staff energized them at a very critical moment and had an important effect on management practices throughout the Medical Center. Nancy Sanchez said, "There is nothing more uplifting to a staff member than when Ken remembers their past conversations. I have told managers time and time again, money is important, benefits are important, but what really makes the most difference is the day-to-day thank you, the public acknowledgment that you did a great job, and the fact that you are willing to stop and have a conversation. That is Ken's philosophy, which I follow and always encourage all leaders to do the same."

Richard Tsien, the director of the Neuroscience Institute, offered yet another testimonial to Langone's impact: "Ken is a magnetic, charismatic believer." Tsien added that this attitude has rubbed off. "If you ask the average person that you meet in an elevator how you like it here, you get a very positive answer. Almost every nurse you meet, every janitor, every doctor says, 'I really like it here.' That is palpable." This attitude inevitably translates into people doing their jobs more effectively and treating patients better.

While Langone is often a highly visible presence at NYU Langone, he said that he is careful about where and how he involves himself in the Medical Center's activities. "The worst thing I could do is to encroach or insinuate myself unless I am asked," he said, "but if I am asked, I will go the extra mile."

MARTIN LIPTON

In addition to Langone, the other crucial board member has been Martin Lipton, who recruited Langone. Lipton was a crucial intermediary in the relationship between NYU Langone and the university. He could call upon a vast network of influential and affluent individuals he knew from his law practice, which was centered on mergers and acquisitions involving major corporations.

Lipton was a classic example of a student who had a strong desire to give back to an institution that he felt had given him much. Lipton, who was born in 1931, graduated from NYU Law School in 1955, and over the course of six decades, he would go on to be a faculty member, a board member of the university and Langone Health, a confidant of several NYU presidents, and a significant donor. Indeed, Lipton played every imaginable role that loyal sons and daughters could play for their alma mater.

Lipton says of the troika—Grossman, Lipton, and Langone: "We have become very close. So we discuss issues all the time." Indeed, he said that there is not only a close relationship between Grossman,

Langone, and Lipton, but also between "the Langones, the Liptons, and the Grossmans," three couples who see each other socially.

> "Our board and its leadership have been critically important. If you do not have a supportive board, then everything is a battle. You can never get to the finish line. You lose traction and use up a lot of energy uselessly."

Because of the close interactions between Grossman and Langone and Lipton, Bob Berne said, "The boards of the Medical Center and the university permitted us to take prudent risks and to do the things we needed to do." He added, "Ken Langone has been a phenomenal leader at the Medical Center. Marty Lipton has been a phenomenal leader at the university. They understand each other and get along very well. We have been very fortunate. Our board and its leadership have been critically important. If you do not have a supportive board, then everything is a battle. You can never get to the finish line. You lose traction and use up a lot of energy uselessly."

INCOME FROM REMICADE

Langone's background in business and his involvement as a political donor have both been put to good use at NYU Langone Health. His financial expertise and proactive management style were demonstrated in negotiations over the drug Remicade. Johnson & Johnson, the company that held the license and rights to sell Remicade, offered to give NYU Langone $80 million as a final royalty payment. Langone chose to personally look into this offer: "I asked for a meeting with representatives of the company. At the meeting I said, 'Okay, help me out. How did you come up with the number $80 million?' They said, 'Well, the drug will have sales of $100–$200 million a year, and you will get four-and-a-half percent. Eighty million dollars is the net present value for that royalty stream.'"

At that point Langone said, "'Let me get back to you after I do some more research.' I called ten Wall Street analysts that cover the drug business and asked them what their estimate of future sales of Remicade were likely to be. Their projections were all very much higher than those given to us by Johnson & Johnson. I knew that meant that the value of the future royalties would very likely be much more than $80 million."

Langone said, "I then called the folks at Johnson & Johnson and said, 'Help me out. We know these analysts run these numbers by you. There is a big gap between their assumption about future Remicade sales and the ones you gave us. How do you square that?' The reply was, 'Well, you are an educational institution. You are depending on the money. We were concerned about you not taking more risk.' I said, 'Do us a favor. We are big boys. We will take our own risk. We are not interested in selling. Thank you.'"

Langone added, "At the time, the financial team at the university did not fully agree. Tensions will exist between a professional staff and the guys like me, always. They tried to persuade the trustees to accept the offer. I called Marty Lipton and said, 'Marty, we cannot do this.'" Lipton agreed, and since then, NYU Langone went on to sell the future stream of revenues for some $650 million, plus additional contingent royalties in the event that royalties exceed a threshold.

"Ken was absolutely right," Berne said. "Johnson & Johnson low-balled us."

THE UNIVERSITY

In addition to the board of trustees, the other center of leadership and power that had the potential to advance or retard NYU Langone's revitalization was the central administration of the university. NYU president John Sexton played an important role in setting in motion structural changes that brought together the hospitals and the medical school under a single leadership team. Sexton also made the final decision, in conjunction with the board of trustees, to choose Bob Grossman. Then he essentially gave Grossman the freedom to do his job. What was most important about NYU's role in many ways was not what it did, but what it did not do. The university did not interfere with or countermand Grossman's decisions.

NYU president John Sexton played a major role in the transformation of NYU from what was essentially a commuter school whose student body was composed largely of New York City residents into a leading national research university.

Sexton, who had been dean of the NYU Law School, was named president of the university in 2002 and held that position until 2015. He played a major role in the transformation of NYU from what was essentially a commuter school whose student body was composed largely of New York City residents into a leading national research university. As Sexton was preparing to take office as president, he recalled, he and his deputy, Bob Berne, "worked over the summer of 2001 to plan the Medical Center's future. We developed a plan, which, over time, could bring excellence." The plan they were developing went far beyond the Medical Center, Sexton noted: "We ultimately developed a mature strategy for achieving excellence in science. One of the things I am most proud of is the attitude toward science here at the university that has developed in the last fifteen years."

Sexton acknowledged that "our initial strategy was primitive. In retrospect, it was more a pathway than a strategy. The two big decisions were first to stay in medicine and second to de-merge our hospitals from Mount Sinai. The next decision was to find new leadership for our medical activities. Simultaneously, we decided to unify the chief executive officer of the hospital and the dean of the medical school."

Sexton added, "I give Bob Berne credit for maybe ninety-nine percent of that decision." He said they reached the decision to hire a single CEO and dean "during the search for a new dean."

BOB BERNE

Once a new structure and new leadership had been put in place, Sexton said Bob Berne became his day-to-day eyes and ears on what was essentially the university's wholly owned subsidiary. Early in his tenure as university president, John Sexton said, "I conceived the idea that Bob Berne should be my alter ego for medical affairs. When we started, there had never been such a post."

Sexton had known Berne for many years. Berne had been the dean of the Wagner School of Public Service when Sexton was dean of the NYU Law School. Sexton added, "Even more important, we were almost brothers. We trusted each other completely. I decided that he should be responsible for medical affairs. I said, 'Listen, what I want you to do is be on this seven days a week, twenty-four hours a day.'"

Berne did not have a medical background, Sexton said, "but I knew he and I thought the same way. In the beginning, we spoke every day for at least a half an hour. He brought me into real time with the situation. For the first six or seven years, we continued to speak at least half an hour every day. If there was an acute situation, I would jump in with him."

From NYU Langone's perspective, there were times when Berne would take actions that went beyond the scope of what NYU Langone executives could do on their own. For example, when there were issues with the accounts payable system at the university and with getting bills paid, Berne stepped in to navigate between the two institutions and helped to integrate the School of Medicine's and hospital's finances.

Berne's office was next to Sexton's, and Sexton said, "I made it clear to the dean of medicine, the chief executive officer of the hospital, the dean of dentistry, and the dean of the nursing school that they reported to him as if he were me." Berne kept this role until he retired in 2017.

In many respects, Sexton and Berne were most important to the transformation of NYU Langone because of several things that they did not do: They did not block the efforts of Grossman and Langone to transform NYU Langone, or second-guess Grossman's strategy, or offer refuge for those within the Medical Center who took issue with Grossman's approach and were seeking to go over Grossman's head and appeal to the central university leadership. Grossman said, "I think the university felt they had so many other things going on that as long as I did not want a dime from them, everything I did was okay."

As Grossman saw it, "Being left alone is a great thing. All I needed was their tacit support. I did not want any end runs, the type that typically happen early on. People get hold of the president and say, 'Grossman is trying to destroy the institution. He is destroying tenure.' If you can manage that part of it, then you can do what is needed. John Sexton and Bob Berne did a really great job in not letting the faculty disrupt what we were trying to do." He added, "It helped that, in contrast to a lot of reformers who want money from the university, I did not ask for a dime." Instead of asking the university for help with raising money, Grossman noted, "we built our own fundraising program."

> As Grossman embarked on his sweeping, and controversial, path to transforming NYU Langone, he benefited greatly from the support of both his board of trustees and the NYU administration.

Meanwhile, Sexton said, "Bob Grossman and his dashboards! He is a driven person. But you did not become number one in quality and safety unless you are a driven person. We've got another driven person in Ken Langone. Ken brings here to the Medical Center the same strategic instinct and the same attention to detail that he brings to his businesses. Everything from grand innovative moves to clean floors draws his attention. He is a force of nature."

While the decision-making framework was supportive, Lipton said, "I think the thing that marks Bob Grossman as special is having created an organization that has the culture of, 'We are going to make this the best academic medical center in the world.' Everybody bought into that. The trustees bought into it. John Sexton did. Usually, there is this tension between a medical center and the administration of the university. Everybody bought into it. Also, Bob has worked it hard. By aspiring to being world class, Grossman created a meaningful yet lofty standard, and convinced everyone that they could and must help reach that standard."

As Grossman embarked on his sweeping, and controversial, path to transforming NYU Langone, he benefited greatly from the support of both his board of trustees and the NYU administration. Innovators face the risk of dangerous isolation from those parts of the organization that are hesitant or resistant to change; they can be undercut by appeals to other power centers. But that couldn't happen at NYU Langone.

Sexton said, "We have an interesting dynamic. The two people who drive excellence at the Medical Center are Ken Langone and Bob Grossman. They both are hugely ambitious, in the best sense of the word—ambitious to do good. Bob Berne often brought a dose of reality. Together, the trio was exactly what was needed. Marty Lipton and I supplied support, absolute support, for their decisions. And everybody knew there was no separating us." Sexton added, "Bob Grossman saw us as a team. He had the unwavering support and affection of Ken Langone, Marty Lipton, Bob Berne, and me. That made a big difference."

PART II

Execution

CHAPTER 5

Comprehensive, Integrated, Transparent, Actionable Information in Real Time

To transform NYU Langone into the institution he envisioned, Bob Grossman told me, "My first priority was structural change. My second priority was information technology." From the very beginning Grossman was focused on building a comprehensive, integrated, and transparent information system that, in real time, would enable NYU Langone management to know where things stood, where they were headed, and where they needed to be. This chapter describes the creation of that system.

FLYING BLIND

In 2007, Grossman met with all the departments. He needed detailed performance information to inform these discussions. When he asked those who should know how and where to get the data, he said he was told, "Bob, we cannot do it." He was shown "books and books and books that contained the information" he sought, but "it was impossible to extract the information I needed from those records efficiently. The feeling was like flying a 747 without a control panel." Shortly after he became dean and CEO, he called a group of colleagues together and said, "I feel like I am flying a big jumbo jet blind. The information I need to pilot the institution is not available to me."

It is an axiom of modern management that what gets measured gets managed, and what gets managed gets measured. Without measurement and benchmarking, it is not possible to know how a complex organization is faring or how to improve performance. The focus on information technology originated in Grossman's earlier experiences as chair of the department of radiology. When he took up that position in 2001, the department did not rank among the nation's top forty. Grossman undertook a program of systematically benchmarking a range of attributes from his department against the top five radiology departments in the country. He identified the specific areas where the department needed to improve to achieve world class status. By 2006, the NYU Langone radiology department was one of the best in the country. Grossman was poised to bring the same approach to his new job.

It is an axiom of modern management that what gets measured gets managed, and what gets managed gets measured.

FIND THE INFORMATION

Where was the information Grossman needed? The chair of information technology at the time could not find it. At one meeting Nader Mherabi, then several layers below the chair of his department, pulled Grossman aside and told him that he knew where the information he needed could be found. Mherabi said he knew because he was responsible for installing and maintaining the information technology equipment throughout the Medical Center. He told Grossman that he could solve his problems but had a condition. Mherabi told me, "The chief information officer came to me after I said something that interested him and asked, 'Can you help?' I said, 'I can help, but with some conditions.' He said, 'What do you mean?' I said, 'I ask that the dean commit to meet one hour a month with me and with the team that I choose. We will discuss how to design the system that I think will meet his needs. But we will meet without his direct reports—including you—and the other vice deans.'"

Nader Mherabi, chief information officer,
conducts a training session at the new NYU Langone Hospital–Brooklyn

Mherabi did solve Grossman's problem and is now senior vice president, vice dean, and chief information officer. Grossman still meets monthly with Mherabi's team alone, without his direct reports.

Jonathan Weider, the assistant dean for advanced applications at the

NYU School of Medicine, explained, "Had that stipulation not been made, Nader and his dashboard team—which included individuals from across the institution—would have been exposed to pressure from their bosses, and we would have continued to be confined to a conventional approach."

The successful interaction between the information technology staff and the business units is crucial in creating an information system that assists and advances the objectives of the organization as a whole.

Mherabi added, "Bob agreed to the conditions. . . . In the meetings we began, Bob met directly with the people who knew how things really worked.

"The members of the team that meet with us are not technical experts. They are middle managers who know where the actual data can be found and how things really work. When the dean says, 'I want this,' they know enough to say whether the data exists or it doesn't."

In my experience, the successful interaction between the information technology staff and the business units is crucial in creating an information system that assists and advances the objectives of the organization as a whole. For this interaction to work, the line managers need to articulate clearly their objectives and the information they need to improve their performance.

TRANSPARENT INFORMATION

Grossman said, "I decided to manage the school and the hospital solely on the basis of metrics and benchmarks." The information technology team needed every manager or team leader to identify the data that could be marshaled or developed to provide that information.

In discussing what he needed to accomplish, Mherabi said Grossman expressed a clear vision of what he wanted. Integration of the system with operations was a must. According to Mherabi, "Integration has very specific connotations in the world of information technology. An integrated system is one that works seamlessly as a whole, whether a doctor is in his office, using advanced technology, conducting a clinical trial, applying for research funding, or ordering hospital or laboratory supplies. All the functions must be connected. They all must be one thing. In an integrated academic medical center, doctors can have what they want. The hospital can have what it needs. Scientists can have what they want. The finance team can have what they need."

The system Grossman wanted was to provide both vertical and horizontal transparency. That meant it would need to provide information up and down the chain of activities in various departments, but it would also need to make that information accessible horizontally, to people doing similar jobs throughout the Medical Center.

"Bob's vision of cross mission integration was unique. Nobody else had done it." Many information systems work in a series of silos, making data available up and down a unit, but not between units. Grossman put equal emphasis on offering "horizontal" as well as "vertical" transparency.

Mherabi said, "We call it 'cross mission integration,' which means that all of the underlying information is integrated whether you are teaching, doing research, or providing patient care. . . . It was about connecting all the parts for better results for our patients."

What Mherabi called a "vision of integration of all aspects of an academic medical center" would drive the technology. He added, "I understood it right away. I understood his commitment to technology and how critical it was to the realization of his vision." According to Mherabi, "Bob's vision of cross mission integration was unique. Nobody else had done it." Many information systems work in a series of silos, making data available up and down a unit, but not between units. Grossman put equal emphasis on offering "horizontal" as well as "vertical" transparency.

HARDWARE AND SOFTWARE

Before Bob Grossman's appointment, NYU Langone was working to improve information systems. The inpatient Eclipsys electronic medical record system was installed in 2005 at a cost of $40 million. Grossman said, "I decided to rip Eclipsys out and put in a more comprehensive information system. I wanted to install an enterprise-wide electronic health record that encompassed ambulatory care, inpatient services, scheduling, and billing. People thought I was crazy. We had just spent all this money on Eclipsys, and now we were proposing taking it out and putting in a whole new system. It was going to take three to four years and cost almost $100 million. I said, 'Yes, but we need an integrated information management system.' What can kill you in information technology is managing the interfaces. The cost of the people you need to manage the interfaces is high. It never works. It drives you crazy. I decided we must have a single integrated information management system."

When NYU Langone issued a request for proposals, Epic Systems, a Verona, Wisconsin, private company specializing in medical software, emerged as the leader. Grossman and his information team worked with Epic over a period of several years. They were first to optimize the enterprise system, developed originally for hospitals, for use in an academic medical center. NYU Langone spent more than $180 million on this new system. Grossman maintains this was substantially less than other institutions had spent on similar systems, particularly those that had attempted to build rather than buy systems.

Mherabi noted that Grossman was deeply involved in choosing Epic. Beyond the initial expenditures for Epic, Mherabi said, "We invested quite a bit of money in information technology. Over the past five to seven years we have invested about $700 million in technology. The investment of $700 million is not just for the dashboard! It includes everything: all the systems and the processes, the phones, the Epic electronic health record across all practices, the corporate systems, purchasing, a centralized processing system, the human resource systems, and grants management systems." Mherabi explained, "We built everything from the ground up because there was so much that we needed to invest in when I arrived."

Pristine real time data is essential to the function of any medical information system. The system also needed to be easy to use and easy to update.

The tasks were Herculean, Mherabi recalled. "In 2011, I built what I call a service-oriented advanced information technology department to implement the vision. To build the department, we had to change some of the people and help them find positions elsewhere. We built a new team. Almost everything changed, from gutting the former network, installing advanced systems electronics, to corporate systems, revamping research systems, and connecting all of them."

DATA STORAGE

Pristine real time data is essential to the function of any medical information system. The system also needed to be easy to use and easy to update. Mherabi approached this problem by building a unified data warehouse. His team created straightforward processes, data input, and updates.

Jonathan Weider, assistant dean for advanced applications and assistant professor of educational informatics, emphasized that the starting point for any good management information system is a robust data warehouse "in which all the data from everyone are entered and stored coherently." By "everyone," he meant data from the most routine maintenance tasks to the most complex medical procedures. Moreover, Weider sought to ensure that there would be no need to make any changes in data once it had arrived in the warehouse. All data would be rigorously vetted before it entered the data warehouse. The information management team was not to be responsible for the integrity of the data. That would be the responsibility of those producing the data. Weider explained that "if you have a problem with any of these reports, you do not call Nader. You click on the little question mark symbol to get the name of the metric data owner, and you call her and ask your question."

According to Mherabi, this was one of the major strengths of the Epic system. "I think we did three things right. We invested hundreds of millions of dollars to build a system that is integrated into one big platform. That was essential to our success in every subsequent effort, including the dashboards." But Mherabi went on to say, "The second thing we did is shift responsibility for the integrity of the data from information technology to 'the business,' operations and management.

Information technology is not where issues with data integrity start," he said, "that is ultimately the responsibility of the business."

As Weider put it, "God help the manager who says, 'The data are wrong. I have the right data here in this spreadsheet.'"

If there is a problem with the data, Mherabi said that "the manager—with the assistance of the relevant operations head, if necessary—must investigate and offer a solution. They cannot call analytics and the data warehouse and ask them to 'fix it on the dashboard.'"

According to Mherabi, the third thing they did that "is very important: To work properly, the architecture of the system must be correct . . . We work with the people who originate the data to assure that the data are entered correctly." Workflow, the way people actually do their work and enter the data, is critically important, he said, as is data management. "If the system is functioning properly, the data on the dashboard are reflective of the data from the source system, which in turn means that the dashboard provides an accurate view of what is actually happening in the enterprise."

It is a never-ending process of continuous improvement
and response to change. Without workflow reorganization
to assure correct and current data entry,
the entire enterprise will fail.

STRUCTURED WORKFLOW

Restructuring workflow around real time data entry is critical. Excellent hardware and software is necessary but not sufficient to provide the accurate timely information needed to implement Grossman's vision.

Each process in the entire medical and research complex needs to be compatible with real time data entry.

Mherabi's information team includes over one hundred doctors, nurses, and technicians with the full-time responsibility of working throughout the Medical Center to adjust workflow to optimize data entry. This is the most time-consuming and difficult aspect of the entire information revolution that occurred at NYU Langone. It is a never-ending process of continuous improvement and response to change. Without workflow reorganization to assure correct and current data entry, the entire enterprise will fail.

"In healthcare, people usually try to optimize the information systems to serve special needs. That is not patient centered. You want things to work for patients and the caregiving overall."

In developing the system, Mherabi said, the emphasis was always on system-wide solutions. "In these discussions, enterprise integration trumps everything. We do not optimize the system to meet the needs of one department. The information flow and integration take precedence over individual needs. In healthcare, people usually try to optimize the information systems to serve special needs. That is not patient centered. You want things to work for patients and the caregiving overall."

For example, he said, "in the past, a chairman might ask what is the best cardiology system for his department? That might be locally optimal for cardiology, but then how do you schedule the patients across their entire hospital experience using a system designed for cardiologists? What would the patient do? Telephone each office? Use multiple systems?" He added, "Because technology is deeply integrated into operations, properly integrating our technology systems reinforces enterprise business integration, which is of course one of the dean's great objectives. It also allows reporting to become a byproduct of normal operations rather than a separate activity."

By way of example, Mherabi said, "If I want to hire an employee, I do not call Human Resources. I go to the *atNYULMC* portal and click the button labeled Hire. I fill out the job requirements, and I hit send. If someone in my department wants to hire, say, an engineer, she similarly submits her request electronically, which likely goes through two levels of review before the originator sees it again. As CIO, I ultimately accept it or reject it electronically."

As the system was being developed, Grossman would ask for continual improvements in data collection and analysis. Grossman insisted that the task of building this information system could not be relegated to the information technology department nor delegated to others.

More importantly, he added, "We apply the same principles to patient care. We do not call a nurse to fill out paperwork for the request for a medication. Doctors now order the medication directly online. Doctors also order diagnostic imaging online. They do not call Radiology to schedule the appointment. If a doctor orders medication for the patient, that order goes to the pharmacy electronically. The pharmacist's job is not to rewrite orders or to transcribe them as they used to do, but rather to check the integrity of the order and make sure the medication is safe to give to the patient. The system automatically checks for drug interactions. Once the pharmacist determines the order is safe, a robot fills the order in our automated pharmacy. The medication is dispensed and is placed on a medication cart on the ward. The cart and the drugs are locked down until the nurse arrives."

As the system was being developed, Grossman would ask for continual improvements in data collection and analysis. Grossman insisted that the task of building this information system could not be relegated to the information technology department nor delegated to others.

DASHBOARDS

The centerpiece of Grossman's information technology initiative was the dashboard. Like the dashboard of a car, system dashboards provide an overview of the status of every variable critical to success. Dashboards display information that flows in real time and present graphic displays of aggregated results. Just as medical charts summarize a patient's vital signs, a dashboard does the same for the activities and attributes of the entire enterprise, and in real time.

It is abundantly clear from his enthusiasm that Bob Grossman is very proud of his dashboards. He is like a piano virtuoso at his keyboard. When showcasing the dashboards for me in person, he said, "The management dashboard was my idea. I sat down in a room every month for two years with all the people who had the data. They went through the information with me each month. I did not let anyone else from my administration in the room. There had to be one idea. If you have everybody with an idea participate, nothing gets done. They think they know it all. Then it becomes unintelligible." Grossman explained, "I built the dashboards myself. I said, 'This is what I want. These are the things I need.' I had a lot of people working with me. They offered a lot of feedback and ideas. The dashboards are still dynamic today."

"There had to be one idea. If you have everybody
with an idea participate, nothing gets done."

Grossman developed a master dashboard for himself, which summarizes a wide range of attributes throughout NYU Langone. He is proud that "everyone has a dashboard now. The place is totally wired. You name any particular component of the hospital, and they have their own dashboard customized to their specific jobs."

I will add that from my personal experience as chair and CEO of Human Genome Sciences, Inc., a company heavily dependent on massive amounts of data, building an enterprise-wide information management system requires that it be directed by a single mind, that of the ultimate user, the CEO. I attribute the multiple repeated and very expensive failures of many local and national health information systems to a lack of such single-minded direction.

INTEGRATION

While various NYU Langone managers each have their own customized dashboard, Grossman added, "Some of the information rolls up to my dashboard, and everyone is looking at it. The whole hospital is managed through dashboards." The various departments have an incentive to both feed Grossman's dashboard and use it because it has so much of the outcomes information they need, things like data on mortality, morbidity, and infection. The dashboards allow everyone to see how they fare as compared to the very best national and sometimes international standards.

Grossman noted, "A benefit of creating the dashboard that I did not fully anticipate has been to facilitate integration. The dashboards help to create integration because everyone who was sitting around this table owned their particular source of data. Data is usually power. All of a sudden, everyone had to share their data. Everyone had to work together. When somebody said, 'I need this particular data to flow into here, the dean wants it,' all of a sudden, it got done. The process required more than the vision. It required leadership to say, 'This is the way it has to be.' We did that. The system took three-and-a-half years to build. Managing through the transition was rough." The dashboards bust silos in real time.

The dashboards bust silos in real time.

The dashboards offer value to most of the senior managers at NYU Langone by providing an early indication of where managers are not meeting performance goals. The dashboards highlight successes and help managers make more timely decisions. Robert Press, the former chief of Hospital Operations, said the dashboard played a valuable role in moving NYU Langone up from number sixty to number one in quality and safety rankings, because it helped management make better decisions in real time. Said Press, "We analyzed the data that was used to determine the rankings. We developed plans on how to improve our performance on each measure. We identified champions to assume responsibility for each of the measures. We developed an engagement plan for the entire clinical team. We set clear goals in each of the critical areas."

The dashboard played a valuable role in moving NYU Langone up from number sixty to number one in quality and safety rankings, because it helped management make better decisions in real time.

Press pointed out that there are national measures defined by the Centers for Medicare and Medicaid Services, "so we analyzed our performance for each of those measures. Martha Radford, our chief quality officer, played a central role in meeting the challenge."

According to Press, "She is a very good example of a person Bob enabled by giving her the direction and resources needed to do the job. Martha created a task force to identify clinical leaders to serve as point people for each of the critical measures. We would meet at least monthly to review the data and where we stood in national rankings on specific measures as of that moment. We analyzed the data and determined what we needed to do next to improve our results. Originally the data was not as up to date as it is now, because we were still developing the dashboard. As the dashboard improved, it became very important for our work."

Because they provide comprehensive, real time measures, the dashboards have played a significant role in improving the quality of services being provided. Mherabi said, "Quality measurements are very important for our internal use. We want to practice the highest quality of medicine. Quality measurements are becoming increasingly important to payments. The government wants to know what they are buying for all the money they spend."

THE HUMAN INTERFACE

Dashboards have changed the way people do their work at NYU Langone Health. It is not sufficient to install the most up-to-date hardware and software. The hardest part of the transition to a truly modern information-based organization is changing the way people do their work so that it is automatically compatible with the flow of real time information into the information system.

Mherabi insisted, "We do not change how medicine is practiced. . . . We do change how doctors do their work. We train people to work digitally. A doctor must enter all prescriptions digitally. A doctor cannot ask a nurse to fill in the order for a prescription. The system assists doctors. For example, if a resident has already ordered an x-ray, the system will inform the doctor that the patient had a recent CT scan and ask the doctor if she really wants to order the x-ray."

"We do not change how medicine is practiced. . . .
We do change how doctors do their work."

Mherabi continued, "We are also adding what we call advanced decision support. The decision support system may help the doctor avoid errors and make more informed decisions. I will give you one example. Intravenous lines are a source of infections, so we now ask the doctors whether they wish to continue to deliver medications intravenously once a patient begins to eat. The minute a diet order for a patient is ordered, the doctor receives a prompt to consider switching all medications for that patient to oral delivery. That is decision support. The doctor still has the final say."

Brotman also said, "The system does require more work by the doctors, but the advantages are so great that they tolerate the extra work and the patient-friendly results. A patient who sees a doctor at three in the afternoon may view the results of the visit at home on the same evening. Patients love it."

The transparency of the dashboards helps foster interdepartmental coordination. That has had a positive impact on quality of services. As patients move from one doctor to another, or from one department to another, as from Surgery to Radiology to Neurology, patients used to experience seemingly endless repetition and duplication of exams, questionnaires, and diagnostic tests. These are largely obviated by the integrated system.

Doctors experience just as many benefits from the system as their patients do. For example, Brotman said, "The doctors get more patients, because the patients love the system. They want to be here. Patients who have multiple doctors are especially happy with the system because their care is automatically coordinated. The doctors involved in patient care also love the system because they can see everything that is happening with their patient, including all the work done by other doctors. All the information is transparent." He added, "The integrated information system dramatically improved payment for our faculty practice physicians."

Brotman went on to speak of the financial advantages of clean, comprehensive data. "There is something called the clean claims rate that measures the percentage of claims that are not rejected because of errors. Our rate used to be about 90 percent. With Epic it is 99.3 percent. Having a higher rating accelerates the payments and decreases rejections, which directly benefits the doctors."

The information system also affects the work of scientists. Weider said, "I do believe that the dashboards have influenced how scientists work. We measure grant income for each scientist. We also encourage scientists to submit collaborative grants. Grants supporting collaborative work are usually bigger than individual grants. Over the past few years, the Medical Center has increased its share of grant awards substantially. I believe the measurements do change behavior. Of course, the share of grant support is not a direct measure of the quality of science. We also track the number of publications of each scientist and the number of citations for each published paper."

In addition, he said, "The data also include information about grants received and pending. One of the first dashboards we constructed displayed the grants in aggregate, for each department, and for each scientist. For instance, we can see that as of this moment, for this department, we have $53 million of grants awarded and $41 million pending. We can display the fraction of salary each scientist receives from funded grants, or the amount in overhead received per department. Everybody who has access to the dashboard can view our grant portfolio in its entirety. We share information internally that is not publicly available, in part to incentivize our scientists."

Transparency provides a powerful incentive for doctors and researchers to do their best work. Doctors are competitive. Since their results are visible to their peers, they have an incentive to outperform their neighbor.

Most management books throw up their hands in despair at the challenge of managing researchers. They are seen as individualistic, strong willed, and resistant to directives from above. NYU Langone has created a transformative approach that makes it possible to hold researchers accountable. The result is dramatically increased collaboration and productivity as measured by increases in the number of cooperative grants involving two or more researchers, publication productivity, and total grant income.

Transparency provides a powerful incentive for doctors and researchers to do their best work. Doctors are competitive. Since their results are visible to their peers, they have an incentive to outperform their neighbor. For example, they may strive to reduce complication rates so that they are the best in the system. Similarly, researchers want to notch up as many grants, publications, and citations as their close peers. And medical school faculty want others to see that they get high ratings from their students.

Chandrika Tandon, an NYU Langone Health trustee and a highly regarded management consultant with wide-ranging experience, said, "The NYU database is extraordinary." She added, "The dashboard is the best example of a real time, end-to-end, transparent system that I have seen."

CONTINUOUS IMPROVEMENT

The NYU Langone Health management information system continues to evolve. Mherabi said, "We have built strong governance. We have a monthly meeting with the dean and all the vice deans to discuss information technology. Each mission—clinical care, research, and education—has a governance committee that decides what each project requires and what they should accomplish. The meetings promote transparency and accountability."

Going forward, Mherabi said, "We are now focused on what information systems can do to improve patient experience and what we can do to involve the patient in his or her own care. We believe that information technology, including virtual health, is part of the answer." He also said, "We are trying to engage patients with technology where it makes sense. We know technology is not the entire solution. I would like to find ways to have our patients use analytic tools to understand and manage their medical issues so they can better manage their care."

DATA-DRIVEN ETHOS

A data-driven ethos permeates the Medical Center, Weider said: "We now assume that everyone will follow the work protocols consistent with the requirements of correct data entry. That is the norm, not the exception. Any departure from this practice requires a truly exceptional circumstance. An argument for local rather than global optimization faces a very high bar. This is one way that the dashboard enforced workflow coherence. That was not the result intended or expected. However, the demand for data coherence has made a very big difference in workflow and what people are required to do."

The focus on data comes from the very top. Steven Galetta said, "Bob worships the dashboard. He can tell you things about your own department you may not know. You better be on your game when you meet with him. He will know the metrics of your department cold."

The dashboard has become so essential that using it has become a requirement for being hired at NYU Langone Health. Brotman said, "We tell everybody we are a metric-driven organization and that we measure performance. Everyone we hire must be comfortable with using our information management system. We will not hire someone who insists on using a different system for their work."

> "Bob worships the dashboard. He can tell you things
> about your own department you may not know.
> You better be on your game when you meet with him.
> He will know the metrics of your department cold."

Paresh Shah, a surgeon at NYU Langone, said, "What NYU Langone has that I have not seen too many other places have is a deep strength in information technology, specifically in actionable information. There is a big difference between data and actionable information. Many hospitals have lots of data. Actionable information is a very different thing. The creation of a central data repository that combines not just your financial data and your administrative data but your actual operational data, your clinical data, is a major achievement."

NYU Langone's emphasis on information technology has not been widely replicated in the hospital world. Grossman said, "Other health systems have developed advanced data management capabilities. However, I have not yet found an organization that has a comprehensive, real time, transparent, integrated, interface-free system such as the one developed here."

"We succeed because we are relentless
in the pursuit of excellence."

Why have other medical centers not followed the same course in information technology? Grossman said, "People are trying to do it. People come here all the time and they ask me, 'How did you do it?' But it is hard. That is why they are not doing it. We succeed because we are relentless in the pursuit of excellence."

He added, "You have to be intensely focused on continual improvement of the information system all the time. Our system is changing even if it is mature." The crucial ingredient, he argued, "is not the technology itself. . . . The software is easy. We upgrade the software and it looks better. It is the process we think about. One of the things that made it so successful, I think, was it was just me. If I had ten vice deans making the decisions instead of me alone, it would never happen."

Sheilah Rosen, manager of the office of the dean and CEO at NYU Langone Health, said, "Our technology is state of the art." But she insisted, without Grossman "at the helm, the technology would not mean anything." In her view, he had a completed vision of "what the technology can do for us and where he wanted it to go."

Rosen's point about leadership is supported in a *Harvard Business*

Review essay entitled "The IT Transformation Health Care Needs." This essay, published in the November–December 2017 *HBR* issue, is by Nikhil R. Sahni, Robert S. Huckman, Anuraag Chigurupati, and David M. Cutler. They conclude, "The hurdles keeping organizations from harnessing their IT systems to transform health care are surmountable. What's needed most is the will and support of an organization's leaders and clinicians." Grossman provided the leadership and brought the clinicians along with him. He adapted existing technologies to serve his vision and his dashboard, and he created the organizational incentives to ensure that everyone was involved in providing data and other inputs to the information system and was also deeply involved in noting and responding to the outputs of the system.

The information technology employed by NYU Langone made a vast range of the institution's activities transparent and subject to objective measurement. Everyone could know how well everything was going. To some, particularly at the outset, this was threatening. There were few secrets; there were no hiding places for processes—and people—who weren't performing as expected. But ultimately most came to see the value of extensive and intrusive information management. They knew how others were doing, and they knew how they were doing. It fostered competition, but it also fostered teamwork.

As Grossman put it, "I blew up the silos. I absolutely destroyed them. There were no silos, no hiding. It was one vision, one database, one message all over."

Because everything was measured and monitored, ultimately it broke down the traditional silos and the often vast gulfs between different parts of the organization. As Grossman put it, "I blew up the silos. I absolutely destroyed them. There were no silos, no hiding. It was one vision, one database, one message all over." He added, "By truly integrating the hospital and the school, we created tremendous agility. Agility is very important in decision making."

Chandrika Tandon, a board member of NYU Langone Health and NYU, is also founder and CEO of Tandon Capital Associates, which has provided management consulting and restructuring services to a number of major corporations. Tandon, who donated $100 million to the NYU School of Engineering, said, "The way Bob uses the dashboard has caused me to revise what was a fundamental tenet of my own belief in management. I used to agree with other management experts who argued once a leader gets past managing five or six or ten indices, he is not managing anything. The idea is that there are too many variables to keep in mind. The leader should remain focused on those most important for success." But, she added, "Bob has shown me that it is possible to manage many, many indicators simultaneously and effectively. Bob sees what is happening from the top, middle, and bottom of the organization."

Information is power, and Grossman had plenty of information. But he pushed it down through the organization, and he empowered everyone in the organization to see the information not as a threat wielded by the boss but as a tool to help them in their own work.

Tandon continued, "Bob makes sure his key managers also have the same picture. The information is transparent throughout the organization.

I have never seen such comprehensive use of information by the CEO and key managers in any other organization."

Information is power, and Grossman had plenty of information. But he pushed it down through the organization, and he empowered everyone in the organization to see the information not as a threat wielded by the boss but as a tool to help them in their own work. Ultimately, managers at NYU Langone knew information was being used to judge their work; but more importantly, it was available to guide their work, to help them do their jobs better. Grossman wisely made data more of a tool than a whip.

At NYU Langone Health, the dashboard, and the information technology that underpins it, completely suffuses the institution and everything it does. As a result, the pilot is no longer flying blind. As Grossman put in place his expensive new information technology, and pored over his dashboard, he was also proceeding on the other elements of his strategy, most notably ambulatory care.

CHAPTER 6

Ambulatory Care

In 2007, the NYU Langone Medical Center was almost exclusively a cluster of buildings on the east side of Manhattan, centered on the Tisch Hospital. Ten years later, NYU Langone Health has an entirely different footprint. The hospitals in Manhattan remain the central hub for research and teaching, but these hospitals and laboratories are only part of a much larger whole. A network of more than two hundred and fifty NYU Langone Health ambulatory and family care centers are spread across Manhattan, Brooklyn, and Long Island in addition to two additional hospitals, NYU Langone Hospital–Brooklyn and the affiliated Winthrop Hospital on Long Island.

Ambulatory care centers house doctors' offices and may offer a variety of diagnostic services and medical treatments that were once available only in hospitals. They run tests, offer x-rays and other imaging services, perform surgery, and administer infusions. Many of the ambulatory care facilities focus on delivering specialized care such as cancer treatment, cardiovascular interventions, and rehabilitation.

The creation of a network of ambulatory care centers is the realization of Grossman's vision for the transformation of the Medical Center.

He realized from the outset that new technologies combined with advanced information services opened up the possibility of providing many procedures as outpatient services that were previously performed only in hospitals. He foresaw that hospital care, though still central for major ailments, is diminishing in importance, as minimally invasive surgery and other treatments are increasingly being offered beyond the walls of the traditional hospital. Grossman was a pioneering entrepreneur who saw this as an opportunity for NYU Langone.

Andrew Brotman, chief clinical officer, senior vice president, and vice dean for clinical affairs and strategy, is the key architect and manager of the ambulatory care network. His relentless energy has turned the dream of high-quality distributed patient care into a reality. He and his team have driven much of the way NYU Langone delivers healthcare today.

I believe the distributed patient care model perfected by NYU Langone is the model all countries, regardless of economic status, must adopt if they are to deliver patient centered, high-quality, low-cost care to their citizens.

> The distributed patient care model perfected by NYU Langone is the model all countries, regardless of economic status, must adopt if they are to deliver patient centered, high-quality, low-cost care to their citizens.

THE HOSPITAL OF OUR PAST

Hospital-centric care has been the guiding principle of healthcare delivery in the United States throughout most of the twentieth century.

The idea of hospital-centric care still prevails throughout much of the world, especially in countries such as China, India, and sub-Saharan Africa. Classical ideas of industrial economics and private sector economics guide these decisions. Economies of scale permit the high cost of complex equipment and specialized professionals to be spread across a larger base of patients converging on a hospital. Scale also lowered the unit costs for hospital services. For example, consolidating all the radiology equipment at one site allowed one facility to serve many patients.

Under Bob Grossman's leadership a new view emerged. Patient centered, not hospital centered, healthcare would prevail. That meant bringing care to neighborhoods where patients live. It meant building a network of closely related health centers offering high-end services throughout local communities. It meant replacing hospital centered services as much as possible with ambulatory care centers for the safety of the patient and cost reduction. It meant using advanced information technology to link hospitals and the network into an indivisible whole for patient management and administration.

As Grossman told me, "Healthcare has totally changed. Minimally invasive surgery has become a big part of medicine. This means shorter lengths of stay. Think about heart surgery and valve surgery. These are complicated procedures. People used to be in the hospital two weeks, three weeks. Now some valve replacements or spine surgeries or hip replacements are being done percutaneously. The hospital recovery period is only one or two days. The recovery time for hip replacement surgery at NYU Langone is less than twenty-four hours."

It is an open secret of modern medicine that hospitals are dangerous places. "You can get infections in hospitals," Grossman said. "We want our patients to be in the hospital for the shortest time possible, or better yet, not be in a hospital at all. We try to keep them in the ambulatory setting."

It is an open secret of modern medicine that hospitals
are dangerous places. "You can get infections in
hospitals," Grossman said. "We want our patients to be
in the hospital for the shortest time possible,
or better yet, not be in a hospital at all."

Grossman concluded that the way forward for NYU Langone was through ambulatory care rather than more and bigger hospitals. "From a patient's perspective, a hospital is not the ideal environment for a routine checkup or a minor procedure," said Vicki Match Suna in our discussion on the growth of NYU facilities. "So we focused on how we could move those services outside of the hospital setting. This gave us the opportunity to create more suitable environments for the patient experience with better outcomes; and, at the same time, facilitated the growth of our ambulatory network and inpatient facilities."

Before Grossman became CEO, Bob Berne noted, "We had been building the ambulatory network, but at a very low level. Bob Grossman said we should double down. We must decide which medical specialties to emphasize. We should think strategically about the geographies we cover. We must analyze the payer mix. We have to know all these things in addition to the all-important issue of quality of service."

To create an ambulatory care facility, NYU Langone Health rents or builds space, then installs the necessary equipment and offices. The out-patient centers typically are equipped to perform many different types of surgery and physical therapy, but each one often focuses on specific medical specialties. For example, "We are leaders in ambulatory cardiac surgery, orthopedic surgery, vascular surgery, and neurosurgery," Grossman said.

One of these NYU Langone facilities was set up in the historic Trinity Building, an office building in lower Manhattan. Meanwhile, in March 2017, NYU Langone announced plans to build a fifty-five-thousand-square-foot, $33 million ambulatory surgery center on the Lower East Side of Manhattan. The largest ambulatory care centers are located within hospitals. These include the musculoskeletal and the cancer centers. Indeed, the Perlmutter Cancer Center has two facilities, seamlessly linked. These facilities link diagnosis, testing, and treatment.

I will share a story from my own experience at the Perlmutter Cancer Center, one of the NYU Langone ambulatory care facilities. I noticed a persistent lump in my neck while traveling in Asia. On my return, I scheduled an appointment for the next day with my primary care doctor at NYU Langone. He sent me for a biopsy the next day. The outpatient facility I visited is a ten-story building in downtown Manhattan that specializes almost exclusively in head and neck cancer. The biopsy room is adjacent to the clinical laboratory. The results came back in five minutes. Because I am a biomedical scientist with a background in cancer research, head and neck cancer specifically, they allowed me to view the biopsy specimens myself. I rose from the biopsy chair, walked twenty feet to the lab, and peered through a microscope at the cancer cells that had recently been mine. There was no doubt about the diagnosis. That was the start of a journey many before me had taken. I am pleased to say that, due to the rapid diagnosis and to the flawless execution of therapy by a group of specialists who have been working together for many years, I am now cancer free.

The Perlmutter Cancer Center on East 34th Street in Manhattan

A more typical experience in a large hospital would have been very different. If a biopsy were required, it would have been done in a doctor's office and the tissue sent out for evaluation. Several days later I would have had to return to the doctor's office to learn the results.

By 2018, NYU Langone Health had more than two hundred and thirty ambulatory and community care centers. According to Grossman, the ambulatory care strategy "differentiates us from other hospitals in the city." Others may try to emulate the NYU Langone ambulatory care strategy, he told me, "but it is hard to do. Part of our success in building a strong ambulatory care network derives from the fact that we now have an integrated medical center. Part of our success comes from the fact that we have been doing it a long time, so we know exactly how to do it. In many ways, ambulatory care facilities are like a box. We superimpose information technology on the box. Everyone is connected and understands what we are doing."

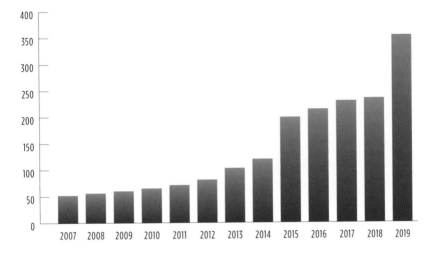

Total number of NYU Langone ambulatory care locations from 2007 to 2019

AN AMBULATORY CARE NETWORK OF DOCTORS

The development of an ambulatory care network was interwoven with a drive to move from consulting physicians with the right to use NYU hospital facilities to doctors employed full time by NYU Langone. For many years, NYU Langone had relied on doctors who maintained their own offices and practices. They would send their patients to NYU Langone if they needed to be hospitalized for tests or procedures. Grossman sought to dramatically enlarge the network of doctors employed by NYU Langone to control both quality and efficiency. Over the past ten years NYU Langone Health has added about two thousand five hundred doctors to the ambulatory care network. These are full-time employees of NYU Langone. About one-quarter of these joined the faculty as a result of the merger with two regional hospitals, Lutheran in Brooklyn, now NYU Langone Hospital–Brooklyn, and Winthrop Hospital on Long

Island. The remainder chose to leave their practices and join as full-time staff members of NYU Langone.

NYU Langone does not purchase these independent practices. Rather, the independent physicians are offered the opportunity to upgrade their practices with better facilities and equipment. For many, the cost of keeping abreast of the changes in technology and equipment is greater than they could afford on their own. Acquiring a physician practice does require a capital investment. As Richard Donoghue, senior vice president for strategy, planning, and business development, told me, "Do not think that acquiring a physician's practice is cost free. Our standard terms when acquiring a new practice are to allow them to keep all their account receivables and their cash on hand at the time of acquisition. We begin paying their salary immediately. There is a forty- to sixty-day lag before we realize any real cash flow. Acquiring each practice requires a substantial investment of working capital. Physician practices come to us for help when they think that they do not have the cash flow needed to invest in necessary technology."

In our conversation, Andrew Brotman revealed one of the secrets of NYU Langone's success in building their ambulatory care practice. "Most hospital administrators know how clinics or inpatient services work, but they do not know how doctors' offices work. We do understand and we meet their needs." This is one reason why NYU Langone is able to work well with doctors, he said, adding, "All our leadership are doctors, from Bob Grossman down." As an example of this understanding, he went on, "We understand that the doctors we hire have a local network of patients. We do not ask them to move from one place to another."

Initially, most of the ambulatory care doctors were recruited from private practice. More recently, about half of new recruits are doctors who have already been employed by a hospital. Brotman said, "Our recruitment is effective. Doctors check the market. They find we are reliable for both the short and long term. We are clear about our initial commitments. We do not commit to promises that we cannot deliver. If a doctor calls us with a problem, we answer the phone." He added, "We do not ask for noncompete agreements. We do not want anybody here who is not happy. Very few of our doctors leave, less than ten a year."

NYU Langone compensates the faculty practitioners with a base salary and supplements based on the specific type of medicine they practice and their productivity. The total compensation usually exceeds that which they would earn in private practice. As Donoghue observed, "Generally speaking, our faculty practice doctors have a base salary. The base salary is supplemented. The supplement depends on their specialty. The salary is supplemented by what we call the relative value unit model."

"Our recruitment is effective. Doctors check the market. They find we are reliable for both the short and long term. We are clear about our initial commitments. We do not commit to promises that we cannot deliver. If a doctor calls us with a problem, we answer the phone."

Donoghue continued, "For example, the relative value unit for radiologists depends on the type and volume of images they are reading. For surgeons it depends upon the number of cases plus time spent on office work. For hospitalists, the relative value unit is determined by the number of patients on the floor you supervise. For community-based cardiologists, it is based on the number of patients under your care. There is a productivity component built into the compensation package."

A NETWORK-WIDE INFORMATION SYSTEM

While NYU Langone ambulatory care facilities are widely dispersed physically, they are all integrated into the NYU Langone information system. The physicians in the ambulatory care centers follow the same rigorous standards of data entry and quality monitoring as do the doctors in the hospitals. The performance of the faculty practitioners is carefully monitored for quality and safety. NYU Langone's information system provides the structure to make a distributed ambulatory care system work.

The NYU Langone Ambulatory Care Center in midtown Manhattan

Once again in the words of Richard Donoghue, "Quality is something that we measure on a regular basis. It is often hard to measure quality at the level of the individual doctor. We mostly measure quality and other outcomes at the division level. Quality and patient outcomes are not part of the relative value unit and generally not part of the compensation model. Of course, all of our doctors must maintain very high standards for quality and safety to remain on the faculty."

ADVANTAGES FOR DOCTORS

Both medical centers and physicians can derive significant benefits from the staff doctors model. For medical centers, the principal benefit is improving the overall quality of medical services while reducing costs. NYU Langone could monitor and measure every aspect of its doctors' activities.

For doctors, being an NYU Langone employee means they are relieved of many of the burdens of running an office. They do not have to hire and manage staff, select and maintain office space, or involve themselves in patient records and endless insurance company forms and issues. NYU Langone central staff do much of the work, leaving the doctors free to focus on their patients. "The people who work in ambulatory care facilities feel liberated," Grossman said. "They can fulfill their aspirations."

For doctors, being an NYU Langone employee means they are relieved of the burdens of running an office. They do not have to hire and manage staff, select and maintain office space, or involve themselves in patient records and endless insurance company forms and issues.

The economics of ambulatory care are attractive. The fixed costs of operating a hospital seven days a week, twenty-four hours a day are significant. The overhead of ambulatory care facilities is much lower than that of hospitals. These facilities are only open during working hours, typically from early morning to early evening. They have no need for sizable nursing staffs or staff and facilities to provide meal support for bedridden patients. The costs of providing ambulatory care are significantly less than the same procedures provided in hospital. Today about two-thirds or more of all surgeries at NYU Langone are performed in ambulatory care practices. Considerably more than half the surplus of hospital operations comes from ambulatory care.

THE BIG PICTURE

Ambulatory care has transformed care at NYU Langone while also transforming its income statement. In the 2016 NYU Langone Health annual report, Brotman wrote, "We are really an ambulatory-care network with several hospitals, rather than the other way around." Some sixty-five percent of NYU Langone revenues now come from its ambulatory services, and seventy percent of surgeries take place in ambulatory settings.

The ambulatory care revolution reverses a century of centralization in medical care. Grossman and NYU Langone were prepared to look to the future rather than the past, and they were not hesitant to pursue the medical and economic logic that suggested turning away from the grand hospital to the neighborhood medical facility.

> Ambulatory care has demonstrated the potential to improve the quality of medical care while costing less than hospital care.

The devolution of healthcare from centralized hospitals to distributed, community-based ambulatory care centers is an important theme in terms of both the technology and the sociology of American medicine. It is also proving to be an important economic theme. Ambulatory care has demonstrated the potential to improve the quality of medical care while costing less than hospital care. NYU Langone is ahead of the curve and a leader in this transformation.

I believe it is critical for medical care in the rest of the world to follow this lead to ensure that patients everywhere receive high-quality care at an affordable cost.

CHAPTER 7

Financial Success

When Bob Grossman joined NYU Langone in 2007, he developed a road map that called for nothing less than a campus transformation, which would include a new hospital and a new science building. The question became how to achieve those aspirations given the precarious finances at the Medical Center. At the time, the hospital and medical school taken together had a negative operating margin. Together they lost $90 million in 2009.

Under Grossman's leadership, NYU Langone completely transformed its financial picture from substantial losses to sizable surpluses. A decade after Grossman took office, NYU Langone had hundreds of millions of dollars in the bank.

As in other aspects of NYU Langone's transformation, Grossman played a crucial role in reshaping the financial status of the Medical Center. Restoring financial health required improving income and controlling expenses. The ambulatory care strategy created an important new revenue stream. Meanwhile, Grossman reduced costs where possible without compromising on quality. Income from research grants and contracts rose rapidly. Major donations also played an important role.

Under Grossman's leadership, NYU Langone completely transformed its financial picture from substantial losses to sizable surpluses. A decade after Grossman took office, NYU Langone had hundreds of millions of dollars in the bank. The institution now has an enviable credit rating and is able to issue bonds to finance new projects at a modest spread over U.S. treasuries.

MEDICAL ECONOMICS

Sustainability and profit are central to the operations of any enterprise. Many of the steps NYU Langone took to regain its financial footing and thrive are applicable to many for-profit and nonprofit enterprises, especially those that rely on a mix of public and private financing. The finances of healthcare institutions are famously complicated. Most hospitals and medical schools are nonprofit institutions. Nonetheless, these institutions must be financially sustainable and, it is hoped, generate a surplus. Otherwise they will disappear.

The cost side of a medical institution's financial statement is reasonably straightforward. Money is spent on salaries and benefits for employees; on development, maintenance, and improvement of facilities and equipment; and on all of the expenses associated with running an organization, from phone bills to office supplies.

The revenue side of hospitals and medical schools is very different from that of most businesses. There are five sources of income: fees for medical services; research grants; medical school tuition and fees; royalty income from intellectual property; and charitable contributions. Each is complicated.

FEE FOR SERVICES

Hospitals charge for each of their services. We have all seen complex and nearly incomprehensible hospital bills. There is a fee for seeing a doctor, for staying in a hospital, for receiving each pill, and for each treatment. In recent years there has been some movement toward what are called bundled payments, a fixed sum paid for treatment of specific conditions, say a broken arm. Nonetheless, fee for service payments still dominate.

While the concept of fee for service is straightforward, the way medical fees are actually paid is complex. Sometimes the fee is paid by the patient. More typically, some or all of the fee is paid by a private insurance company or by a government agency. In almost every case, the payments come long after the service was rendered. Often the insurance company that is billed may pay part but not all of the charge. Then the patient is billed. The patient may be incapacitated or unable to pay the entire sum, so payments may arrive much later and piecemeal. Government agencies may also question bills and are often slow to reimburse. The payment process may involve Medicaid, Medicare supplemental insurance, and the patient; or an employee benefit plan, a private insurer, and the parents of the young patient. Both the billing and payment processes are often sequential, not simultaneous.

RESEARCH GRANTS

Research grants are another source of revenue for medical schools. These grants may come from government agencies (mostly from the National

Institutes of Health), foundations, and individual donors. The grants usually support the work of one or more investigators. Research grants are given to the institution, not to the investigator directly. Institutions collect payments called overhead for providing services such as laboratory space, in addition to the money they transfer to the investigators. Overhead may run as high as ninety percent of the direct payments.

TUITION

Most medical schools charge tuition. Medical students may pay tuition personally or receive scholarships from the school or external foundations. Medical schools may also receive federal capitation payments on a per-student basis. In addition to having students seeking degrees, medical schools often provide a number of postgraduate fellowships.

ROYALTY PAYMENTS

Research results can sometimes be commercialized: New drugs or devices may be discovered. When this happens as a result of research conducted by employees, the revenue is shared between the school and the inventors.

PHILANTHROPY

Hospitals are beneficiaries of a vast array of charitable contributions. These range from the revenues generated by bake sales and "fairs" to multimillion dollar gifts from individuals, foundations, and corporations.

From this array of sources, academic medical centers seek to develop an overall income stream that pays for expenses and leaves something over, not only for a rainy day but also to finance the growth and development of the institution. Medical institutions can issue bonds for capital projects, either under their own name or through various public sector healthcare credit facilities. Meanwhile, the surpluses are reinvested to pay for smaller-scale expansions, as well as to meet the inevitable increases on the cost side of the balance sheet.

ENVIRONMENT

NYU Langone Health is located in one of the most expensive cities in the country. Operating costs are high. NYU Langone's professionals are among the highest paid in the country. NYU Langone is located in a state and city that provide substantial medical benefits to the poor, but the government agencies are bureaucratic and slow moving. Insurance company reimbursement levels that might seem adequate, even generous, in the rest of the country often do not cover the charges incurred by a New York hospital.

How could NYU Langone improve its finances in this complex setting? Grossman and his colleagues pursued several broad avenues for improving the finances. These included enhancing the efficiency and quality of the revenue cycle, creating a seven-day hospital, pursuing the growth of ambulatory care, and increasing the level of philanthropic contributions.

REDESIGN OF THE BILLING SYSTEM

Grossman quickly recognized that the hospital was not billing correctly. Early on, analyses revealed that NYU Langone was simply not levying charges for a substantial number of reimbursements, because the services being rendered were not documented properly.

The first step in improving the finances of NYU Langone was ensuring that it collected what it was owed.

By failing to bill for various services that had been provided, NYU Langone was forgoing a significant fraction of the revenues to which it was entitled. Grossman quickly concluded that the first step in improving the finances of NYU Langone was ensuring that it collected what it was owed. Improvements could be made even without a new billing system, just by changing processes and procedures.

Lapses in billing are a common problem at many academic medical centers. The chief financial officer at NYU Langone from 2008 to 2018, Michael Burke, explained it to me this way: "The first-year resident, who is typically on the front line, is charged with documenting everything that is being done to a patient. These residents are the most tired people on the planet. They work at least eighty hours a week. The last thing they want to do is document each and every procedure. Sometimes people forget." As a result, Burke went on, "our services were not documented properly. Not all the necessary information for payments was being entered into the medical records. I calculated we were missing out on about twenty percent of reimbursements for work we actually did. They never charged for it."

The situation was improved through a two-pronged effort. NYU Langone created and deployed teams of people to improve documentation and billing, and it armed them with a highly sophisticated information management system.

IMPROVING COST RECOVERY

Burke explained that to improve documentation, "we instituted concurrent documentation reviews. We brought in new teams to help. We trained the team members and put them on the hospital wards. They observed and queried the residents while the patients were still present. They would say, 'I notice your patient is being given medicine to treat diabetes. If your patient does have diabetes, have you forgotten to document that in the record?'"

There are now thirty observer teams, composed of nurses and doctors who were recruited and trained for this specific job. They can recognize what the frontline doctors might have done or should have done, and they can see if it is recorded. Doctors and nurses review the charts after they are coded. After the procedures are documented, the charts are sent to a team that assigns specific billing codes. The hospital charges for procedures that are coded properly. If a procedure isn't coded, the hospital will not be paid for it.

NYU Langone brought in a team of people from IRM, a company in California, to provide staff training. Burke said, "We found the errors and fixed the processes and procedures that created the errors. We really needed to create robust processes. Remember, we have a new group of residents every year. Without good process management and audits, people will revert to bad habits. Technology can help. We have integrated query tools into Epic to extract data and look for what might be missing."

Automated algorithms help staff identify potential lapses in billing. For example, if a physician is prescribing a set of drugs for a particular disorder, the billing team can follow up to ensure that the disorder is properly accounted for in the billing process. The first month the new system was in place, NYU Langone was able to recover more than $600,000 in additional payments. They now have a team of forty-five people auditing medical records. As a result, in 2017 they recovered more than $150 million of additional payments.

The lesson is, "Make sure you charge for what you do and collect what you charge."

The auditing is closely interwoven with the information system. Before Epic, what was billable, what was billed, what was collected, and what was owed by whom and for what was information that existed only in fragmented silos, and it was often incomplete. Burke said, "The decision to adopt Epic was made the summer before I arrived. Bob decided to install the billing part of Epic first, because he wanted that to generate enough cash to help pay for clinical development quickly. That meant we had to build interfaces with our existing clinical systems that we knew were to be discarded once we installed the full clinical interface with Epic."

For a while, NYU Langone managed two parallel billing systems to give them time to perfect billing via Epic. In 2011, NYU Langone converted all its billing to Epic. Once the elements of the new system were put in place, NYU Langone was able to recover between $24 million and $30 million per month that would otherwise have gone unbilled. The lesson is, "Make sure you charge for what you do and collect what you charge," Burke said.

Documentation is much easier with electronic health records. NYU Langone invested in coders and brought documentation down to the house officer level. Each small improvement gradually led to even greater improvements down the line.

Fee for service has continued to dominate medical economics, and NYU Langone has learned how to make sure it charged a fee for each of its services. According to Grossman, fixing the billing process was one of the most important things that NYU Langone did. Grossman said the Medical Center "put in place revenue cycle initiatives, coding, billing correctly, documentation, and all the support functions that we lacked. All of a sudden we started making money. Then we poured that money right back into the institution."

In addition to dramatically improving its process of billing and collecting, NYU Langone also reexamined its charges. Publicly available data showed that other hospitals in New York were charging more for some of their services. For example, NYU Langone was charging too little for outpatient services compared to other hospitals. As a result, NYU Langone systematically raised fees for its various services to market levels.

THE SEVEN-DAY HOSPITAL

NYU Langone also improved its finances by creating "the seven-day hospital." While at first glance, hospitals may appear to be the quintessential 24/7, always open, always active, around-the-clock institutions, in fact, many of the diagnoses and treatments are done nine to five, Monday through Friday, not unlike typical office hours at most institutions. To be sure, emergencies are handled around the clock and patients require observation and treatment day and night. Like most offices, however, weekends at a hospital mean limited procedures and reduced staff.

The returns on the seven-day hospital reflected basic economics: The hospital had underutilized capacity on weekends. By using its operating rooms and radiology facilities on weekends, it could generate significant revenue while incurring modest additional costs.

Grossman set out to change that. In early 2008 he launched the "seven-day hospital." This meant patients could have elective surgery and other treatments or procedures on the weekend. According to Joyce Long, a veteran member of the NYU Langone administrative staff,

"The seven-day hospital was a big initiative, both for improving patient experience and revenue." For patients it meant an end to spending the weekend in the hospital waiting for a procedure or waiting to be discharged when the weekend was over. With the seven-day hospital, Long said, "Patients can be discharged on Saturday and Sunday as well as during the week. They do not need to remain in the hospital over the weekend if it is not necessary."

Meanwhile, this program led to an increase in elective surgery. "In 2010, we performed eighty-nine elective surgeries on weekends," Long said. "In 2011, the number was two hundred and eighty-two." She added that NYU Langone went on to offer imaging services on the weekends as well. The returns on the seven-day hospital reflected basic economics: The hospital had underutilized capacity on weekends. By using its operating rooms and radiology facilities on weekends, it could generate significant revenue while incurring modest additional costs and requiring no new capital expenditures.

SURPLUS FROM AMBULATORY CARE

The third critical financial development was the emphasis on ambulatory care as discussed in this chapter. The attractive economics of ambulatory care was just one of several reasons for moving in that direction, and ambulatory care substantially improved the financial picture at NYU Langone.

Ambulatory care had an impact not only on costs but also on the level of revenues. Ambulatory care centers increase the population base for a medical center. For many problems, patients prefer to see doctors in their neighborhood. Patients and their doctors often prefer nearby medical facilities. A network of ambulatory care centers spread across a wide area significantly expands the number of patients.

Total revenue for NYU Langone from 2007 to 2017

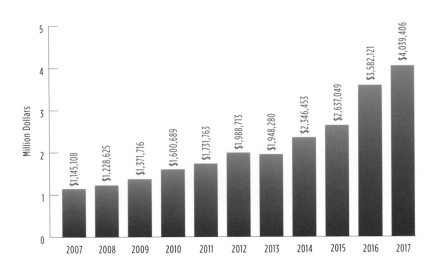

In a wide-ranging interview, Joe Lhota, senior vice president, vice dean, and chief of staff, said, "Bob Grossman understood the changes taking place in patient care and drove them successfully. Our outpatient revenues account for more than fifty percent of all revenues. I do not think there is another academic medical center here in New York that can show outpatient revenues greater than inpatient revenues."

"Our outpatient revenues account for more than fifty percent of all revenues. I do not think there is another academic medical center here in New York that can show outpatient revenues greater than inpatient revenues."

Total surplus for NYU Langone from 2007 to 2017

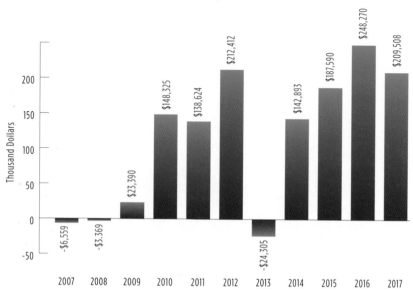

The 2015 merger with the former Lutheran Hospital also generated a significant increment in NYU Langone's revenues. The acquisition strengthened the NYU Langone beachhead in Brooklyn and significantly advanced its market penetration in this rapidly gentrifying section of the city. While substantial numbers of Brooklyn residents already traveled to NYU Langone in Manhattan, thousands more would now have an NYU Langone outpost nearby. The merger with Lutheran, now named NYU Langone Hospital–Brooklyn, and the merger with Winthrop Hospital in Mineola, Long Island, added additional revenue.

PHILANTHROPY

In addition to improving the efficiency of its revenue streams, another major financial thrust at NYU Langone was philanthropy. Ken Langone and Bob Grossman recognized that to achieve the ambitious vision they

144

had for NYU Langone, they would need substantial philanthropic support. They challenged the NYU Langone community to raise $2.8 billion by 2019. NYU Langone conducted a philanthropy feasibility study with extensive input from longtime supporters, physicians, and leaders across the NYU Langone community. Based on the feedback received, Langone and Grossman developed a comprehensive plan that served as a philanthropic road map for institutional leaders and key board members. By August 2018, NYU Langone had raised $2.68 billion and was well positioned to meet their target. The philanthropic effort was a success thanks to the same key values that Langone and Grossman embraced throughout their tenure: clear vision, broad engagement, and transparency.

> The board of NYU Langone Health is composed of a number of philanthropically minded people who donate themselves and help to raise additional support from their friends.

For NYU Langone, the key figure was, and still is, Ken Langone. Langone not only was generous with his own money, but also helped obtain serious commitments from others. While he gave over $300 million to NYU Langone, he raised several times that amount by soliciting sizable donations from his friends and business acquaintances.

TRUSTEES

Trustees are generous in their support of the hospitals and the medical school. The board of NYU Langone Health is composed of a number of philanthropically minded people who donate themselves and help to raise additional support from their friends.

Martin Lipton was active in raising money, recruiting donors from the contacts he had established over the years at his legal practice. Ronald O. Perelman donated $50 million to create the Perelman Center for Emergency Services, which opened in April 2014. In 2015, NYU Langone announced another substantial grant from Paolo Fresco, a trustee of NYU Langone since 2013, who had known Ken Langone since his days at General Electric, where Langone had been a director.

MATRIARCHS AND FAMILIES

Many families have supported NYU Langone over the years—support that is, in large part, driven by women. Larry Tisch, the former chair of NYU, and his brother Preston Robert Tisch were both intimately involved in the university and cared deeply about science and Tisch Hospital. Yet it was their respective wives, Billie Tisch and the late Joan Tisch, who solidified the family's legacy and had a major influence on NYU Langone philanthropy. Larry and Billie Tisch's sons serve on the boards of the university and the Medical Center, along with their daughter-in-law, Alice Tisch. Alice Tisch also founded KiDS of NYU Langone, which is focused on making healthcare better for children and families.

Laurie Perlmutter, who has served on the board of NYU Langone Health for decades, was the driving force behind support for the Perlmutter Cancer Center. She also staffed the gift shop at one point, when she was an auxiliary member.

The late Sylvia Hassenfeld, who had also been a longstanding board member, left a legacy gift to NYU Langone on behalf of her family. The gift from the Hassenfeld family spans three generations and led to the naming of the Hassenfeld Children's Hospital. Sylvia Hassenfeld's granddaughter, Susie Block Casdin, now serves on the board.

Fiona Druckenmiller made a significant gift to the neuroscience institute and continues as co-chair of the NYU Langone Health board. Lori Fink serves as a trustee, along with her husband, Larry Fink. Both have been generous supporters of many areas, including the Perlmutter Cancer Center, which Lori chairs. Trudy Gottesman has given significantly and named the Sala Institute for Child & Family Centered Care after her mother, to advance the practice of family centered care.

Helen Kimmel, a trustee of NYU Langone since 1984, was also instrumental to the transformation of NYU Langone Health. In November 2008 she donated $150 million toward the construction of a new patient pavilion at NYU Langone. Construction of the pavilion was scheduled to begin in 2012 and was completed in 2018. Its 840,000 square feet will increase the space for inpatient care by fifty percent. This contribution followed Helen Kimmel's $10 million contribution in 2005 to establish the Helen L. and Martin S. Kimmel Center for Stem Cell Biology. That was followed a year later by an additional gift of $15 million to establish the Helen L. and Martin S. Kimmel Center for Biology and Medicine at the Skirball Institute for Biomolecular Medicine.

Immediately following her gift for the Kimmel Pavilion, Helen Kimmel announced a $4 million contribution to NYU Langone to establish the Helen L. and Martin S. Kimmel Wound Healing Center. Helen and Martin Kimmel also endowed two basic science professorships in molecular immunology and pharmacology, as well as a new professorship in advanced therapeutics. Neither Helen nor Martin Kimmel are graduates of New York University; Helen graduated from Barnard College and Martin attended Syracuse University. According to an article in *NYU Physician*, at a luncheon honoring Mrs. Kimmel for her contribution of $150 million, she explained, "I must say, it was because my husband, Marty, and I became so excited at the way Bob Grossman is leading this medical center that we decided to do this. With Bob's leadership, we're going to be tops in the country."

"Dr. Grossman has galvanized the Medical Center's board, supporters, and longtime donors. The record giving reflects the trust and confidence that this vision has inspired in many supporters of this institution."

FUNDS TO FINANCE A BRIGHT FUTURE

Healthcare Finance published an article in its November 13, 2008, edition under the headline "NYU Medical Center receives $260 million to boost expansion efforts." The article said the two gifts, from Helen Kimmel and another family that wished to remain anonymous, "brought total philanthropic giving to NYU Langone in 2008 to $506 million." It added that this sum is "believed to be the highest amount ever raised by an academic medical center in a single year. . . . Members of the NYU Board of Trustees attribute much of the upsurge in major gifts to the medical center to Grossman, who was appointed dean and CEO in July 2007 after serving as chairman of radiology at NYU for six years."

In the article, Kenneth Langone said, "Dr. Grossman has galvanized the Medical Center's board, supporters, and longtime donors. The record giving reflects the trust and confidence that this vision has inspired in many supporters of this institution."

The year of 2008 was an exceptional one. However in recent years, NYU Langone Health has continued to raise more than $240 million a year from donations. From 2007 to 2018, NYU Langone has raised $2.686 billion through nearly two hundred thousand gifts, including more than $675 million for capital projects, $181 million for faculty recruitment and retention, $353 million for neuroscience, $337 million for children's services, $244 million for cancer, $109 million for cardiac and vascular, and $118 million for musculoskeletal research and treatment.

In addition, to help achieve Grossman's vision of tuition free medical education, more millions were raised to support scholarships and financial aid, including forty-two endowed scholarships. Moreover, NYU Langone had established forty new endowed professorships.

By virtually every measure, the overall financial picture at NYU Langone has improved dramatically over the past decade. As revenues have climbed, surplus has risen. The institution has invested heavily in improving its physical plant.

The creation of a capital reserve, a rainy day fund, proved to be critical to the facility to recover from the damage inflicted by Hurricane Sandy in 2012. In recounting the financial stress of that time, the Chief Financial Officer during that time period told me, "We have been the only organization I know that has suffered such excruciating damage as we suffered in 2012 as a medical center. The previous year we made $240 million and yet even though we were closed for three months and had an emergency room shutdown for fourteen months, [in] that next twelve-month period we still made $47 million in operations. I do not know of any place that would have been able to do that except for this place."

There are few who calibrate an institution's financial strength more carefully than those who invest in the nation's public bond market. Consequently, the bond market's view of NYU Langone is instructive. The NYU Langone bond rating is A-. This is less than triple A, but in the top tier of ratings, a status that not every hospital attains. Investors express their assessment of a bond issuer's financial prowess even more precisely by establishing the size of the premium the issuer must pay above the cost of similar duration U.S. treasury bonds.

In 2012, NYU Langone sold bonds at a spread of 187.5 basis points over treasuries. In 2013, not long after the hurricane, the spread on its bonds went up to 210 over treasuries. But in 2014, the spread was down to 172. When NYU Langone came to the bond market in May 2017, it raised $600 million at a cost of a mere 125 basis points over treasuries.

NYU Langone's financial vital signs are good and getting better. Over the course of a decade, it has grown its revenues from $2 billion in 2007 to $6 billion in 2016. Meanwhile, it has swung from a loss of $150 million in 2007 to a surplus of approximately $300 million in 2017.

Philanthropy combined with increasing revenues and grants, plus financial efficiency, has brought a dramatic change to NYU Langone's financial picture. The financial turnaround has been crucial not only to support the ongoing activities of the hospital, but also to facilitate Grossman's ambitious plans for transformation and expansion. By enhancing each of its disparate sources of revenue, NYU Langone has managed to simultaneously improve the quality of its services and the quality of its balance sheet.

CHAPTER 8

Hurricane Sandy

Hurricane Sandy, the worst storm in more than a hundred years, hit New York City on October 29, 2012. The most extensive damage was to the mid and lower east side of Manhattan Island. NYU Langone's hospitals and research laboratories were in the bull's-eye. The damage was extensive. The storm arrived just as hope in the future had returned. Hurricane Sandy was an extreme test of the resilience and resourcefulness of NYU Langone's leadership and staff. Their response is an excellent case study in managing black swan events that threaten the very existence of an organization.

THE STORM

Hurricane Sandy was the deadliest and most destructive hurricane of 2012 and the second costliest hurricane in U.S. history. The October 2012 storm, often called Superstorm Sandy, became the largest Atlantic hurricane on record, with high winds spanning 1,100 miles. At least 233 people were killed as the storm passed through eight countries, including approximately 117 people in the United States. Sandy caused more than $75 billion of damage in the United States alone, a total surpassed only by Hurricane Katrina in 2005.

Sandy affected twenty-four states, including the entire Eastern seaboard, and had an impact as far west as parts of Michigan and Wisconsin. There was particularly severe damage in New Jersey and New York. The storm hit the city at night with eighty-mile-per-hour winds, a torrential downpour, and a fourteen-foot storm surge. Low-lying streets in Manhattan and Brooklyn were soon underwater while underground roadways and subway tunnels were flooded.

SITTING IN THE BULL'S-EYE

The storm caused the East River to overflow its banks, damaging the Consolidated Edison power station located on the river's edge and plunging most of Manhattan south of 39th Street into darkness. In the space of thirty minutes, more than eleven million gallons of water poured into the Medical Science Building through a ventilation shaft and spread into Tisch Hospital and other buildings on NYU Langone's main campus. The water knocked out the Medical Science Building's fuel pumps for the backup generators and destroyed a vast array of equipment.

Bob Berne said, "The prediction was that the water might reach eleven feet, above flood stage. The flood actually reached fourteen or fifteen feet."

In the space of thirty minutes, more than eleven million gallons of water poured into the Medical Science Building through a ventilation shaft and spread into Tisch Hospital and other buildings on NYU Langone's main campus.

The situation unfolding at NYU Langone as the evening progressed on October 29, 2012, was vividly described in an article in the *New Yorker* by its editor, David Remnick: "By late Monday, the conditions were frightening. The lights were out. There was no water. The toilets didn't flush. There were power failures in the emergency room and the transplant unit."[1]

In my interview with Bob Grossman he remembered his reaction to the storm in vivid detail. He recalled, "The weather reports were all wrong. The situation was totally chaotic. None of the systems worked. None of the backups worked. There was no communication. The walkie-talkies did not work. The emergency lighting did not work. We had a life or death situation."

I believe NYU Langone's leadership and staff response to this disaster contains valuable lessons for any enterprise facing a sudden and unexpected existential threat.

VISIBLE LEADERSHIP

As soon as Grossman recognized the potential magnitude of the storm's impact, he created a command center. He moved all of the senior staff to the central lobby of the hospital. He said, "This was an incredibly important decision. The command center was the first thing everyone saw. There was a big table with the management team making decisions in real time."

The command center conveyed a sense of stability along with an aura of decisiveness, he said. Despite the apparent chaos, someone seemed to be in control.

---

1   See "Leaving Langone: One Story," *The New Yorker*, October 30, 2012.

The command center conveyed a sense of stability along with an aura of decisiveness, he said. Despite the apparent chaos, someone seemed to be in control. The command center also enabled Grossman and his management team to observe the staff and monitor conditions as they were unfolding.

A blurry shot of Dean and CEO Robert Grossman at the command center in the lobby, taken the night Hurricane Sandy hit

PRIORITIZE AND ACT

Grossman told me, "We prioritized first getting the patients safely out." As the storm worsened, many patients were sent either home or to hospitals in parts of the city that were predicted to be safe from flooding. For those who remained, if a total evacuation became necessary, they gave each patient a detailed medical record to make sure that receiving hospitals had the information they would need if they were transferred. They notified family members where to find their loved ones in case the worst happened and they needed to be moved. And the worst happened. The facilities flooded and the power, including backup generators, failed.

View of the lobby as NYU Langone is evacuated of patients the night of the hurricane

The sickest and most vulnerable patients were moved first, including twenty infants from the neonatal intensive care unit, some of whom required battery-powered respirators. The hospital staff had printed out tags for each of the children in the pediatrics department containing their entire medical history up to the last hour. They put these histories into plastic sleeves and pinned them on to each bed. The doctors and nurses carried every child downstairs, because the power failure had knocked out the elevators, and put each one into a waiting ambulance. Every child's family was there and was ready to go with them.

Evacuation of adult patients followed. Many were in critical condition. Some walked down the stairs from their hospital room, but many had to be carried down through pitch-black stairwells. They were met by an armada of ambulances, many of which were driven by volunteers who had come from miles away to help out. Over the course of more than twelve hours, 322 patients were safely evacuated.

> The sickest and most vulnerable patients were moved first, including twenty infants from the neonatal intensive care unit. . . . Doctors and nurses carried every child downstairs, because the power failure had knocked out the elevators.

Medical workers assist a patient into an ambulance during the evacuation

THE MIRACLE ON 34TH STREET

It turned out that one of the patients in NYU Langone that night was its namesake, the board chair, Kenneth Langone, who had been hospitalized for pneumonia. When he learned the hospital was being evacuated, he got dressed and walked down the stairs to the command center, where he watched the institution's senior management orchestrate this historic evacuation.

"I am glad I was there," Langone said. "It was a gift for me because I was able to see what a Herculean effort the nurses and doctors made, especially for the premature babies and other patients." After watching patients being carried down numerous flights of stairs on stretchers, often with only flashlights to show the way, then safely evacuated, Langone dubbed the process "the miracle on 34th Street." Later that night, Langone walked out of the hospital, waded through the water surrounding the hospital, and was driven home.

"The attitude was 'Okay, let's look at the problem. Here is what we have to do today. Who do we need to call? What do we need?' Our leadership team came to the hospital every day, seven days a week, even when there was no power and it was freezing cold."

"It was all hands on deck throughout much of the storm," said Richard Tsien, director of the NYU Neuroscience Institute and chair of the Department of Physiology and Neuroscience. "Graduate students helped patients get out of hospitals. I took a series of buses to Columbia University to get dry ice to save the reagents of some of our scientists. There was a sort of attitude that we could all pitch in."

CENTRALIZED COMMAND

As NYU Langone management sought to assess the damage and formulate a recovery plan, Grossman said, "We operated from the lobby for a few days, and then moved into a semipermanent command center on the campus, even though we were without electricity. Everybody was at the table. It was no politics. It was all business. The attitude was, 'Okay, let's look at the problem. Here is what we have to do today. Who do we need to call? What do we need?' Our leadership team came to the hospital every day, seven days a week, even when there was no power and it was freezing cold."

The semipermanent command center on the NYU Langone campus

As Grossman toured NYU Langone with officials from the state and federal government, he estimated that the cost of repairs would be well over a billion dollars. While most of NYU Langone's campus had to be closed, its senior executives were determined to keep the institution functioning in whatever ways possible.

SUPPORT THE STAFF

A day after the storm, Bob Grossman called Ken Langone and said, "You know, a lot of our staff do not know if they have homes. Their whole lives have been discombobulated. I think that we ought to assure them that for as long as we are shut they should not have to worry about income. We'll keep paying them."

Langone agreed, saying, "Bob, that is the smartest decision in the world. We will make an executive decision. Let's do it."

> Without exception, all those who had experienced the hurricane told me the same thing almost in the same words. . . . "We will never forget how the senior management promised to keep paying our full salary even though we were closed."

In the course of my research for this book and during my own medical treatment, I spent many hours with the management and staff. Without exception, all those who had experienced the hurricane told me the same thing almost in the same words: "We will always remember how we all pulled together during this difficult time." "We will never forget how the senior management promised to keep paying our full salary even though we were closed."

BACK TO WORK

In the immediate aftermath of the storm, senior management made a concerted effort to allow as much of the staff as possible to get back to work. Many activities were simply relocated to NYU Langone's network of what was then more than ninety ambulatory care centers. Doctors and nurses who could not be relocated to other NYU facilities were offered jobs in other hospitals during the interim. In a remarkable testament to loyalty, virtually all of the professional staff that found temporary jobs in other New York hospitals returned to work at NYU Langone as soon as they could. Medical school lectures were initially suspended in the aftermath of the storm, but they too were relocated to other facilities and resumed a week later.

As for research, Dafna Bar-Sagi, the vice dean for Science and chief scientific officer, said, "We put the highest priority on placing people back in a lab as soon as possible so that they could start to work again. We accomplished this by moving research teams from the affected buildings to laboratories in unaffected sites on the Medical Center campus. Some of our scientists moved to laboratory space that was temporarily unoccupied in the downtown NYU campus." She added, "This is where investment in cultivating a strong sense of community paid off. The collegiality and the willingness of people to accommodate and help others were critical to enabling us to get back on our feet."

> "The number one lesson about leadership is to be there, on the spot," Grossman said. "It was important that people know that we would emerge from the crisis in better shape than when we began."

The NYU Langone leaders began carefully planning which functions to restore and in what order. Shortly after the storm, Grossman asked the chief of radiology whether he could get an MRI unit up and running within two weeks. Grossman was told that it could be done if there was a way to clear all the red tape. Grossman made it happen. Similarly, NYU Langone would end up being without an emergency room for fourteen months, but in its stead, Grossman proposed opening an urgent care center. Burke said, "Over a weekend, he built it and opened it."

As the work of NYU Langone resumed in makeshift quarters, management set to work rebuilding its own facilities. While plans were being formulated by senior managers in the command center, Grossman continued to hold weekly meetings with NYU Langone staff, where he was constantly explaining and updating ongoing developments and plans.

"The number one lesson about leadership is to be there, on the spot," Grossman said. "It was important that people know that we would emerge from the crisis in better shape than when we began. Everybody had to understand that we would come out of this stronger and better."

FEMA AND INSURANCE FUNDS

Grossman and the senior leadership team knew that support from the federal government, the Federal Emergency Management Agency (FEMA), would be absolutely essential to recovery. One of the first tasks was seeking out insurance and federal disaster relief money. Grossman told me, "We had FEMA here right away. We hired people to work just with FEMA. We had teams working with our insurance companies." At the time, FEMA was coming away from the Hurricane Katrina aftermath in New Orleans and, Grossman said, "the administration in Washington knew they had to do things differently."

FEMA's standard practice had been to pay for replacing damaged buildings and equipment. As Grossman put it, FEMA would say, "You decide what was damaged, you figure out how much it costs, you build it, you replace it. Then we audit the hell out of it. Then there are big fights about the money five, ten, fifteen years later. An army of people measure and audit the cost and so on."

After Katrina, however, an alternative approach emerged: Determine a fixed price for the repair of damage based on the work of estimators and reach an agreement with FEMA on the total. Then FEMA provides an amount equal to ninety percent of the cost.

With this approach, Grossman explained, "If you go over the estimate, it is on your dime. If you spend less than the estimate, you can apply to reprogram the money: for example, to cover the costs of other mitigation matters—subject to Federal Emergency Management Agency approval. In theory, they will not nickel and dime you on the estimate. They will ask if you used the correct specifications and did all the things you needed to. After about a year and a half of discussions, we opted to go with the fixed-price option. We were the guinea pig for the fixed contract."

As the discussions with FEMA unfolded, Grossman said, "Ken Langone was there from day one, urging politicians to get us the Federal Emergency Management Agency money." He added this was "a total political process. If you do not have people like Ken and advocates like New York senator Chuck Schumer in your corner, you are finished. Senator Schumer was on top of the process." Grossman added, "Ken, who is a Republican, totally supported Schumer, who is a Democrat. We also had the support of Eric Cantor, a Republican from Virginia, and the then-majority leader of the House of Representatives. That is the best of American politics."

Although the discussions with FEMA were protracted, the Chief Financial Officer at the time, Michael Burke, said, "The federal government really came through when we needed them." By contrast, Grossman said, "The insurance company took a hard line. We had to sue it." While NYU Langone estimated total damages at $1.5 billion, it filed insurance claims totaling about $1.4 billion, and since then it has been in litigation and discovery.

PRUDENT RISK

Thoughtful risk-taking had become typical at NYU Langone under Grossman. "Let me place the Federal Emergency Management Agency discussions in a broader context," he said. "One theme that emerged from all our work in restructuring NYU Langone, the medical school, and the hospital is that we take prudent risks. We took prudent risks in dealing with the Federal Emergency Management Agency and opting for the new reimbursement system."

UNEXPECTED OPPORTUNITY

As NYU Langone set about cleaning up and rebuilding its facilities, Grossman's message was that the storm was to be viewed not simply as a disaster but also as an unexpected opportunity. Grossman said, "Every decision regarding the hurricane was a long-term decision. We were not just going to solve the problem. We were going to solve it for the long term."

Some facilities, like the emergency room, already needed to be brought up to date and were able to be renovated and expanded during recovery, saving time and money overall. Although reopening its emergency room quickly could have generated much-needed revenue for NYU Langone, Grossman chose to reopen it in the broader context of the reemergence of the entire hospital so that its facilities could be reconstructed.

Bob Berne pointed out, "Strange as it may seem, Hurricane Sandy, in late October 2012, helped us implement the new information system." Berne explained, "We had scheduled the launch of Epic for clinical inpatient services for December 2012. When we closed the hospital in late October, we were able to clean out the old system. When we opened again in January 2013, we also initiated Epic. We did not have a midnight changeover. We were able to use the downtime to do thousands of hours of classes and training. The flood did not affect the NYU

Langone Orthopedic Hospital, which is the musculoskeletal hospital on 17th Street. They were open the whole time. We implemented Epic there first. We used it as a training site. Then, when we opened up in January, we opened up with Epic."

OPENING DAY

After eight weeks of cleaning, refurbishing, and building, NYU Langone reopened on December 27, 2012, two months after Hurricane Sandy, and well ahead of most predictions. That day, surgeons performed fifty-five procedures, and many of the hospital's other departments were back to full capacity. However, the Emergency Department, which had typically been handling some one hundred and eighty patients per day and had suffered particularly severe damage during the storm, would remain closed well into 2014.

There were several keys to its successful reopening. One was the decision to pay employees, as mentioned earlier. There would not have been fifty-five surgical procedures on opening day if there had not been a trained surgical staff on hand. Had NYU Langone not paid salaries, many staff members likely would have drifted off to other jobs. Indeed, other healthcare institutions were seeking to "pick off" NYU Langone staff and hire them at the time. While the policy of paying salaries was expensive, it would have cost more if NYU Langone had to recruit and train new staff, and this would have inevitably been accompanied by a much slower reopening process.

PLAN FOR THE UNEXPECTED

Money in the bank was essential for survival and rapid recovery. The storm had bombarded both sides of NYU Langone's financial statements. While Sandy would create an enormous repair bill, the Medical

Center was not generating any revenues, yet it was running up a vast range of ongoing daily costs, from phone bills to interest payments, as well as the cost of the salaries paid to nonworking staff. Hurricane Sandy caused NYU Langone to forgo around $500 million dollars in medical revenues that the hospital would otherwise have taken in, as well as many millions more in other losses.

Fortunately, NYU Langone had the foresight to create a rainy day fund. The Medical Center had saved $10 million a month for the prior four years. By the time the storm hit, they had $480 million in the bank and access to an additional $300 million in royalties from Remicade. There was an additional $700 million in the university endowment, which was never used. Burke explained, "To cover our expenses during that time, we spent $150 million of the Remicade money and another $50 million from insurance. NYU Langone also received $200 million from the Federal Emergency Management Agency as an advance on payments that would come later." As these funds were marshaled, Burke said, "We lived on that for eighteen months while our emergency room was still shut down."

The improvements that had been made in NYU Langone's financial condition ensured that they could weather the financial storm. Bob Berne said, "If Hurricane Sandy had hit in 2005, closing the hospital permanently would have been part of the conversation. By 2012, it was never part of the conversation. The only conversations we had were focused on reopening the hospital as soon as possible."

While the hospitals and medical school were able to resume and restart their activities, research was more difficult. Dafna Bar-Sagi said, "The research community was decimated. It is hard to put into words how difficult this was for us. We were unable to access the laboratories in the affected buildings in some cases for over a year, and for many investigators, many years' worth of work was destroyed." She added, "Under the directive of Bob Grossman, every affected researcher received institutional funds to jump-start their research operations. This commitment was made way before we received any money for disaster relief from the federal government. It was instrumental in accelerating our recovery."

Bar-Sagi said the NYU Langone response compares very favorably with the disaster recovery process at other institutions: "One of the first things I did, within a few days after Sandy hit, was to bring in a person from Tulane. He had been in a position similar to mine during Hurricane Katrina and its aftermath." She said this visitor "ended up having a very positive effect on the community. It was uplifting for all of us to hear him speak. He said, 'I know it looks horrible now, but you will recover.' Then he took me aside and told me, 'I know that right now it seems that the most important thing is to bring back functionality to the facilities. Do not worry, the recovery of the infrastructure will happen. What you need to pay most of your attention to is the morale of the faculty.'" Tulane's medical center lost about forty of two hundred fifty faculty members after Katrina. How many faculty did NYU Langone lose after Sandy? "Very few, if any," Bar-Sagi said.

A CASE STUDY

The impact of the hurricane and the way NYU Langone bounced back was such an epic tale of disaster and recovery that it prompted preparation of a Harvard Business School case study entitled "Weathering the Storm at NYU Langone Medical Center," by Robert S. Huckman, Raffaela Sadun, and Michael Morris (February 3, 2016). NYU Langone has also prepared an eight-minute video recounting the storm and NYU Langone's recovery.

Hurricane Sandy had an impact on the NYU Langone organization that went beyond storm damage. Steve Abramson said the hurricane and its aftermath made it particularly clear that Grossman "is extremely skilled as a leader." He added, "The example I will cite, and we all saw firsthand, is the impact and recovery from Hurricane Sandy. Bob was on the ground immediately, helping to evacuate patients on the night of the storm. Subsequently, he led the leadership team in an unheated room, hour after hour making decisions, saying to people, 'We are going to get back and running in ninety days.'"

Despite the massive disruptions that Sandy caused, the following year NYU Langone was ranked first in quality and patient safety among all academic medical centers in a national ranking survey.

Abramson said, "At the time, everyone thought it would be a minimum of six months. Through his efforts, daily leadership, skill, and by working closely with Ken Langone, NYU Langone achieved the ninety-day goal, and is now stronger than ever." Abramson also said, "Bob was a leader during a crisis. Yes, prior to Hurricane Sandy he shook up the old and sclerotic system through his management skills, but he was deep in the trenches during a crisis when we really needed his support. That really made a difference in people's attitudes."

Looking back at Sandy, Grossman said that as a chief executive officer, "you know you are going to be faced with a black swan event. You do not know what it is. But it is going to happen." The issue is how well a manager deals with it. In Grossman's case, he said, "The truth is, in my heart, I absolutely believed we were going to be better. In retrospect, maybe I was overconfident, but I was confident that we were going to get through it. I was almost serene. I was sure we would emerge stronger than we were before."

Despite the massive disruptions that Sandy caused, the following year NYU Langone was ranked first in quality and patient safety among all academic medical centers in a national ranking survey. Moreover, Burke said, "We actually generated a surplus of $47 million at the Hospitals Center in the first twelve months post Sandy. Then we produced a surplus the next year, also, of $100 million."

Hurricane Sandy was a stress test for the revitalized NYU Langone. It created enormous challenges for the institution's management as well as for its finances. NYU board chairman William Berkley said, "If there ever was an event that could have derailed us, Hurricane Sandy was it. We could not and did not plan for such a disaster. Yet when it happened, we managed it and emerged even stronger than before. We did it through sheer force of will. Bob focused on what was essential to take us through the crisis, which was focusing on people first and the physical plant second. I am in the insurance business, and I can tell you how he handled that horrendous crisis was a great success. All of Bob's leadership skills were on show."

Visit www.youtube.com/watch?v=3z078ak7_sc to view an
NYU Langone video highlighting recovery efforts after Hurricane Sandy

Despite Hurricane Sandy occurring less than five years into the Grossman regime, NYU was in a much stronger fiscal situation than it was when Grossman became CEO and dean. It was making money. Its fundraising operation was a well-oiled machine, and so were its billing and collection activities. Most importantly, there was widespread agreement that it was doing high-quality work. It stood the test of a legendary hurricane and emerged in ways that enhanced its reputation, its morale, and its understanding of the need for resilience.

PART III

Taking a Closer Look

CHAPTER 9

Quality and Safety

P *atient centered* are the first words of the NYU Langone vision state-ment. Quality and safety are essential elements of patient care. When Bob Grossman first became CEO and dean, NYU Langone was rated in the bottom third of academic medical centers for both quality and safety, number sixty of the ninety academic medical schools then rated. In recent years NYU Langone Health is rated, by the same ser-vice, as having among the best quality and safety records in the country. How did this transformation happen?

PATIENTS FIRST

Improving quality and safety flows from the desire to put patients first. From the very outset Grossman and his team put the patient experi-ence front and center in all their efforts. That had not always been so. In a series of interviews, Martha Radford, chief quality officer at NYU Langone Health, provided a firsthand account of the transformation. She recalled, "When I arrived at NYU Langone, the quality and safety score was about two-thirds the way down the list for academic medical centers. I was here before Bob Grossman became dean. I was starting to measure quality—for example, the acute myocardial infarction measures. I knew they would be publicly reported eventually. I suspected, and I was right, that they were going to be used for financial incentives in the future. I went to senior management and showed them our performance, which was terrible. We were only giving around sixty percent perfect care back then. I said that was not good. The hospital president at that time responded, 'Sixty percent is fine. These things do not matter.'"

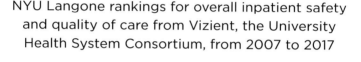

NYU Langone rankings for overall inpatient safety and quality of care from Vizient, the University Health System Consortium, from 2007 to 2017

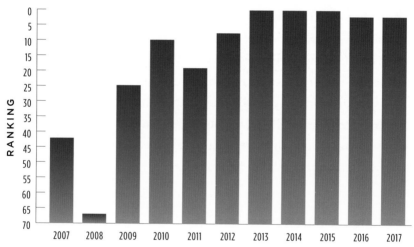

The situation changed quickly under the new leadership. Radford told me, "I went to the person who then became the functional hospital president, Bernie Birnbaum. I said, 'We are not doing well.' He said, 'Martha, you are right. What do you need?' I said, 'I need an executive team to focus on quality.' He said, 'Go ahead and create the team.'"

Birnbaum had come with Grossman from the University of Pennsylvania radiology department. When Birnbaum became her boss, Radford said, "It was a breath of fresh air."

While leadership drove the improvements in patient care, technology played a crucial role in guiding this leadership. The quality of patient care was yet another realm at NYU Langone in which what got measured would be managed, and consequently, the development of measures and benchmarks to assess every facet of patient care was crucial to the improvement process.

Improving quality and safety flows from the desire to put patients first. From the very outset Grossman and his team put the patient experience front and center in all their efforts.

According to Martha Radford, research has identified four attributes that correlate with success in improving the quality of medical care: *managerial leadership*, *clinical leadership*, *timely and actionable data*, and *shared goals* throughout the organization. "Here at NYU Langone we have all four in place," she said.

LEADERSHIP

The drive for improved quality in patient care at NYU Langone began with the creation of a quality control team. With Birnbaum's support, Radford said, "I convened an executive group that included leaders of the constituencies that needed to deal with quality improvement across the board." This executive team would go on to meet every three weeks. Focusing the attention of this high-level team led to quick results.

For example, Radford remembered that "we moved from sixty percent error free to ninety percent error free for all of the processes that were being measured in the first year." One of the factors that helped Radford's team deliver results was that Bernie Birnbaum came to the first meeting of the committee and "gave a five-minute pep talk, basically saying that this was important," Radford recalled. All of the team members take ownership of their roles when an organizational leader lets them know how important their work is.

TECHNOLOGY

Radford emphasized, "Technology was key to our success." Technology would become "the backbone of a well-developed and multifaceted effort to improve quality," Radford said, because "it was the key to measuring and benchmarking." Efforts to measure quality require establishing quantitative measures in three areas: structure, process, and outcomes. Structure includes fixed parameters, such as the number of beds, staffing ratio, policies and procedures, and equipment. While it is generally clear how to measure the structured costs of medical services, measuring quality or processes is more difficult.

MEASURING OUTCOMES

In discussing initiatives to improve quality and control cost, Paresh Shah, the vice chair of Quality and Innovation in Surgery and the chief of the Division of General Surgery at NYU Langone Health, said, "Our initial metrics measure patient satisfaction and hospital-acquired conditions. We are now creating a metric to evaluate department and disease-specific measures of quality, as the initial metric is very blunt." Shah added, "We have very good measures for some diseases. For others we do not. And we are asking our clinical departments to provide guidance." Outcome measures are usually associated with a time period, such as thirty days after release from the hospital. Shah also said, "Readmissions within thirty days is a quality measure for anybody. There are some generic quality measures."

Many quality measures related to outcomes are beyond the purview of a hospital. Shah said, "The really positive outcomes that we are looking for," such as return to work status, return of functional status, disease free intervals, and overall survival, "are not measurable in the context of an episode of care." These take place after, sometimes long after, the patient has completed his or her medical care. He told me that although NYU Langone measures of quality meet or exceed the best in the country, there is still room for improvement.

Measuring process can also be complicated. Shah added, "Most quality measures that are assessed in the healthcare delivery system today are negative measures. There are very few positive quality measures."

In addition to establishing metrics for a process or a procedure, such as a coronary bypass, NYU Langone also established goals for quality improvement. Hospitals are required to have their own yearly quality improvement plans. Each year, NYU Langone staff create a plan to meet internal goals, critique the plan, and then move forward with implementation. The quality improvement goals are reviewed every year.

Radford said, "We can measure our own processes internally. We are trying to automate process measurements by using our electronic health record system. That is a challenge because electronic health records are not built for such measurements. The electronic record systems are transactional; they are not analytical platforms. We must reengineer the system to allow us to measure process. You must have someone with a critical eye to oversee this work—someone like me."

Once measurements were established for a full range of activities at NYU Langone hospitals, they provided indications of how well various processes and procedures were doing their jobs and offered guidance in where to focus attention on improving quality. As these metrics were developed and applied in a variety of areas, NYU Langone sought to develop improvements in a host of processes. Radford said, "We executed on many different projects. Many were long-term projects. We proceeded gradually, gradually, gradually."

One general focal point was variability in results: Why were there significant differences in the results achieved by the same procedures? How could this variability be reduced or eliminated? Shah said, "I focus my attention on areas of high variability. I see reducing variability in healthcare delivery as one of our great opportunities."

Sometimes simply measuring results could bring changes—and improvements. That was a conclusion of an essay in the November–December 2017 *Harvard Business Review*, cited earlier, entitled "The IT Transformation Health Care Needs." The authors of this article looked at information technology at NYU Langone, and they noted that providing additional information "increased the willingness of department chairs and administrators to challenge norms and to design and implement improvements. For example, the need to establish data fields in the information technology system forced discussions about the definition of 'excellence' and the best ways to assess the impact of frontline staff."

> Sometimes simply measuring results
> could bring changes—and improvements.

Many of the changes designed to improve quality did not involve new technology, new equipment, or new staff members. Improvements resulted from thinking about ways in which existing processes could be performed better.

ACTION

As an example of the interplay between data collection and aspirations for improved quality, Radford explained how NYU Langone dealt with in-hospital mortality rates. "When I first came here in 2005," she said, "our hospital mortality was higher than expected. We were not very good. The usual response is that we are not properly coding all relevant comorbidities." Comorbidity is the simultaneous presence of two chronic diseases or conditions in a patient.

Hospital mortality at NYU Langone, from 2008 to 2018

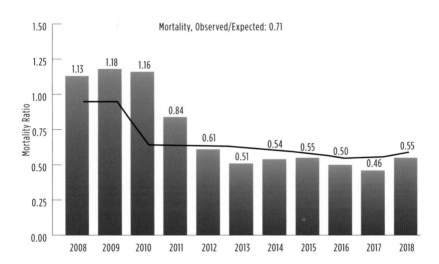

Radford added, "We launched a project to capture all the comorbidities. We saw a bit of a drop in our observed mortality, but not much." Meanwhile, she added, "We noticed from our case reviews that we had a number of cases—not a lot, but a number—where it seemed as if patients were languishing for a time before any interventions were applied. This is what I call a failure to recognize and respond to deterioration."

Hospital acquired conditions at NYU Langone, from 2011 to 2018

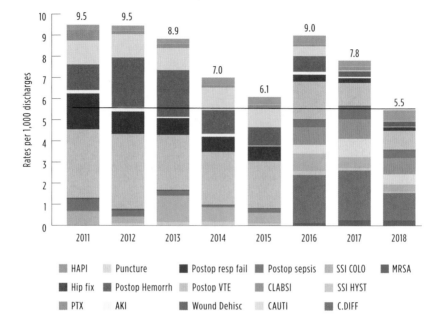

■ HAPI	■ Puncture	■ Postop resp fail	■ Postop sepsis	■ SSI COLO	■ MRSA
■ Hip fix	■ Postop Hemorrh	■ Postop VTE	■ CLABSI	■ SSI HYST
■ PTX	AKI	■ Wound Dehisc	■ CAUTI	■ C.DIFF

NYU Langone's solution? "We created a rapid response team," Radford said. "This helped improve in-hospital mortality a little bit more." Nonetheless, she said, "Still, there was languishment going on. What was happening was adherence to an ethos of, 'Oh, I cannot call anybody for help because I am tough, and I can do it myself.' We decided to ask all the departments to develop escalation policies to encourage their nurses, their residents, and their junior people to call for help early on. These response teams are like gold. They provide immediate assistance when you need it. You get zero kudos for trying to tough it out yourself. That really changed the culture. It is now no longer acceptable not to call a response team when you first think one may be needed. I count this shift as a major success."

"Response teams are like gold. They provide
immediate assistance when you need it. . . .
You get zero kudos for trying to tough it out yourself."

This approach helped bring two distinct drops in mortality at two different times. "The first drop occurred in 2010," Radford said. "This is when we were working on coding and documentation. We put in response teams throughout, but the policies and procedures happened here too. . . . That is when the rate really dropped. Then the rate began to climb again when the data for NYU Langone Hospital–Brooklyn, which we acquired, began to be included." To help this new hospital rise to the level of the rest of NYU Langone, Radford explained, "We did exactly what we did before: coding and documentation, response teams, and policies and procedures for all departments. Now their mortality rate is coming down quickly."

PROMPTS

Like the rapid response teams, the inauguration of prompts was another innovation in the processes used across NYU Langone. "There are very few things that have been shown to change physician behavior," Radford said, but one thing that does is prompts, which are reminders. NYU Langone has tweaked its technology so that "the information system prompts you to do the right thing," Radford explained. For example, if a physician admits a patient with pneumonia, she said, "you have a pneumonia order set. Embedded in that order set are orders that tell you the right antibiotics to prescribe. That is a prompt."

Infections related to surgical procedures
at NYU Langone, from 2008 to 2018

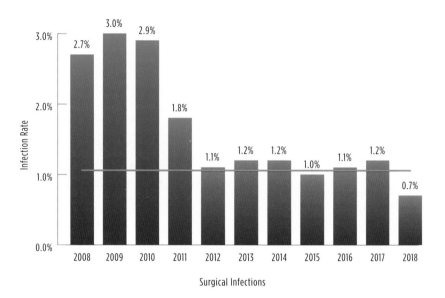

Surgical Infections

The initial response was resistance, she said: "I asked the house staff, outside the team meeting, 'How about those questions?' Half of them loved the prompts, and half of them hated them. Meanwhile, our performance was going up, up, up. I realized that the prompt still served its function even for the half that hated it. They would answer 'No, the patient does not have pneumonia,' even when they did. Nonetheless, the physician would still do the right thing. It did not matter whether they answered yes or no. Because of the prompts, they were aware of what they should do."

Radford emphasized that doctors deliberately refused to answer the question correctly: "They would tell the computer a patient did not have pneumonia even though they knew they had pneumonia. They did not want to be bothered with all the prompts." Radford said: "They would do their history and physical, and their impression would be pneumonia, and they would do the right treatments. They just did not want to do it with the computer. Part of the learning was we had to make these prompts easy and fun, not a burden. Anything people do with computers always involves more clicks. People hate more clicks. You have to figure out how to require the minimal number of clicks."

"Anything people do with computers always involves more clicks. People hate more clicks. You have to figure out how to require the minimal number of clicks."

DOCTOR-NURSE PARTNERSHIP

Partnering for Quality is yet another small innovation that boosted quality. Press said that when he was chief medical officer, he initiated this program along with the chief nursing officer. The goal of this program was to create a partnership between the nurses who supervise the care for each unit and the physicians staffed in the unit in order to improve the quality of care. Press explained, "We already had nurse managers, and sometimes even assistant nurse managers, but we did not have doctors serving as medical directors for them. There was no leadership from the physicians. To address that gap, we created a medical director program. We assigned a doctor to each unit as a medical director."

He noted, "We had the medical directors partner with nurse managers to create duos of medical director-nurse manager on each unit. A primary task of the duos was to supervise quality improvement. At the beginning we let them focus on any quality metric they wanted. Later, they chose one of three quality metrics. We measured their performance, and our quality measures improved on each unit. The collaboration between our doctors and nurses also improved."

BEST PRACTICES

As NYU Langone staff created a variety of new approaches and sought to introduce them, it quickly became clear that they had to combat both lethargy and resistance in order to encourage acceptance of the new best practices.

A key element of this process has been a system of representatives who make sure that new ideas and processes are implemented. These representatives include a variety of people, ranging from a young hospitalist who worked with other hospitalists, to a chief surgical officer. Radford explains, "After each meeting every member of the oversight group had homework to finish before the next meeting. The homework was slightly out of their comfort zone. Gradually, people's comfort zones expanded. Then they became real change agents."

TRANSPARENCY

Transparent patient outcomes allow one doctor within NYU to compare his or her own results to those in the system who treat similar patients. The doctors' dashboard allows them to view their performance and NYU Langone's performance against national and global standards. Transparency brings out the best competitive instincts of doctors and nurses. Doctors are healers by profession. They want to do the best for their patients. Transparent data allows them to know exactly how their patients fare when compared to others. That ignites an internal drive to improve.

Many of the quality improvement initiatives were data driven:
They were activities in which measurements showed poor
results and clearly required attention and analysis.

INCENTIVES

Another element in motivating changes in physician behavior was the creation of financial incentives. Paresh Shah told me, "A system of gain sharing was created at the department level to reward clinical departments for the improvements in value they achieve."

Radford agreed with Shah that although information systems and financial incentives are valuable in disseminating and implementing best practices, they were not the only determinants. Often gains in quality were achieved simply because doctors took note of suggestions about best practices.

Innovation for quality improvement is not necessarily costly nor complicated. Radford pointed out, "Our success was all about aligning vectors and having the right people in the room." In the case of many innovations designed to improve quality, there were "no additional resources, no people, no money involved. Nothing. That project was accomplished through the collaboration of busy people focused on the goal," she said.

BEYOND SIX SIGMA

Many of the quality improvement initiatives were data driven: They were activities in which measurements showed poor results and clearly required attention and analysis. Many of the new efforts came under a Lean Six Sigma program. "Six Sigma is about precision and accuracy based on data-driven decisions," Joyce Long explained. "Lean is about speed and efficiency." Starting in 2008, NYU Langone began to train "Lean Champions," who then trained their colleagues and inculcated the goals and values of the Six Sigma program. "The Lean Six Sigma approach was implemented across all departments and operating rooms," Long said. "We were able to improve our processes and eliminate waste and inefficiencies."

NYU Langone also sought to improve quality through several other systemic undertakings. "We have four levels at which we implement quality improvement," Radford said, with one being "big, organization-wide projects" such as "training all of our care sites in High Reliability techniques and installing value-based management."

Grossman described High Reliability techniques "as having to do with communication, teamwork, scripts for calling out when there is a safety threat, and making alerts acceptable, among others." Grossman added that part of the "High Reliability initiative" was to "create a no-fault culture, one where people talk about near misses so that we can learn from them."

> "We take the defensiveness out of people admitting to errors. Reducing defensiveness—that is the key."

He told me that as part of this effort, "We had a person from the nuclear power industry speak to us about how to avoid accidents. The industry in the United States has not had an accident since Three Mile Island. We want to be that reliable." He added, "How do I go about it? Every week at the chairs meeting I have people present cases that are near misses. Everybody learns from the experience of others. We take the defensiveness out of people admitting to errors. Reducing defensiveness—that is the key." In discussing this with me, Grossman returned to his focus on culture: "Cultural change is critical. People have to be willing to talk about errors."

VALUE-BASED MANAGEMENT

Value-based management is an operating principle of NYU Langone. Grossman and Shah both describe it as value and outcome divided by cost. One aspect of the drive for value is the realization that over time, more and more people will be covered by government insurance, Medicare, and Medicaid. Medicare and Medicaid payments sometimes don't even cover the cost of the necessary treatment. The concern over how to deliver high-quality care at a cost affordable to providers is a central question in American healthcare today, as it is in many countries.

Average length of stay at NYU Langone, from 2008 to 2018

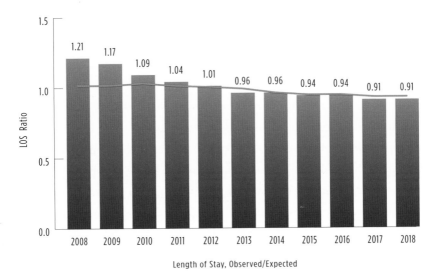

Length of Stay, Observed/Expected

It is possible to do great things if cost is no obstacle, but cost is almost always a critical factor in determining what is possible. Three years ago, NYU Langone hospitals were judged to be number one in quality and safety, but were among the worst performers in terms of cost of care. Grossman spearheaded a wide-ranging set of initiatives that sought to harness two different, and sometimes conflicting, aspirations: to be the best in quality and safety and to control costs at the same time.

It is possible to do great things if cost is
no obstacle, but cost is almost always a
critical factor in determining what is possible.

To advance these objectives, the former chief of Hospital Operations, Robert Press, said, "We needed to engage the doctors. Our method was to show the doctors comparative data from other hospitals. I prepared a presentation tailored to each group to show them where there was room for improvement." For example, he said, "the data showed that our doctors were using more units of blood for transfusions than were many other hospitals. Blood is expensive. In addition, the more blood used in a transfusion, the higher the risk of transfusion-related complications. Our team then encouraged the doctors to come up with corrective actions. I knew that if they devised the corrective actions themselves, they would do their best to make sure they were implemented. I think having the doctors propose the solution to a problem is a powerful approach. If what they come up with is logical, and they assist in the process design, they invest themselves in making it work."

To integrate this kind of thinking, Press said, "We engaged the doctors in each of the clinical areas. We selected a champion to drive change for each area. The champions must be respected by their peers and have good interpersonal skills. For example, for orthopedics the doctors analyzed the orthopedics guidelines and reviewed the literature in their specialty. They learned what the benchmarks for excellence were, and that allowed them to understand their performance as compared to others in the field. We created evidence based guidelines based on data."

NYU Langone also improved the way they controlled costs associated with surgery preference cards, or the list of the preferred instruments and supplies to be available in the operating room. At the time, the number of instruments and supplies on the card varied widely depending on the surgeon, even for the same procedure. Some of the instruments and supplies on some of the cards were never even used. With the agreement of the surgeons, NYU Langone started standardizing surgical preference cards to save money.

NYU Langone also initiated a program designed to increase the number of patients that are discharged from the hospital to their own homes rather than to another medical facility. This goal was defined in response to Medicare efficiency metrics, with a set percentage of home discharges for each department to reach.

Grossman also set a goal to increase the number of patient discharges from the hospital that occur before noon each day. A prime benefit of discharge before noon is that the hospital can refill the bed and get the next patient in early in the afternoon. Early checkout means that hospital resources are used more efficiently. This simple change can reduce the hospital stay by a full day on average. Length of stay is an increasingly important metric for hospitals in the eyes of government and private sector payers.

According to Press, Grossman told him, "'Only ten percent of our patient discharges occurred before noon. I think we can do better. We should have thirty-five percent discharges before noon.' Nobody thought it was doable. We have now surpassed that goal. Forty-two percent of our hospital discharges occur before noon."

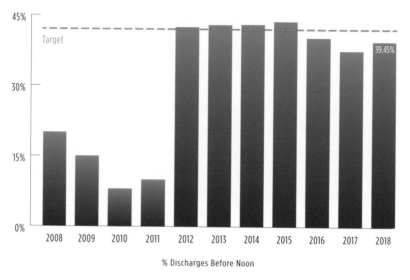

Discharges by noon at NYU Langone Health, from 2008 to 2018

% Discharges Before Noon

Early discharge "is better for the patients being discharged, because the longer a patient is in the hospital, the more likely they are to sustain an adverse event," Press said. "Additionally, patients discharged earlier can pick up prescribed medications and have more time to get everything set up if they have a homecare agency." Meanwhile, as more patients depart earlier in the day, more new patients can be admitted early enough to have a full workup, including diagnostic tests, on the first day of hospitalization.

Press said, "Nurse participation in meeting the goal was critical. The nurses are the ones who spearhead getting the patients ready to be out before noon." In addition, "the dashboard was also critical, as we were able to identify specific nursing units that needed to improve. The dashboard allowed us to provide real time feedback to each unit on its progress."

Reducing length of stay is important not only to government agencies and insurance companies, Shah said, but also to the hospital's own economics because of the role of variable costs. "In our value-based management world," Shah explained, variable direct costs are expenses directly linked to taking care of a patient. "They are something that we can control because variable costs are dependent on the decisions that individual physicians make. Will I use this tool or that tool? Will I use this drug or that drug? Will I choose to keep the patient in the hospital for two extra days? Will I draw labs every day that a patient is in the hospital, just because they happen to be in the hospital?"

Shah's analysis of these costs has meant that NYU Langone could track the individual choices made by groups and physicians to the cent and see in which category each patient had variable direct costs. This information allowed them to compare variable costs attributed to a specific physician for a specific patient and then to the peer group of physicians treating patients with the same diagnosis.

If this analysis identifies a physician who is performing below his or her peer group, Shah said, "we try to remediate them. We incentivize the departments to improve their overall performance and the performance of their individual members. We have created a value-based management department incentive program linked to the amount you save, the amount of cost reduction you achieve. What is really important is that the incentive is linked to the value proposition, not just cost, which means that quality has to be as good, if not better, for the cost reduction."

The value-based management program incentivizes the department on the basis of the cost reduction achieved and the quality improvement achieved simultaneously.

Shah stressed that quality cannot be compromised. The value-based management program incentivizes the department on the basis of the cost reduction achieved and the quality improvement achieved simultaneously. It is a complex formula.

HIGH-QUALITY AFFORDABLE CARE

Paresh Shah's comments touch upon a critical issue. Are efforts to achieve both improvements in quality and value-based management in conflict? Shah agreed that improving quality can sometimes raise costs. He added, "One of the challenges in value-based management and in assessing projects is where are we going to spend money? There is a willingness to add costs when the quality improvement that it achieves is worthwhile."

Shah said, "We have added cost to improve quality outcomes at many levels. I am particularly proud of a program that we started last year, the medical comanagement of complex patients." Whereas once it was assumed that doctors "had to know all the medical diagnoses, and we had to understand how to manage all the medicine, today the growth rate of information and knowledge in medicine is too great for any one doctor to understand entirely."

Whereas once it was assumed that doctors "had to know all the medical diagnoses, and we had to understand how to manage all the medicine, today the growth rate of information and knowledge in medicine is too great for any one doctor to understand entirely."

There is too much to know for anyone to know everything, Shah said. "We did not do as good a job as we could and should do in managing the medical comorbidities of our surgical patients. We saw that as a clear opportunity for medical comanagement."

Shah said, "We looked retrospectively at all of our patients on all surgical services. Which ones had the highest readmission rates? Which ones had increased lengths of stay? What were their medical comorbidities? We use an algorithmic model to look back and then look forward to be able to predict where it is going to be. Now, when a patient gets admitted to surgery, we have fifteen medical comorbidities that we have identified and stratified by relative impact. If a patient flags two or more of those and has an aggregate score higher than X, they are flagged on the comanagement dashboard. A full-time medical hospitalist is assigned to such patients. They make sure that all the other things are actually being taken care of the way they are supposed to be." In short, at NYU Langone, value-based management is an important tool, but it remains subservient to quality management.

To implement value-based management, Shah said, "Our structure is such that we have an overarching value-based management task force, which Bob Press chairs and I am on. The task force has a number of subcommittees that report to it." He added, "I chair the surgical committee—all surgical services at all sites. Our committee has strong support from strategy and project management groups. We work directly with the department chairs and their liaisons to identify these opportunities. We develop specific solutions to problems. We set specific goals and measure performance."

According to Shah, "How each department actively manages it is going to be up to each department. I think the departments that recognize the opportunity, and have the bandwidth to be able to dedicate some resources to it, do it more aggressively, and are doing a good job. The data are especially valuable to departments where there is the biggest variability. We push them to make intensive use of the data that are at their fingertips. We see huge potential in rectifying outliers."

Shah said, "I empower all the department heads in all the surgical service lines to use their data. Here are the data. Here is an easy way for you to look at them. Here is an easy way to understand them. If you want to deep dive and segment the data, you can. We track dashboard use by individual physician. Are people actually using the dashboard? Increasingly the answer is yes."

To ensure that value-based principles are applied, Shah added, "We now have a departmental incentive program. I can say, 'If you fix this problem, it will translate into $300,000 back to the department at the end of the year.'" In seeking to incentivize individuals to achieve their goals, he explained, "We intentionally made it a departmental incentive so that the chairs could unite their departments toward that singular objective. If you make the incentives individual, then someone is always going to be willing to say, 'Hey, it does not matter to me. I can only make an extra five hundred bucks, so I do not really care.' But it does make a difference at the level of the department." The department chairs can use the money at their discretion.

"If you make the incentives individual, then someone is always going to be willing to say, 'Hey, it does not matter to me. I can only make an extra five hundred bucks, so I do not really care.' But it does make a difference at the level of the department."

Shah holds meetings with department chairs to ensure that they will see "exactly what contributed" to their incentive payments. "I personally met with the departments of orthopedics, neurosurgery, surgery, and cardiology. These are the big dollar driver places," he said. The first of these incentive payments began to be paid out in the fall of 2017, and will be based on evaluations undertaken every six months.

NEXT STEPS

Radford knows there is still a lot of work ahead to improve quality outcomes and value-based management. The growth of ambulatory care, with treatments on an outpatient basis, presents quality measurement issues. Radford said, "To be honest with you, I was not crazy about the rating scheme for ambulatory care about a year ago. It was really based on productivity. Productivity is not everything." She noted that Grossman had expressed similar concerns. Now, a year later, she said, "We have three measures for ambulatory care. They are drawn from about fifty measures I would like to see deployed. As we develop more of them, we will have a relatively more complete assessment of the quality of the care we give to our outpatients."

Radford said, "Medicine is moving toward ambulatory care. It is important that we measure the quality of ambulatory care properly." Despite the complexities in developing benchmarks for ambulatory care, Press noted, "We are rated for the quality of our ambulatory care. I am pleased to say that we are number one in national ambulatory care rankings."

Shah said, "Right now, my primary focus is on improving the value of inpatient services, because that is our primary loss driver. We do alright with our private payers. We do not do very well with governmental payers because of our large indirect costs that are not chargeable, that are not offset-able." Payments from government health insurance programs are often viewed as modest, even stingy, making it difficult to fully recoup costs. "The impetus to the creation of value-based management was a recognition that we were losing money at an unsustainable rate with our governmental payers," Shah said. "We needed to bend that curve very aggressively. We have been remarkably successful."

In fact, Grossman said, "Lutheran Hospital, which we acquired recently, has the highest level of Medicaid patients in the United States. Yet we still turned a profit with our hospital services there while improving the quality of patient care significantly. We are learning how to profitably manage a hospital that deals mostly with Medicaid patients. That is very important for the future."

MANAGE CULTURAL CHANGE

Despite the emphasis on technology and measurement, Shah insisted, "The most interesting part of improving quality is culture. It is philosophy. It is more than just lip service. What I have been really thrilled by at NYU Langone is a top down culture of change. When I look back at what this institution has achieved under Dean Grossman's leadership, I think it is fair to say that everyone I have spoken with attributes this culture change to Bob Grossman and to Ken Langone. What they envisioned, what they articulated, they actually made happen. They created a belief in achieving excellence and a belief in not accepting mediocrity."

"How do you change a culture without inciting a revolution? You have to be fair. You have to communicate like crazy so that everybody understands what you are doing. You make sure everyone understands what is in it for them . . ."

To pursue and achieve excellence, Grossman said that managing cultural change was critical: "The culture today is a meritocracy. It is a culture of accountability. It is totally different from what it was when we started. When I became dean and CEO of NYU Medical Center, the way was 'nothing happens here.' I changed thirty-one of the chairs. I fired all the senior management and others who were not performing. Took away laboratory space. Cut salaries. Yet, we did not have a revolution."

Grossman said, "That is the challenge. How do you change a culture without inciting a revolution? You have to be fair. You have to communicate like crazy so that everybody understands what you are doing. You make sure everyone understands what is in it for them, and why the changes are to their own personal advantage." Grossman added that staff also need to feel wanted and important. "If everyone feels important, then they learn. If they learn then they do a better job. If our people were just nine-to-five workers, we would never change anything."

Grossman described his philosophy. "People want a purpose. People want to know they are important. Everybody is important—I tell them that. Somebody who does not wash their hands in the cafeteria can put us out of business. Think about that. Everybody is critical." He went on, "People, including doctors, need to feel that they control their own destiny. It is very frustrating to be in a status quo situation where nothing improves. It is really important to set an aspirational agenda. You need to show people the journey they are on. Everybody wants to be part of a great thing."

Shah emphasized that "Excellence is what we are driving for. I believe Bill Gates said perfection must be our goal. If we set a lesser goal, we will always accept results that are less than perfect. Nothing less than perfection is worth achieving. It may take us time to get there. We are willing to take the time. That is the goal. Our goal must be perfect quality. I think striving for perfection is a cultural issue."

Radford pointed out, "There are some areas in which we are never going to score very well. Just like NYU Langone, people in New York City are never completely satisfied. Our patients will never tell us they 'always' receive the best care. Someone will always say they are unhappy.

Our patients are very different in voicing their opinions from those in Minnesota, for example." Nonetheless, Radford said, "We have really diffused an ethos of quality improvement and change management throughout the entire organization. Everyone is doing quality improvement all the time."

As evidence of that, she went on, "Nine years ago, a couple of us got together and decided to have a Quality Safety Day where we would celebrate our improvements. We organized a presentation by a national-level speaker and some breakout sessions. Everybody was invited to submit projects. We awarded prizes. The first time we held Quality Safety Day, thirty projects were submitted. This year, our ninth, three hundred thirty projects were submitted. Ten times as many. One hundred more than last year. The quality of the projects was wonderful."

CHAPTER 10

Education

Bob Grossman made it clear from the outset that his goal was to become world class in patient care, research, and teaching. In 2007, the NYU School of Medicine was ranked thirty-fourth out of the one hundred and twenty medical schools in the country by *U.S. News & World Report*. Today it ranks number three in the country, just behind Harvard and Johns Hopkins. Unlike the other major medical schools, the NYU School of Medicine will be the only top ten medical school in the United States that covers the cost of tuition for all medical students, regardless of merit or financial situation, beginning in fall 2018. The same principles of leadership and execution that transformed patient care at NYU Langone transformed education at the School of Medicine.

Steve Abramson, senior vice president and vice dean for Education, Faculty, and Academic Affairs, played a leading role in educational transformation. As a former professor at Harvard Medical School, I was very interested in what he had to say. In recounting the story of transformation of medical education at the School of Medicine, he recalled his very first conversations with Bob Grossman just after he had become CEO and dean.

Abramson said, "Early on, Bob Grossman asked me, 'What do you want to do?' I said, 'I want to have a curriculum for the twenty-first century.' Bob replied, 'Fine. But if you are going to do it, make sure it is something that the country will see as important and that will make us better.'"

Abramson set out to create a medical school curriculum for the twenty-first century, which he called C21. "Our goal was to create a new, flexible curriculum tailored to the needs of individual students. I had in mind an education system that was not one-size-fits-all," he said.

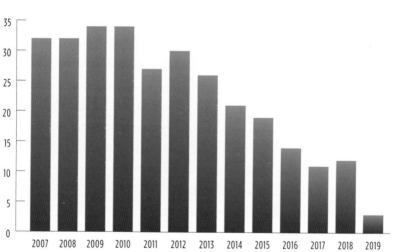

U.S. News & World Report national medical school rankings for NYU School of Medicine

PATIENT CENTERED EDUCATION

Central to the reform of medical education is the idea that medical students need more intense and earlier contact with patients. Traditionally medical students do not interact with patients until after they complete two years of intense academic studies. A focus on early, direct contact with patients is integral to NYU Langone's *patient centered* approach.

To allow earlier contact with patients, Abramson said, "The first step was to reduce the first two full years to an eighteen-month program. That allowed us to have our students begin to work with patients the very first year by providing students with the opportunity to experience working in a doctor's office." The revised curriculum enables them to experience patient interactions immediately. Shortening a traditional two years to eighteen months was a bold step in a conservative medical education environment.

The new curriculum also ties the course material to experiences with patients suffering from the diseases the students are studying. Patient experience and classroom studies are aligned. According to Abramson, "We aligned the patients that the students saw with what was being taught. For example, if we were teaching insulin signaling, we wanted them to see a patient with diabetes. We wanted them to understand what an insulin infusion is actually like. I had hoped—and it turned out to be true—that students would return to class to learn about insulin in a way that they had not before. Shortening the basic set of courses all students needed to take from two years to eighteen months gave us the freedom we needed."

Shortening a traditional two years to eighteen months was a bold step in a conservative medical education environment.

ADAPT TO CHANGE

The practice of medicine is rapidly changing. Those involved in planning education reform feel those changes acutely. Tom Riles became a leader in adapting medical education to changing medical practice. Riles is professor of Surgery; associate dean, Medical Education and Technology; director, Office of Continuing Medical Education; and executive director, New York Simulation Center for the Health Sciences. While walking around the simulation laboratory, Riles explained what motivated his desire to reform medical training. He told me, "During my training, patients remained in the hospital for several days before surgery and for many days during recovery. That gave medical students the opportunity to meet the patients, witness the surgery, and care for the patients during recovery. This was no longer the case. In many cases, patients are in and out of the hospital the same day, or at most one or two days later."

The training for students and residents had not adapted to this cultural shift; indeed, it was still hospital based. "Our students were missing most aspects of care. These were all taking place in outpatient services, not the hospital. The students did not have anything like what I saw during my training. Our medical students were not receiving the same level of historical patient exposure they needed to understand the basics of patient care. There simply were not enough patients in the hospital. I knew that medical education had to change."

Marc Triola agreed. Triola is associate professor, Department of Medicine, as well as director of the Institute for Innovations in Medical Education and associate dean, Educational Informatics at NYU Langone Health. As he put it, "Today, a patient having their gallbladder removed will have arrived on the morning of the surgery and go quickly into anesthesia. The student will rarely speak to the patient. The students will watch the laparoscopic procedure on a monitor. The patient will go home that same evening."

Abramson said there was a growing need "to create a better way to train residents or students in the ambulatory care setting."

In response to the changes he saw, Riles and his team devised what is now known as WISE-MD. WISE-MD is a series of web-based modules created to enhance the surgical education of medical students, as well as other healthcare professionals, by providing high-quality content on common surgical conditions. These modules blend text, live action, animation, and charts and graphs. Riles noted, "We and others have replaced lectures in surgery with online instruction via WISE-MD." Instead of giving lectures, Riles said, "Professors hold tutorials in which they discuss what the students have learned online. Now there is much more interaction between the students and the faculty."

The WISE-MD modules were developed by the School of Medicine with contributions from physicians from a number of medical disciplines, including members of the Association for Surgical Education and the American College of Surgeons. WISE-MD is a very focused response to the gaps in medical student surgical education resulting from shortened hospital stays and increased use of outpatient facilities for pre- and postsurgical care. The modules were designed to follow the typical course of a patient from the initial presentation to the physical examination, laboratory testing, and radiological imaging, as well as preoperative preparation, surgery, and recovery. Not only do the modules include medical and scientific information about illnesses and medical procedures, but they also discuss patient-physician interactions in sections related to taking the patient's history, performing the physical examination, and preparing the patient for surgery. Most of the modules have self-assessment questions. An editorial board of fifteen nationally recognized surgical educators from the Association for Surgical Education determines the content of the modules and selects editors for specific topics.

There are now thirty-four of these modules, and although initially created to teach surgery, Riles said, "We are now developing training modules for internal medicine." Students can access the modules online and on demand. Currently, two WISE programs are available, WISE-MD for third-year surgery clerkships and WISE-ONCALL for preparing medical students and junior residents for the responsibilities of residency. More than one hundred medical and osteopathic schools use WISE-MD as part of their clerkship curriculum. They are also used for medical training in Singapore, Ecuador, and other countries.

STUDENT CENTERED EDUCATION

The revised curriculum is more student centered and less one-size-fits-all than in the past. In August 2018, NYU Langone announced that every student enrolled in an MD degree at the School of Medicine would receive a full tuition scholarship to cover the majority of their costs of attendance. The scholarships make it possible for aspiring physicians to choose specialties based on their talents and interests, and not on the need to work in a high-paying field in order to pay off a hefty student loan.

The medical education program at NYU Langone also offers the opportunity for each student to receive specialized training in areas of their own particular interest by providing access to specialized courses and research opportunities. Student centered education "meant providing choices early on," Abramson said. "Our students now declare their interests after the first eighteen months—for example, if they want a more science or population health set of courses. We added several months to the program to allow some students to do research and others to choose among twenty selective courses offered by each of our departments. The content of the selective courses ranges from medical informatics to health disparities. The courses are offered once a month, several times a year."

> "One goal was to create better integration between an understanding of basic science and clinical medicine to encourage our students' ability to think more deeply about their areas of interest."

Abramson also said, "Another novel aspect of our curriculum is what we call the five pillars of the curriculum. Five content areas thread throughout the entire medical degree program. These include diabetes, colon cancer, tuberculosis, congestive heart failure, and neurodegenerative disease. Our approach includes an introduction to both the science and clinical treatment of these diseases. We use these as paradigms of what our graduates should know about disease."

In the case of diabetes, for example, Abramson explained that "our students will understand the relationship between intermediate metabolism and cell receptor signals. They will understand the role of the pancreas and kidneys in the disease. We also want our students to understand disease in a social context to understand health disparities, population health implications, and the genetics of each of these diseases. You also gain direct clinical experience with each disease. We have course directors who coordinate the pillars. Each of the pillars is developed by a cluster of one hundred professors. The concept is to use these pillars as examples of how doctors should approach medical problems broadly, not only technically."

To create the pillars, Abramson said that "we added new material to what we were already teaching on the subject. We added a web-based component. Students encounter patients with the disease in class. We show how social and medical issues converge for each disease. One goal was to create better integration between an understanding of basic science and clinical medicine to encourage our students' ability to think more deeply about their areas of interest."

AN MD-MASTER'S DEGREE

Another goal was to train doctors suited to the complex organizational and managerial demands of modern medicine. That meant graduating more doctors with dual degrees—a medical degree plus a specialized master's degree. Traditionally, a master's degree requires an extra year, so the dual degree would require a total of five years of postgraduate work, but the NYU curriculum would enable a student to graduate with a dual degree in four years. The NYU School of Medicine created master's degree programs in public health, public administration, clinical research, biomedical ethics, and business administration. The combined MD-MBA is the most popular.

The NYU School of Medicine created master's degree programs in public health, public administration, clinical research, biomedical ethics, and business administration. The combined MD-MBA is the most popular.

Students admitted to the School of Medicine can choose the traditional four-year program. But students who have been accepted into the four-year program also have the option of applying for admission to an accelerated track within their field of specialization that will enable them to earn an MD degree in three years.

AN MD IN THREE YEARS

Bob Grossman's one-page road map included the words *three-year MD*. For more than a century an MD degree was granted only after completing a four-year course in undergraduate medical education—two years of course work followed by two years of closely supervised patient care. Grossman thought it possible to complete training in three years, a plan that would increase the total number of doctors that could be trained and reduce the cost of MD training by twenty-five percent.

Today, NYU Langone offers students a choice of a three- or four-year degree granting program.

In describing how they implemented the three-year program, Abramson said, "The opportunity came as we developed the C21 curriculum focused on choice. We realized that by shortening the curriculum to allow a four-year combined medical master's degree, we had actually created the opportunity to graduate some students in three years."

Abramson went on to say that clearly a "three-year pathway would have real financial benefits for students, not only by saving them a year's tuition and room and board, but also by making it possible for medical students to go into practice and begin earning an income one year earlier." That has implications that extend beyond the pocketbooks of medical students. Abramson explained: "Medical school costs about $75,000 a year between tuition and room and board. Students typically leave school with a debt of over $300,000. I believe that the debt attracts doctors to higher-paying specialties and away from careers in research and lower-paying fields, such as geriatrics, family, and community medicine. New doctors who are not deeply in debt have more freedom in determining their careers."

Finishing a year early has additional benefits that Abramson highlighted. "We noticed that the average age at which physicians begin practicing has been creeping up. Age creep begins in college. Many students now take one or more gap years before or during college. Then comes four years of medical school. Doctors used to enter practice after two years of residency. What used to be two years of a residency is now three years for general medicine, five years for surgery, and eight years for plastic surgery. Most of these requirements are set by the specialty board examination process. In fact, for most of us, the doctor we become is the doctor we are the last four years of our training, not the first four years. Accelerating the first few years of training suddenly assumed more importance. It's not fair to keep people locked into training that they may not really need."

As the NYU School of Medicine faculty thought about providing training that students may not need, they began to think about more than the calendar. Abramson said, "Competency-based training is a revolutionary way to think about medical education. The concept is that competency is not solely determined by the number of years of training. If a student can show in two years that they have learned all the things they need to learn, they should not have to wait for four years. We wondered: Once the preclinical core content and required clerkships had been completed, there was ample time for certain students to explore electives and take advanced courses without requiring the fourth year of medical school. For many students, the fourth year is not very valuable, as they spend a good part of the year interviewing for residency programs or doing 'audition electives,' but not learning."

Abramson said he was influenced by an article by Ezekiel Emanuel and Victor Fuchs that appeared in the March 21, 2012, edition of the *Journal of the American Medical Association,* entitled "Shortening Medical Training by 30%." The authors advocated shortening the educational process for physicians starting from college on through residency and specialty training. In their view, every segment of medical education can be shortened by thirty percent.

"The idea of a three-year program really emerged from our curriculum redesign," Abramson said, adding, "Bob Grossman enthusiastically endorsed the proposal." In fact, shortening the medical curriculum was part of Grossman's early road map.

Grossman said, "I gave a 2007 investiture speech. In the speech, I laid out the path we were to follow, and we followed it."

"Our three-year medical students did as well as or, in the area of clinical knowledge, even better than the four-year students."

Abramson added, "We decided that a three-year medical degree should be a choice we offered our students. We also decided to become national leaders of a three-year medical education." To implement the program, he said, "each department chair was told to open twenty percent of the student slots for a three-year pathway. Students had previously been accepted into our four-year program."

Does saving a year mean some important components of medical education are shortchanged? The evidence at NYU Langone suggests it does not. According to Abramson, "We evaluated about thirty of our three- and four-year students for competency at the simulation center prior to graduation. Our three-year medical students did as well as or, in the area of clinical knowledge, even better than the four-year students. I think one of the reasons for the outcome is that the four-year students were spending so much time looking for internships and residencies that they had no meaningful clinical experiences in months."

> Does saving a year mean some important components of medical education are shortchanged? The evidence at NYU Langone suggests it does not.

Other institutions may follow the NYU School of Medicine in creating three-year medical degree programs. In 2014 the Macy Foundation awarded NYU a five-year grant to form a consortium of medical schools with three-year programs. The consortium has now grown to seventeen members. Abramson said, "According to our information, there are about thirty-five medical school deans who are either now planning three-year programs or seriously thinking about doing so." The innovative idea of shortening the medical degree at NYU Langone has the potential to dramatically alter the academic landscape—and affect thousands of medical students' lives.

FULL TUITION SCHOLARSHIPS

It costs NYU medical students around eighty-five thousand dollars a year to attend the School of Medicine. Tuition makes up nearly two-thirds of those costs, with the rest made up of other costs, like books, supplies, and room and board. The rising cost of tuition leaves many students with debts in the six figures upon graduation. In 2018, more than sixty percent of the medical school's most recent graduating class had student loans averaging $184,000.

In August 2018, NYU Langone announced that it will offer full tuition scholarships for all medical students, no matter their financial situation. As *The Wall Street Journal* reported the day the news was announced, "The move dwarfs efforts by other schools, including Columbia University and the University of California, Los Angeles, to alleviate the financial strain of a medical education. Earlier this year Columbia's Vagelos College of Physicians and Surgeons announced it would eliminate loans for all students who qualify for financial aid, while UCLA's David Geffen School of Medicine expects to provide more than 300 full scholarships between 2012 and 2022, based on merit."

Dr. Rafael Rivera, associate dean for admission and financial aid, said in the same article that the move was going to be a "huge game changer for us, for our students, and for our patients." Citing worries that the heavy burden of student loans were pushing doctors into higher paying fields or scaring them off from medical school entirely, Dr. Rivera said there was "a moral imperative" to reduce the amount of debt people have. The NYU Langone press release announcing the move echoed those sentiments:

"This decision recognizes a moral imperative that must be addressed, as institutions place an increasing debt burden on young people who aspire to become physicians," says Robert I. Grossman, MD, the Saul J. Farber Dean of NYU School of Medicine and CEO of NYU Langone Health.

Overwhelming student debt is fundamentally reshaping the medical profession in ways that are adversely affecting healthcare. Saddled with staggering student loans, many medical school graduates choose higher-paying specialties, drawing talent away from less lucrative fields like primary care, pediatrics, and obstetrics and gynecology. Moreover, the financial barriers discourage many promising high school and college students from considering a career in medicine altogether due to fears about the costs associated with medical school.

The scholarships were made possible thanks to a groundswell of philanthropic support from more than 2,500 backers. NYU Langone estimated that it would cost roughly $600 million to fund the tuition package in perpetuity. As has been the case in years past, the trustees provided visionary support, with a $100 million contribution from Ken Langone and his wife Elaine, and other substantial contributions from the Berkleys, Buckleys, Druckenmillers, Vilceks, Silversteins, and the Finks. As of August 2018, more than $450 million had already been raised.

TECHNOLOGY

While revamping the broad contours of the overall curriculum, NYU dramatically reconfigured what went on in the classrooms and laboratories. Well before Grossman arrived at the Medical Center, the School of Medicine was becoming an early advocate of using computers for medical education.

Marc Triola is a driving force in the application of technology to medical education. He recalled, "While in medical school, I began to see the power of technology as a disruptive, transformational force for change in medical education, in medical research, and in clinical care. I became fascinated by this." He added, "I was attracted to the field because I knew that technology had the potential to break down traditional hierarchies."

Triola said, "About 2006 we started doing really interesting things; the environment was exciting and changing. We found faculty who were open minded. Things were just beginning to happen. Then Dr. Grossman showed up and everything accelerated." The key people in driving change were Grossman and Steve Abramson. According to Triola, "Steve Abramson shared our vision: He understood that informatics-based education was a differentiating factor for NYU School of Medicine. At the time, there were only three schools, including us, the University of California at San Francisco, and Vanderbilt, that were on a similar path."

In 2008, NYU School of Medicine established the Division of Educational Informatics, which served as a technology and software start up group for educational innovations. Over the subsequent years, the division took on the task of creating several new technologies and e-learning resources in support of the curricular reform efforts occurring in NYU's undergraduate medical education programs. In 2013, NYU Langone established the Institute for Innovations in Medical Education to develop, validate, and support teaching, learning, and assessment innovations across the continuum of undergraduate, graduate, and continuing medical education.

In 2013, NYU Langone established the Institute
for Innovations in Medical Education to develop,
validate, and support teaching, learning, and
assessment innovations across the continuum . . .

DASHBOARDS

Dashboards and a data-driven approach to achieving excellence are an increasingly integral part of the education process throughout the NYU School of Medicine. In addition to designing and implementing new mechanisms for collecting, reporting, and analyzing data to support operational and administrative needs, the school's sophisticated data infrastructure fosters curricular change that takes advantage of the informatics expertise available at NYU Langone. For example, Triola noted that with support from the American Medical Association and the Association for Surgical Education program, the medical school has introduced a new Health Care by the Numbers curriculum. Key to this curriculum is the use of big clinical data sets abstracted from public sources, combined with de-identified data from NYU Langone's own data warehouse. Using a customized database of millions of inpatient discharges in New York State, Triola said, "Students are instructed to generate a hypothesis, abstract a large clinical data set, do their analysis, then present to the class potential implications for the healthcare system based on their findings." This paves the way for medical student exposure to a health systems approach to patient care that teaches important principles in evidence based medicine and population health.

Additionally, Triola said that technology has also assumed a substantial role in facilitating continuous quality improvement in NYU's learners, faculty, and educational programs. Assessment is now based on learner progression and competency development. "The data we collect as part of our longitudinal, workplace-based assessment initiatives are intended to be formative, actionable, and must ultimately meet our goal of supporting individualized pathways."

SIMULATION

Tom Riles told me that "the other big idea that came out of our thinking at the time was the simulation laboratory." A skills laboratory is the med school equivalent of the flight simulator used to train pilots. In both cases, developing hands-on skills by practicing is important, but the tasks are too fraught with risks to permit actual experimentation.

Riles noted, "I began thinking about a skills laboratory in 2001. We knew that surgery was becoming more complicated. The technology of surgery was advancing rapidly. We decided to build a surgical skills laboratory to teach skills that the students needed in a safe environment."

The skills laboratory was opened in 2005, when Riles was the chair of the Department of Surgery. He recalls, "It was a real struggle to get these things going, to find funding to get them off the ground. The big change came when Bob Grossman became dean. He and Steve Abramson were open to new ideas." After listening to Riles's ideas about the surgical skills laboratory, he recalled, "both Steve Abramson and Bob Grossman said, 'That is a great idea. Go with it.'"

Riles was not the only one interested in building simulation laboratories. Other faculty members wanted to build their own simulation labs. "Grossman recognized right away this was not the way to do it," Riles said, adding, "Grossman told the various departments, 'Let's build one simulation laboratory for everybody.'" Grossman and Abramson put Riles in charge of a committee to design this laboratory. Six months later, Riles concluded that NYU School of Medicine needed ten thousand square feet of space and $10 million to do the job properly.

As the planning process was proceeding, Riles said, "Something amazing happened. A person from the City University of New York approached me. He said they had just received $20 million to build a medical simulation laboratory. It was a beautiful marriage." The New York Simulation Center is a joint facility of NYU School of Medicine and the City University of New York. Half of the money for the Center came from the State of New York and half from the city. The Simulation Laboratory is used by both institutions.

Riles noted that Bob Grossman understood right away that working with City University was the way to go. "It was a bold decision. I remember Steve Abramson's and my anxiety in preparing the presentation for Bob. The first year operating budget alone was projected to be $2 million. After listening to the presentation, Bob just said, 'This is great. Let's do it.' That was it. Bob's response was totally unlike that of previous administrations. He gave us the green light just like that. His mind was prepared. He immediately saw the value of what we were doing."

Armed with organizational support and funding, Riles learned from the best. He and his staff visited ten or fifteen simulation laboratories in the United States, including highly regarded facilities at Stanford University, the University of Pittsburgh, Johns Hopkins Medical School, the University of Maryland, and Harvard University. Riles adapted many of the ideas he saw.

The 25,000-square-foot New York Simulation Center for Health Sciences opened in 2011. The simulation laboratory is designed to give doctors, nurses, emergency medical technicians, and other healthcare personnel the opportunity to confront an assortment of real-world medical scenarios. The key elements of the simulation center include trained actors, state of the art manikins, and an assortment of body parts that can bleed, be sedated, or even give birth.

One way to simulate interaction with patients is by using trained actors. "We have about two hundred actors that we can draw on, depending on what is needed," Riles said, adding, "We train the actors to simulate specific ailments." The actors, some of whom have been involved in the program for a decade, may not display the vital signs of someone suffering from a particular ailment—they may not actually run a high temperature or have lesions on their legs—but they can give responses to questions posed by medical students.

Medical students examine these patients and propose treatments. As the students conduct their examinations, faculty members evaluate how well the students perform: Are they asking the right questions? Displaying the right bedside manner? Requesting the appropriate tests? Are they making the right diagnosis and proposing the right remedies? The simulated examinations are videotaped so that the students can review their actions and be advised as to what they might have done differently.

The center also has some twenty manikins that can sweat, urinate, vomit, and mime assorted other bodily functions. Moreover, these manikins, cousins to the familiar crash test dummies used for studying auto safety, can simulate a variety of medical conditions. They can, for example, change their heart rate or simulate a maternal hemorrhage during childbirth. They can also answer medical student questions. Or, more precisely, an instructor, using a remote microphone, can speak through a dummy's mouth. Here too, the students are evaluated as they diagnose and treat these "patients," and afterward the taped interactions are reviewed.

The center also has some twenty manikins that can sweat, urinate, vomit, and mime assorted other bodily functions.

The Simulation Center offers a number of settings, including a disaster training room, a five-bed intensive care unit, two operating rooms, trauma rooms, a labor and delivery room, and fourteen "doctor's office" style examination rooms. Many of the rooms are fitted out with one-way glass permitting students to be observed by faculty. Moreover, the center is equipped with more than one hundred cameras that can provide live feeds or record training sessions from a variety of angles and produce recordings that can be played back for debriefing sessions.

Since the Simulation Center opened in 2011, Riles said, "It has been fun to watch how simulation is incorporated into the curriculum. Simulation changes how we teach, and how we teach influences what happens in the simulation laboratory. It is a process of constant adjustment." The Simulation Center is used not only for training, but also for testing and assessment. Most of the students' activities in the Center are observed and evaluated. Students receive extensive feedback on their performance. In addition, Riles said, all the students "go through a big simulation event during the third year" in which they are presented with ten different cases, and they have twenty minutes to work on each case.

THE VIRTUAL MICROSCOPE AND A BIODIGITAL HUMAN

The NYU Langone Institute for Innovations in Medical Education pioneered the development of the Virtual Microscope and the Bio-Digital Human. The Virtual Microscope brings digital technology to a longstanding component of medical education: looking through a microscope at slides showing various tissues, bacteria, and indications of diseases at the cellular level. Under Marc Triola's direction, NYU Langone staff scanned more than three thousand microscopic pathology slides. These are now fully digitized.

The Virtual Microscope brings digital technology to a longstanding component of medical education: looking through a microscope at slides showing various tissues, bacteria, and indications of diseases at the cellular level.

Triola and his team adapted the tools developed by Google to navigate the earth to navigate these images. Students can zoom in, tag, place queries, and share images. Students and teachers can view the same slides at the same time.

NYU School of Medicine's information technology specialists also developed BioDigital Human. Using three-dimensional glasses and an iPad, students can view a fully digital human body in three dimensions. "The BioDigital Human allows our students to gain a deep understanding of anatomy prior to actual dissection," Triola says. "They have the iPad with them during the dissection itself."

The Virtual Microscope and BioDigital Human, like WISE-MD, were developed by the Institute for Innovations in Medical Education. This institute, and those that preceded it, has been playing a central role in increasing the role of data and digital analytics in the medical curriculum for two decades.

The NYU School of Medicine has been and will continue to be a leader in medical education, adapting education to the needs of future patients and students. I am confident that with the progress they have made they will quickly adapt advances in technology to education. I believe pioneering advances made in education at NYU will spread far beyond medical education there and elsewhere. Someday soon we will see them in all aspects of education, and reeducation, of a revitalized skilled workforce—one prepared for the challenges of the information age.

CHAPTER 11

Infrastructure

G rossman's road to the future envisioned expanding and rebuilding the NYU infrastructure to provide the modern hospital and research facilities necessary for a world class institution. Rapidly changing medical technology places heavy demands on infrastructure. Old buildings need to be refurbished and new ones built.

RENEWING THE CAMPUS

The renewal and expansion of the main campus was guided by a plan that grew out of Grossman's original road map, and this plan was executed in stages. The NYU Langone campus has generally been defined by its main campus as the area bounded by 34th Street on the north, 30th Street on the south, the FDR Drive to the east, and First Avenue on the west. However, in recent years it has not only been building on its original campus, but has also been spilling across those borders, putting down roots south along First Avenue and onto other nearby city streets.

TISCH HOSPITAL

The initial rebuilding centered on Tisch Hospital. The NYU Langone website describes Tisch Hospital, which opened in 1962, as "the long standing heart of NYU Langone," and its renovation was a central component of the campus transformation project. The building was essentially a 1950s structure. A half century later, it was in need of substantial renovation.

The first step was the Tisch Hospital elevators and lobby project, which added a new four-car elevator bank inside a freestanding structure that was connected to the hospital's eighteen-story tower. This increased the total number of elevators serving the hospital to twelve. This proved to be an early win for the new administration. The inefficient elevators had been a long-festering frustration for patients and staff. Grossman used a significant philanthropic donation to fast-track the project and make it a priority for the institution.

I can personally attest to the efficiency of the new elevators. I timed them myself. In no case was any wait longer than twenty-five seconds at a busy time of day. The elevator project also included the expansion and renovation of the Tisch Hospital's main lobby, which dramatically improved the overall flow of foot traffic.

Meanwhile, the expansion of Tisch Hospital's intensive care unit was completed in April 2010, doubling the size of the unit and redesigning it to provide state of the art holistic care. The space offers thirty-five beds configured in layouts that incorporate the latest hospital technology in a design that seeks to maximize both efficiency and patient comfort.

A few months later, in October 2010, NYU Langone opened a new 7,500-square-foot pharmacy. It featured advanced robotic storage and dispensing technology, and an automated retrieval system that streamlines medicine delivery to patient units. Reflecting the emphasis on being patient centered, this system was not only more convenient for patients, but also safer. Because it is automated, it is less subject to human error.

After that, in early 2011, NYU Langone opened the Bone Marrow Transplant Unit in Tisch Hospital. Because the immune systems of patients in this unit are often suppressed, the 4,500-square-foot, six-bed allogeneic unit features carefully filtered air with relative air pressures closely monitored. The renovation added substantial new patient and visitor amenities, both to the main lobby, including a new reception area and meditation room, and to each of the upper inpatient floors. In addition, the new tower and lobby offered visitors a welcoming entrance on the first floor and cheerful spaces on all patient floors. Again, the renovations were focused on the needs of patients in terms of both comfort and avoiding infections.

NEW INPATIENT FACILITIES

The next phase was completion of the 830,000-square-foot Helen L. and Martin S. Kimmel Pavilion. That facility opened in the summer of 2018. Planning the Kimmel Pavilion from scratch allowed senior clinical and administrative leaders at NYU Langone to rethink how an inpatient facility could best accommodate the latest technologies and innovative clinical practices while also providing a better patient experience. The layout is designed to limit moving patients around by bringing patient care equipment to the bedside. The Kimmel Pavilion's single-bed inpatient rooms help limit the spread of infections while also facilitating a more efficient workflow for staff and help accommodate a patient's family and visitors. As Vicki Match Suna, NYU Langone's senior vice president for Real Estate Development and Facilities, told the *New York Post*, "It will be patient- and family-centered."[1] The Kimmel Pavilion and Tisch Hospital facilities offer what is inevitably described as a "seamless" patient experience: The buildings are designed to be directly connected on several

---

1   See "NYU Langone hospital's dramatic revamp is nearly done," by Lori Weiss, *New York Post*, April 23, 2018.

floors, and on the lobby level. The two facilities also share central sterilization and other support services. Plans call for extensive remodeling of the
upper floors of Tisch Hospital, which will eventually reconfigure patient
care units to offer all single-bed rooms, like the new Kimmel Pavilion.

Entrance to the new Kimmel Pavilion

The Hassenfeld Children's Hospital, which opened in 2018, is part
of the Helen L. and Martin S. Kimmel Pavilion, rather than a free-
standing facility. Located at the corner of 34th Street and First Avenue in Manhattan, the Hassenfeld Children's Hospital is designed to
address the special medical and psychological needs of sick children.
The building is designed to be both child-friendly and family-oriented.
It will also feature all private rooms, and it will offer overnight accom-
modations for parents during a child's hospital stay. Hassenfeld, which

has a separate street entrance and elevator lobby exclusively for pediatric services, will also provide a family center, a "teen room," and a library, plus consultation rooms and a lounge area.

NEW FACILITIES

In addition to reimagining of the Tisch Hospital with the addition of the Kimmel Pavilion and the Hassenfeld Children's Hospital, the NYU Langone campus was also being revitalized through the construction of three new facilities:

THE RONALD O. PERELMAN CENTER FOR EMERGENCY SERVICES

The Ronald O. Perelman Center for Emergency Services, also known as the Perelman Emergency Center, opened in April 2014 at Tisch Hospital. Located on First Avenue at 33rd Street, the 22,000-square-foot facility more than tripled the size of the former NYU Langone emergency department. It is equipped with forty treatment spaces, including three triage rooms, three resuscitation rooms, and three negative-pressure isolation rooms. An on-site pharmacist is on duty twenty-four hours a day, seven days a week.

Plans for a new, larger, and more modern emergency room began to be developed a number of years earlier, but in 2012, Hurricane Sandy, which forced the existing emergency room to close, provided an opportunity to accelerate construction of the new facility. The design of the Perelman Emergency Center, which opened eighteen months after Hurricane Sandy, incorporated flood mitigation measures that will help protect the facility against severe storms. The Perelman Emergency Center's innovative features include spacious treatment rooms, bedside registration, state of the art imaging facilities for quick testing and diagnosis, and efficient intake and discharge processes to make treatment areas available sooner for incoming patients. It has a new KiDS Emergency Department, which provides a child focused and family centered environment. It also provides direct access to NYU Langone's Comprehensive Stroke Care Center, a nationally recognized program. The Perelman Emergency Center was designed to be flexible and scalable so that its space can be adapted to fluctuations in patient volume.

THE SCIENCE BUILDING

Construction of NYU Langone's new Science Building provides more than 365,000 square feet and ten floors of laboratory space dedicated to research, as well as conference space and public amenities. It will be home to the school's Neuroscience Institute. The building, which brings together researchers who had been scattered among several buildings, is designed to integrate a variety of research facilities and services so that researchers, students, faculty, and clinicians can work more efficiently and collaboratively. The laboratories are designed to be easily adaptable, with shared equipment. The sizable new Science Building will enable the NYU School of Medicine to accommodate new recruits and projected growth in funded research. It incorporates an assortment of environmentally friendly green-design approaches and sustainable technologies.

Research scientists often spend day and night in their labs. As the *New York Post* explained, "That's why hospital leadership made a conscious decision to add a large pantry and café hangout area with its own calming and beautiful river views to encourage mingling and discussions among the scientists." Several existing facilities were demolished in order to make room for the Science Building and enable it to anchor the transformation of the southernmost end of the main campus.

The new Science Building at NYU

THE ENERGY BUILDING

NYU Langone began construction on a new Energy Building in 2012, and it was completed in 2016. The Energy Building is the centerpiece of NYU Langone's plan to become both a more resilient medical center and a leader in sustainability by reducing its contribution to global warming through clean and efficient energy use. The Energy Building was being planned prior to Hurricane Sandy, which caused a devastating power outage in 2012, but that storm underscored the need for an assured supply of power. The building's combined heat and power plant, emergency generators, and boilers mean NYU Langone will be completely self-sufficient in the event of an interruption in the power supplied by Consolidated Edison, the local electric utility. In fact, the building will have two different sources of backup power for critical areas.

The new facility also advances NYU Langone's energy conservation program. Since this program was launched in 2007, NYU Langone has reduced its aggregate greenhouse gas emissions by twenty-two percent. The new plant is expected to enable NYU Langone to achieve its goal of reducing emissions by fifty percent. The 71,000-square-foot energy facility will provide the primary electric service to the campus and accommodate the anticipated growth in energy consumption while employing advanced generation technology to produce energy that is cleaner as well as more economical.

The facility has an 11-megawatt cogeneration, combined-cycle plant. It includes a dual-fuel-fired turbine that produces 8 megawatts of power. The waste heat from the turbine enters a heat recovery steam generator, which powers a steam turbine generator, creating 3 additional megawatts of power. The steam is distributed throughout all medical center buildings for heat, hot water, sterilization, and humidification. Ultimately, the steam is pumped back to the facility to help create more steam. This cycle substantially reduces the need to purchase electrical power from outside sources.

Two additional backup boilers can supply steam to the campus when the gas turbine steam turbine system is shut down for maintenance, thus ensuring the medical center always has steam. The Energy Building also houses a 7.5-megawatt diesel-fired emergency power plant if the main system fails for any reason; and it is designed to withstand severe flooding conditions that exceed those of Hurricane Sandy.

The Energy Building, which is adjacent to Tisch Hospital, also houses the Department of Radiation Oncology, and allows easy movement between Tisch Hospital and the Kimmel Pavilion, both of which will use the new radiation oncology facility.

The Energy Building also houses a 7.5-megawatt diesel-fired emergency power plant if the main system fails for any reason; and it is designed to withstand severe flooding conditions that exceed those of Hurricane Sandy.

A REVITALIZED CAMPUS

As it was constructing new buildings, NYU Langone was also reconfiguring existing buildings and facilities. The hospital's administrative offices were moved to One Park Avenue, and the aging building housing NYU Langone's well-known, but aged, Rusk Institute of Rehabilitation Medicine was demolished. Ambulatory care patients were moved to East 38th Street and inpatient rehab was moved within the Schwartz Health Care Center. A significant amount of work was done to improve conditions for students. Match Suna told me, "We substantially increased study space for the students, which is extremely important for them. We also added student lounge spaces with amenities and a fully reimagined library. We acquired a new dormitory and demolished an old, outdated residence building, which was a point of dissatisfaction for many students when they considered attending our medical school." Students were relocated nearby to a newly renovated Vilcek Hall on East 26th Street. As the *New York Post* put it in an April 23, 2018, article headlined "NYU Langone hospital's dramatic revamp is nearly done," "A decade long master plan for NYU Langone is finally coming to fruition."

NYU Langone has spent more than a decade dramatically extending its physical presence by developing a network of hundreds of ambulatory care centers. But the main campus remains important. It is the symbolic center of gravity for NYU Langone Health as well as the headquarters and nexus for a variety of administrative and managerial functions. It remains the focal point for the most complex medical services as well as the epicenter for medical education and research.

NYU Langone has spent more than a decade dramatically extending its physical presence by developing a network of hundreds of ambulatory care centers. But the main campus remains important.

As a result of a massive redevelopment and construction project, NYU Langone's new approaches and new spirit would be housed in new or renewed facilities. NYU Langone's revitalized physical plant was equipped to deal with the constantly changing infrastructure needs of contemporary medical care, and it was poised to integrate whatever additional changes would inevitably come along.

NYU Langone now looks like the complete twenty-first century medical center. It has modern buildings filled with modern accoutrements, from USB outlets to fiber optic cables. The modern facilities serve to impress the casual observer, but the revitalization is in fact a meaningful renewal and updating of the main campus in ways that affirm a commitment to being patient centered and enable it to accommodate rapidly changing medical technology.

While it is important for leaders of an organization to focus on culture and process, these efforts benefit from a setting that facilities achieving an organization's objectives. The rebuilding and reimagining of the NYU Langone campus made major strides in providing that setting.

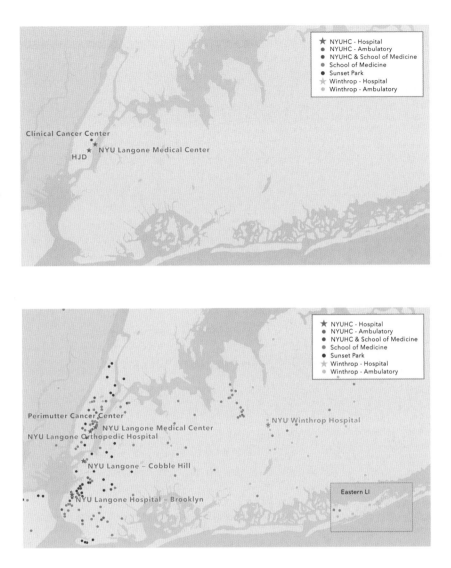

NYU Langone Health's footprint in New York in 2008 and 2017

CHAPTER 12

Research

Research, the third component of NYU Langone's mission, is notoriously difficult to manage. Most books on management deal only tangentially with managing scientists and engineers vital to the continued survival of many businesses and to the economies of nations. Research scientists by their very nature are strong willed and independent minded in any enterprise, especially in universities where individual freedom is prized. I believe NYU Langone's success in increasing the quality and productivity of its scientists is well worth understanding by every business and university that depends on research for success.

In the 1950s and '60s, NYU School of Medicine was a national leader in biomedical research. A half century later, NYU Langone was a far less important research institution. Research at the medical school had stagnated. By 2007 pockets of excellence remained, but many other universities and academic medical centers far outperformed NYU Langone in terms of funding and the productivity of the professional staff.

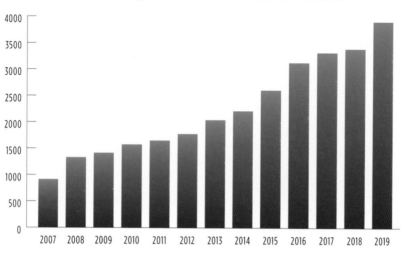

Total number of faculty group practice physicians at NYU Langone Health from 2007 to 2019

Cutting-edge biomedical research is a complex and expensive activity. Excellence requires that an institution recruit the best scientists and research physicians in the world. Laboratories and medical research facilities require expensive infrastructure and equipment. Much of the work is done by very young researchers and doctors in training who come to leading research centers from all over the world. Recruiting such talent depends upon the international reputations of the leaders as well as the reputation of the institution itself. A reputation that attracts the best takes many years to build.

A reputation that attracts the best takes many years to build.

MEASURING SUCCESS

Transforming research and discovery at NYU Langone was one of Bob Grossman's three principal goals. Measuring the success of a research and discovery enterprise is not straightforward, as the true importance of a discovery may be realized only many years after the fact. Nonetheless there are meaningful ways to measure success. One such measure is the overall standing of a medical school in national rankings. The *U.S. News & World Report* annual rankings represent a broad consensus of the academic community regarding both the comparative quality of education as well as the quality of research. In 2007 the NYU School of Medicine was ranked thirty-fourth in the nation. In 2018 it was ranked third, a rapid and unprecedented rise.

U.S. News now ranks NYU Langone as the best graduate school in New York State. Other measures of success include the amount of research grant support and the number of reports published in leading scientific and medical journals. By these measures NYU Langone Health has been a remarkable success. In 2007, NYU Langone ranked thirty-ninth in receipt of National Institutes of Health funding. By 2016, it had risen to twenty-first place. Meanwhile, total research funding had climbed from some $187 million in 2007 to more than $341 million in 2017. The number of reports published in leading scientific and medical journals almost doubled over the same period.

Two graphs here show the increase in total funding and NIH funding.

Grants received from the National Institutes of Health by NYU Langone from 2008 to 2017

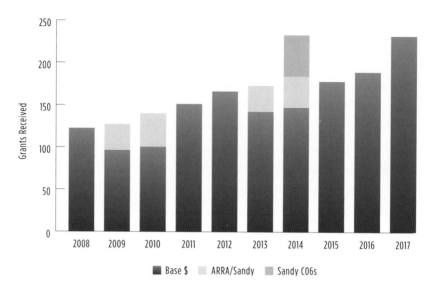

NYU Langone grant funding from 2009 to 2017

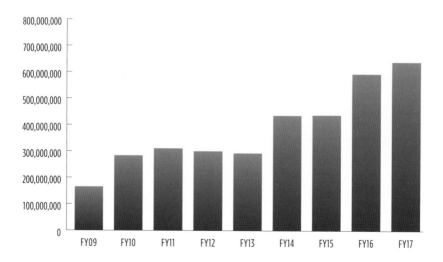

A CULTURE OF ACCOUNTABILITY

As I interviewed those involved in the transformation of research and discovery at NYU Langone, it became clear that the most important determinant in improving research and discovery was a change in culture, a change from a culture of laissez-faire to a culture of accountability. All those I spoke with—from Grossman on down to the department chairs—emphasized the importance of the culture change in the turnaround of research and discovery.

In 2007, a significant number of the research faculty received little or no external research funding. Many had done good work in the past. Their best days were behind them. Academic tenure and the guarantee of lifetime employment made replacement difficult.

Andrew Brotman, the medical school's vice dean for Clinical Affairs and Strategy and chief clinical officer, said Grossman "turned around the research culture at the medical school." According to Brotman, "He took the whole research enterprise by the horns and basically said, 'You folks think you are good and productive. Let me show you the data and demonstrate to you that you are not as good or productive as the people we want to be compared to.'"

One significant aspect of accountability was to significantly reduce the salaries of those who were unable to obtain competitive grant support. The transitions were not abrupt and were managed carefully with concomitant programs to ease those who were not productive into retirement. The specifics of these programs are described in chapter 3.

While many in academia may believe they hold their researchers to standards of accountability, I can say from my many years in academia that most such standards are qualitatively different from those of NYU Langone. NYU Langone quantitates scientific productivity in terms of grant and the income received, grants applied for and rejected, the number and quality of papers published and rejected, and the numbers of citations per research article, as well as several other measures. The data are displayed on the dashboards of the individual researchers and their department chairs and are prominently displayed for all to see on what I heard described as "a wall of fame and a wall of shame." While this may seem discouraging to some, scientists, like all top professionals, are competitive and strive to be among the very top visible performers.

The unofficial motto for researchers seems to be:
The more you deliver to the institution,
the more the institution delivers to you.

Dafna Bar-Sagi said, "We have created a culture of accountability among our researchers. We have a dashboard that displays key indicators of performance across multiple spheres: research, clinical, education, and financial." The unofficial motto for researchers seems to be: The more you deliver to the institution, the more the institution delivers to you. Bar-Sagi said, "For us, accountability is more than just measuring and metricizing performance; it is about gauging trajectory. When I look at faculty performance data, I think less about whether the stated goals and objectives were achieved and more about the path forward."

"What do the researchers think about this system?" I asked.

Bar-Sagi said, "Most do not like it. Scientists are typically independent minded, and most feel that they should be left alone to do whatever they want to do." Be that as it may, the research ethos at NYU Langone Health is that everybody needs to be productive.

Grossman's efforts to change the paradigm ultimately "took five to seven years to achieve," according to Abramson. The change management process was marked by what were sometimes slow yet always deliberate steps designed to infuse a sense of accountability.

ALIGNING FUNDAMENTAL AND CLINICAL RESEARCH

One of the keys to the creation of an integrated academic medical center is close ties between fundamental and clinical research, aligning the work of scientists seeking to explore the origins of health and disease with physicians treating those very diseases. Bar-Sagi has led a major effort to "focus on strengthening our research in areas where we believe there are gaps, especially those that align with our clinical practice. For example, we would like to build strengths in metabolic disorders, neurological diseases, human genetics, human immunology, and infectious diseases."

Scientists and physicians throughout NYU Langone
are encouraged to work together to approach a
problem from multiple perspectives.

Another means of strengthening the ties between fundamental and clinical research, and to encourage collaboration among scientists in different areas of research, is an emphasis on collaborative research projects. Scientists and physicians throughout NYU Langone are encouraged to work together to approach a problem from multiple perspectives. Specifically, scientists and doctors are encouraged to apply for what National Institutes of Health designate as program project grants. These grants typically require that three or more researchers collaborate on a common research proposal. Those that include research physicians as well as scientists are especially encouraged. Program project grants bring people together with different backgrounds and favor the integration of fundamental and clinical medicine. They contribute to busting silos between departments and research specialties. They also tend to be significantly larger than grants received by single scientists or research doctors.

In describing the focus on collaborative research Grossman said, "I will encourage big science research involving teams of scientists from different disciplines working together to solve big problems." This collaborative approach extended beyond NYU Langone.

Bar-Sagi said, "I believe there are more opportunities for synergy between the research at the Medical Center and the Washington Square campus of NYU." She has sought to develop greater linkages with the science departments at NYU as well.

SUPPORTING LESS COMMON PROJECTS

NYU Langone does not depend upon metrics alone to judge the merit and value of research programs. Judgments regarding the quality of a researcher and a research program must be more nuanced. Some cutting-edge projects that go against established ideas may be important but difficult to fund. Some may require years of investment. In our discussions, it was clear that Bar-Sagi not only is aware of these issues but also nurtures such work. She told me, "We certainly understand that making fundamental breakthroughs in science may take many years of research that might not be competitive for extramural funding." Consequently, she added, "We make provisions for that type of research and provide institutional support for personnel and equipment." In addition, she noted, there are medical school faculty members who are devoted entirely to teaching and are not expected to be involved in research.

CLINICAL TRIALS

Bob Grossman's road map included an increased emphasis on clinical trials. After a promising drug or medical technique is developed, it must be tested to determine whether it is safe and effective. Testing involves using the drug or technique on healthy people as well as those with a specific disease under carefully controlled conditions. Such clinical trials are the way new drugs and experimental medical techniques are approved for use and for coverage under various insurance programs. For Grossman and his team, patient centered care means playing a central role in developing new and better ways to treat and cure disease.

Being involved in a clinical trial puts an institution and members of its faculty and staff at the cutting edge of developing treatments and remedies. Bar-Sagi said, "The opportunities for support of clinical trials from the National Institutes of Health are significant." She added, "We are investing heavily in building the infrastructure that our clinical investigators need to develop those trials." As a result of these efforts, the number of active clinical research studies has increased from fifteen hundred in 2008 to twenty-five hundred in 2017. Revenue from industry sponsored clinical trials—which is considered a good proxy for the level of people and resources involved in this work—has nearly tripled from $7.6 million in 2008 to $20.6 million in 2017.

> Being involved in a clinical trial puts an institution and members of its faculty and staff at the cutting edge of developing treatments and remedies.

RESEARCH INSTITUTES

The creation of new research institutes is a prominent feature of the 2009 road map. Research institutes generally focus on one central aspect of biomedical science such as cancer, neuroscience, heart disease, or diabetes. Research institutes are different from academic and clinical departments and typically draw their staff from both. Most if not all researchers in an institute have departmental appointments.

Research institutes have several advantages. They contribute to the overall goal of integration of fundamental and clinical research as institutes' staff come from both sectors and work on common problems. The creation of a new research institute is often an attractive way for a major donor to fulfill a wish to make a difference to an area of medicine of special interest to them personally.

In our discussion of the research enterprise, Bar-Sagi said, "Bob Grossman and I realized that there were certain areas of research that we wanted to expand, but that the scope might not justify the establishment of a department." Institutes, which are smaller than academic departments, address that need. "They provide the opportunity to engage existing faculty and to add new faculty devoted to focused areas of research."

NYU's former president John Sexton was pleased with NYU Langone's plan to enhance existing institutes and create new ones. He said, "At the time, the sciences throughout the university, including the medical school, were weaker than they should have been. There were terrific individual scientists but few real centers of excellence. The only major exception was the Center for Neuroscience, which was a little boutique operation in the Faculty of Arts and Sciences." Sexton added, "We had some neuroscientists that were good in the Medical Center, but neuroscience at the Square and neuroscience at the Medical Center did not work closely together. This situation could not be tolerated, could not continue, if we were to be great. We knew we had to build science, but we had to build systematically." The creation of a new Neuroscience Institute has been a major success. (This was made possible, as mentioned earlier, by a gift from Fiona Druckenmiller, a member of the NYU Langone board of trustees.)

Building a new institute requires significant upfront funding followed by a concerted effort to recruit world class talent. Thus, a top priority was recruiting a director. This task fell to Bob Grossman. His choice was Richard Tsien. Tsien, then a professor at Stanford University, had a job he described to me as "nirvana-like." How could he be convinced to leave such a position and come to NYU Langone? The answer was a firm commitment by NYU Langone to providing financial support and freedom. Tsien said, "The money came with very few strings attached. The money was to support fundamental research in neuroscience."

Tsien recalled that he was told that he could be both the chair of the Department of Neuroscience and Physiology and director of the Neuroscience Institute. He could "have a life partly independent from the department but use the department as the academic home." By running both he could solve several problems at once, have control of what the future of the department would be, and have control over space that the department holds.

The offer included thirty faculty positions—but not all at once. According to Tsien, "They very cleverly said, 'Bring them in one at a time, and we will judge them. We do not want to give you a lump sum. You can make the case for every one of them. You will do better that way.'"

Tsien's original title was chair of the Department of Physiology and Neuroscience, but later "the names have flipped. It is still the same department started by my predecessor, but we have built something very different, something less insular, something more unifying."

When Tsien arrived in 2011, he said, "I came here with the excitement of starting something new . . . that is, to be part of something more idealistic, something like the Peace Corps." Tsien added, "I am here partly out of a sense of challenge, partly out of a sense of idealism, and partly because my family likes New York very much."

In a half dozen years, Tsien has built an institute that now has almost the full quota of faculty members. Reflecting on his move, Tsien said, "I like the upwardly mobile, restlessly ambitious, slightly chip-on-the-shoulder immigrant feeling of this place that is embodied by

Ken Langone, being an Italian-American, and Bob Grossman, being a Jewish boy from the Bronx who went to Tulane and had the attitude that there were a lot of snobbish people in this world, but that nothing couldn't be overcome with a mix of zest and street smarts and energy."

"I like the upwardly mobile, restlessly ambitious, slightly chip-on-the-shoulder immigrant feeling of this place that is embodied by Ken Langone, being an Italian-American, and Bob Grossman, being a Jewish boy from the Bronx . . ."

When Grossman became CEO, NYU Langone already had two distinguished institutes. Perhaps the best known was the Rusk Institute of Rehabilitation Medicine, established in 1948, which is the world's first and largest university-affiliated center devoted entirely to inpatient and outpatient care and research and training in rehabilitation medicine. The Rusk Institute has been voted the best rehabilitation hospital in New York and among the top ten in the country since 1989, when *U.S. News & World Report* introduced its annual "Best Hospitals" rankings.

In addition to Rusk, NYU Langone also had the Skirball Institute of Biomolecular Medicine, which opened in October 1993. Bob Berne recalled, "The Skirball Institute was a way to focus what was then thought to be the highest-quality researchers and to encourage interdisciplinary research." The Institute also includes the Helen L. and Martin S. Kimmel Center for Stem Cell Biology. The Institute's administrative staff works with some thirty different research groups within the Institutes.

FROM BENCH TO BEDSIDE

Over the past ten years NYU Langone has made a concerted effort to translate discoveries made by its scientists and doctors to new ways to treat and cure disease. After all, it was research from an NYU scientist, Jan Vilcek and his team, that led to the development of the drug Remicade that revolutionized the treatment of several autoimmune diseases and brought NYU close to a billion dollars in licensing and royalty payments.

Dafna Bar-Sagi oversees this activity. In describing the renewed efforts to assist the scientists and doctors to focus on the practical aspects of their work and to create new companies, she said, "We have a robust legal and scientific team that collaborates under the umbrella of the Office of Industrial Liaison and the Office of Therapeutic Alliances. The intent of the latter is to transform the process of commercializing discoveries from being strictly a legal operation to one that supports the investigators in their efforts to translate their discoveries into useful products."

She explained, "We do much more than file patents on behalf of the inventors. We help inventors to develop their discoveries further right here at the Medical Center so that we and they obtain greater value when the discoveries are licensed. We use institutional resources to invest in inventions that we predict will benefit from additional development."

NYU Langone is now prepared to use its own funds to support the early work needed to bring a new drug, diagnostic test, or device to the market. As ideas are developed, Bar-Sagi said, "The Office of Therapeutics Alliances has an advisory board that reviews the inventions and provides recommendations about their commercial potential. The advisory board of external experts is assembled on an ad hoc basis, depending on the nature of the invention and the type of expertise needed. We draw heavily on experts from the pharmaceutical industry and on practicing physicians who can provide input on the clinical relevance of the invention."

NYU Langone is now prepared to use its own funds to support the early work needed to bring a new drug, diagnostic test, or device to the market.

The Office of Therapeutics Alliances is overseen by Robert Schneider, who is a member of the Department of Microbiology and who has started several companies himself. Bar-Sagi said that "his team includes individuals who go door to door to look for inventions. We decided to take this proactive approach because we find that many scientists do not realize that their discoveries might have commercial value."

Since 2013, the Office of Therapeutic Alliances has reviewed more than fifty projects. Nine of these successfully licensed to industry. This process has raised total financing of $78 million. At the end of 2017, there were twenty-one projects in the "active pipeline," according to Bar-Sagi. The total number of patents NYU Langone has received has grown from 419 in 2001 to 791 in 2017. A total of forty-six new companies have been created between 2007 and 2017 as a result of research conducted at NYU Langone.

To summarize, research and discovery at NYU Langone are thriving.

PART IV

Building on Success

CHAPTER 13

The Transformation of a Brooklyn-Based Safety Net Hospital, and a Long Island-Based Suburban Hospital

My hope writing *World Class* is that hospitals in the United States and other countries will adapt elements of the NYU Langone vision, strategy, execution, and especially information systems to improve the quality, access, and affordability of their own hospitals and academic medical centers.

I am sure that one question my readers will ask themselves is, Can the NYU Langone system deliver the same results with patient populations that differ substantially from people living in midtown Manhattan? Will they work in poor urban areas? Will they work in the suburbs and in sparsely populated regions of the country? Will they work in another country where more than half of the population lives in rural areas? Will they work amid a rapidly developing urban population?

While I cannot answer all of these questions with definitive proof, I can offer two very different examples of how the NYU Langone management system has been successfully adapted: one to a hospital serving a low income population in Brooklyn and another to an upscale suburban hospital in Long Island. I am personally convinced that the process and procedures developed by NYU Langone, particularly the patient centered, information intense, integrated approach, is the recipe for successful transformation of underperforming medical systems in many contexts, not just New York and not only in the United States.

NYU LANGONE HOSPITAL–BROOKLYN

In April 2015, NYU Langone acquired what was formerly known as Lutheran Hospital and has since been renamed NYU Langone Hospital–Brooklyn. NYU Langone Hospital–Brooklyn has a very different patient base than the rest of the NYU Langone hospitals. In the two area codes that surround the Brooklyn hospital, eighty-five percent of the population are either covered by Medicare, Medicaid, or are uninsured, the highest percentages for the patient mix of any hospital in the country. As we shall see, NYU Langone transformed this hospital in less than two-and-a-half years from one that was losing money to profitability, and from one with a poor quality and safety record to one with one of the best quality and safety records in the country.

How did NYU Langone, which had stood apart from the hospital merger mania of the past ten years, come to acquire the former Lutheran Hospital? The hospital merger grew out of NYU Langone's emphasis on treating patients through ambulatory care facilities rather than in hospitals. As NYU Langone built an ambulatory care network, it made sense to expand into Brooklyn. Richard Donoghue, senior vice president for Strategy, Planning, and Business Development, said, "Only one-third of our patients at Tisch Hospital live in Manhattan. About twenty-six percent of our patients live in Brooklyn. We deliver more babies at Tisch Hospital who go home to a zip code in Brooklyn than go home to a zip code in Manhattan. Brooklyn has always been an important market for NYU Langone."

Joe Lhota, senior vice president and vice dean, explained, "People want to stay in their neighborhood for treatment. People will ask, 'Why do I have to travel to Manhattan for treatment if I can receive the same high-quality care nearby and be home by evening?'" So, to bolster its growing ambulatory care penetration of Brooklyn, NYU Langone was interested in having a hospital in Brooklyn to serve the patients receiving outpatient care locally.

Meanwhile, Lutheran Hospital, established over one hundred years ago, was struggling. According to Donoghue, "People on Medicaid populations accounted for about forty percent of its business; Medicare was about thirty-five percent, and the uninsured about ten percent."

The former Lutheran had been designated a safety net hospital. Safety net hospitals are those that offer access to care regardless of a patient's ability to pay and whose patient population includes a substantial share of those who are uninsured or on Medicaid. Most safety net hospitals receive subsidies from Medicaid and Medicare. Given the reimbursement rates, Donoghue said, "It was very difficult for them to break even, and even harder to generate the surplus needed to reinvest in updated, modern facilities, equipment, and technology."

Donoghue pointed out that in addition to a 450-bed hospital, the Brooklyn hospital "also had forty-two ambulatory sites. Most of the ambulatory care sites are located throughout Brooklyn as well as some in Staten Island, Queens, and a couple in Manhattan. They have a large school-based program. Almost all of these are primary care facilities. They did not have sophisticated ambulatory care capabilities. Lutheran did not have ambulatory infusion therapy, ambulatory surgery, cancer, or high-end ambulatory imaging centers. All of their centers were focused on primary care."

Lutheran and NYU Langone entered into an agreement under

which NYU Langone assumed control in April 2015. NYU Langone did not pay anything to acquire the hospital. Lutheran was in a difficult financial situation, and they were looking for a partner that would help them build new facilities. Donoghue said, "The financial consideration was our promise to invest in the facility and to ensure that the community received a continuing and improved quality of care. The original plan was to complete a full merger over the course of several years, but we decided we would be better off accelerating that timetable." NYU Langone completed the merger on January 1, 2016.

LEADERSHIP

Leadership was the first thing to change as the merger progressed. Grossman said: "I let go all the people who were not performing well. I replaced them with people from our Manhattan campus, passionate people who share our culture. They blew up the old way of doing things." The change included almost all of the senior management team, the chief executive officer, the chief operating officer, and the general counsel. The chief medical officer and the chief financial officer retired just before the transaction.

NYU Langone also changed almost all of the clinical chiefs. Donoghue explained, "Many of their chiefs were people who had part-time appointments at Lutheran and full-time private practices. That is not the model we use. We look for people who are full-time employees of our organization. The head of the emergency department, the head of medicine, the head of pediatrics are all incredibly important jobs in terms of the quality of service we deliver." In place of the seven who departed, five new chiefs were transferred from NYU Langone and two were recruited from the outside.

Grossman appointed a new head of NYU Langone Hospital–Brooklyn, Bret Rudy. Rudy was vice chair of Pediatrics. He went to Lutheran in August 2015 as chief medical officer, and in June 2016, he was promoted to senior vice president of NYU Langone Health and executive director of the newly renamed NYU Langone Hospital–Brooklyn. The new name symbolized the Brooklyn hospital's new status: NYU Langone Hospital–Brooklyn was to be a fully integrated part of the also newly renamed NYU Langone *Health*, just like Tisch Hospital and the NYU Orthopedic Hospital.

The leadership team at NYU Langone Hospital–Brooklyn,
including Bret Rudy (third from left)

NYU Langone Hospital–Brooklyn also underwent a sweeping transition from a reliance on consulting doctors to staff physicians, the same path that had been carved out in Manhattan. "When we merged with Lutheran," Rudy said, "not only did they not have full-time physicians, but they also relied on outside companies to staff a number of very important areas. For example, the emergency department was staffed by an outside group. In August 2016, we replaced that company and put in full-time physicians. That made a dramatic impact on the quality of care and the operations." In addition, NYU Langone Hospital–Brooklyn had two radiology services, one an on-site generalist, and another at an outside company. "There was a lot of variability. We took over all of radiology as soon as we went live with all of our integrated systems."

QUALITY AND SAFETY

As the new team was being assembled, Rudy said, "The first thing we did was to revamp the safety procedures and root cause analysis of the hospital." Whenever there is what Rudy called a "serious occurrence in a hospital," the hospital must undertake a root cause analysis focused on the processes and systems that may have contributed to the outcome. "We then follow up to make sure that we implement the proper changes and that our changes have the intended effect," Rudy said. "For example, we may discover that there was inadequate communication between care providers. We will then create a format for a more structured hand off and set new requirements so that communication among providers is standardized. We monitor adherence to the new procedures for a period of time to make sure that progress is sustained."

Rudy said, "In safety net hospitals there is a tendency to operate under the assumption that 'we do the best we can with limited resources.'" But Rudy didn't see it that way: "Our approach was not necessarily to throw more resources at improving quality and safety. We approached the problem by creating structures and formats we knew worked well." But he added, "Most importantly, we changed the culture. The accountability standards we applied to everyone at the hospital were very different than what they had seen before." That, he said, "was really my work for my initial two months."

Rudy set out to elevate standards at NYU Langone Hospital–Brooklyn.

Rudy told me that "in Brooklyn we began with the premise that we cannot accept any lower standards for the patients that we care for in Brooklyn than the patients that we care for in Manhattan. The goals around quality of care at the campus in Brooklyn are exactly the same as the goals in Manhattan. There is the perception that a safety net hospital working in a community cannot meet the same standards as an academic medical center. Our plan is to create an academic medical center in a community, not a community hospital with an academic medical center affiliation."

> "The goals around quality of care at the campus in Brooklyn are exactly the same as the goals in Manhattan."

INFORMATION TECHNOLOGY

Within the first year NYU Langone completed installation of its innovative information management system at a cost of $80 million. As the NYU Langone newsletter, *News & Views*, reported in April 2017, "Previously Lutheran relied on a patchwork of record keeping systems, some electronic, some paper, to monitor 1.7 million patients. Now there is a single, comprehensive digital file for each patient treated at any of NYU Langone Hospital–Brooklyn's twenty-two inpatient and outpatient locations, or referred to any NYU Langone facility."

Rudy said, "The information system and the dashboards were and are critical to achieving our goals. I do not think we could have made the progress we have without it. Having data at your fingertips that is accurate, that is actionable, is critical. I probably use the dashboard ten times a day. You can slice and dice the data in many different ways. The chief medical officer at Brooklyn, who reports to me, goes over data from the dashboard at every meeting of the service chiefs."

Rudy went on to say, "It is important when working toward improvement that we are all looking at the same data. Real time data creates the opportunity for detecting a problem quickly and working toward improvement. The dashboards provide the data you need to analyze an issue and to understand where changes are needed. We look at all the factors that impact the outcomes."

"Real time data creates the opportunity for detecting a problem quickly and working toward improvement. The dashboards provide the data you need to analyze an issue and to understand where changes are needed."

To enhance accountability, Rudy went on, "We break the data down by provider, that is to say by individual doctor. Some of our doctors never saw their quality data before the merger. For example, we may ask them why their patients are staying twice as long in the hospital as patients treated by other doctors using the same procedure. We ask them to be responsible for improving what they are doing. We provide them with the necessary analytic and information tools, pathways, and guidelines. Ultimately the doctors must be responsible for their own patient outcomes. When we went live with all of Epic and the twenty-two other information systems, all of the family health centers were included, plus all of the twenty-six school-based clinics, and all the community medicine programs." The community medicine programs provide care in homeless shelters. However, much of this network had become part of the NYU Langone ambulatory care network and was not at that time Rudy's responsibility.

VALUE-BASED MEDICINE

Aided by the sophisticated information system, Rudy said, "We have instituted standardized processes across all our units. Integral to the success of NYU Langone is that every unit follows really the same set of standards. Things fall apart if different units follow different processes. The entire staff is systematically educated to implement standard processes and procedures. If people do not follow the best clinical standards, you wind up having totally avoidable complications. We have standardized our care across all types of surgical programs—C-sections, abdominal hysterectomies, and others."

> "Value-based medicine focuses on improvement in quality of outcomes and reduction of costs. This program has been very successful in saving costs."

But what should those standards be? "As soon as all of the NYU Langone information processes went live at the Brooklyn campus, we had the financial and the quality data at our fingertips so that we could institute the value-based medicine approach. We did the financial analysis and the quality analysis and saw that we had great opportunities to improve in Brooklyn," Rudy said.

He continued, "The value-based medicine approach was put in place" at NYU Langone "to reduce our losses when treating patients covered by Medicare. Value-based medicine focuses on improvement in quality of outcomes and reduction of costs. This program has been very successful in saving costs. For example, we were able to identify less expensive drugs that could be substituted for others without reducing the quality of the outcome. We found ways to reduce the length of stay without compromising outcomes. We discovered how to eliminate unnecessary diagnostic tests."

In implementing value-based medicine in Brooklyn, Rudy said, "We first applied what we know worked to the Brooklyn hospital." As an example, he cited the issue of unnecessary blood transfusions: "Blood transfusions are good if you really need them. If you over-transfuse people, they have a worse outcome. Over-transfusion adds costs and adds risks. Manhattan was able to reduce the number of blood transfusions and show improvement in quality and decrease in cost. That was very easy to institute with immediate impact in Brooklyn."

While an assortment of other analyses were also transferred from NYU Langone to the Brooklyn hospital, Rudy added, "We are now implementing some value-based medicine projects in Brooklyn that are more specific to our population. An example—we found that we had patients that would linger in the hospital for sixty, eighty, a hundred days due to complex issues including immigration status, placement issues, and absence of home support. These patients are challenging. They require a lot of social work and care management time. These patients were not responsive to our initiatives to have patients out of the hospital by noon on the day of discharge. We created a separate team that included a full-time physician, one of our hospital care managers, a social worker, and one of our community physicians to focus on those patients. We have had great success in reducing their length of stay. Earlier discharge from the hospital is better for the patients. They have fewer complications such as bedsores and hospital-acquired bacterial infections. We are an acute care hospital that is not ideally suited to long-term chronic inpatient care." Discerning and implementing best practices is turning into a two-way street, Rudy noted: "We are planning to extend our program for long-term patients to patients in Manhattan."

"Earlier discharge from the hospital is better for the patients. They have fewer complications such as bedsores and hospital-acquired bacterial infections."

ADDING NEW SERVICES

Rudy not only implemented new processes at NYU Langone Hospital–Brooklyn, but also added new services. For example, robotic surgery was never performed at the former Lutheran. Now they are performed regularly. In 2018 alone, they were expected to perform more than four hundred robotic cases. Rudy added, "We are performing microvascular techniques that were never done before at Lutheran, expanding spine surgery and advanced endoscopic surgery."

REBUILDING NYU LANGONE HOSPITAL–BROOKLYN

The Brooklyn hospital is housed in a retrofitted manufacturing building. "It is a very long building that is difficult to manage in terms of patient flow," Donoghue said, adding, "All of the existing patient rooms really need to be modernized. Like Tisch Hospital, which opened in 1963, the fundamental infrastructure needs to be renewed to reflect the many changes in clinical medicine that have occurred over the past forty to fifty years." For starters, he said, they redesigned the patient flow at NYU Langone Hospital–Brooklyn.

"Ambulatory care patients were intermingled with inpatients. We are moving ambulatory care out of the hospital altogether and into facilities in the surrounding community," Rudy said.

Donoghue added, "We will be building a new building adjacent to the main hospital. We will do at Lutheran what we are doing at our main campus. Our new hospital, adjacent to Tisch, will open in June 2018, with all private rooms and technologically advanced surgical and procedure rooms. We will transfer significant activity to the new faculties adjacent to the Tisch and Lutheran Hospitals, and then we will retrofit and update the older facilities. The new rooms will be single-person rooms. We will convert almost all of the rooms at both the Tisch and the Brooklyn campus to private rooms."

Donoghue added, "At present the ten operating rooms at Lutheran treat both elective and emergency surgery patients. We will transfer all ambulatory surgery out of the main facility into a new ambulatory surgery center. We have already created an infusion therapy center for treating cancer patients apart from the main hospital." He added, "The primary surgical and complex ambulatory care service building will be housed in a separate facility just across the street from the main hospital."

INTEGRATION WITH NYU LANGONE

Following the introduction of new staff and new procedures, the Brooklyn hospital has become a full-fledged part of NYU Langone analyses and innovation. In the case of nursing, for example, Catherine Manley-Cullen, vice president of Patient Care Services and Nursing at NYU Langone Hospital–Brooklyn, said, "We have started to integrate all of our strategic goals for nursing among all four sites. We have common goals with Winthrop, Orthopedics, Manhattan, and Brooklyn. We have one strategy and one plan." Manley-Cullen added, "Today all of the programs that we are rolling out in Manhattan are also rolling out in Brooklyn."

There are still different degrees of integration in the system. Rudy pointed out, "Radiology is the most integrated department across our entire health system. No matter what campus you are at, no matter what time of the day, if you need a CAT scan of your abdomen, your film is read by a radiologist sub-specialist trained in body CAT scans. We have all sub-specialty trained physicians, which has really improved the quality of radiologic reads."

OUTCOMES

What has been the result of all these changes? According to Donoghue, "Since the merger, the improvement in quality of care in Lutheran has been remarkable. For example, the in-hospital mortality rate at Lutheran has declined substantially. The ratio of observed to expected mortality was 1.2 when we entered into the relationship, and the first quarter of 2018 the ratio was 0.5. That is just an extraordinary change."

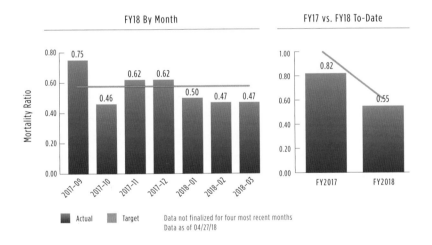

Reductions in mortality at NYU Langone Health–Brooklyn from 2017 to 2018

Donoghue said the rate at Tisch Hospital is also 0.5. He added, "Remember the patient base at Lutheran is drawn from a very difficult population. Eighty-five percent of the patients are Medicaid or

Medicare. Most of these have aged out of Medicaid. Some have aged out of commercial insurance programs. The Medicaid population, whether it is under sixty-five or over sixty-five, has some very significant comorbidities, complexities, and behavioral health issues that make their care complicated. To have the kind of changes that we have had in the quality scores has just been outstanding."

Rudy agreed that "we have made great progress in improving outcomes." He cites improvements in a variety of benchmarks used to evaluate quality, such as observed vs. expected length of stay, surgical site infection rates, and hospital-acquired pressure injuries. Some of these measures seem intuitive, some are complex, but on most of them, NYU Langone Hospital–Brooklyn has been doing much better—and closing the gap with NYU Langone.

One area where it has excelled is the Performing Provider System. Donoghue said, "In 2015 New York State received a Medicaid waiver from the federal government, an $8 billion experiment, to try to change the way in which Medicaid patients were cared for and how they used certain services. The intent was to reduce the number of what are termed potentially preventable admissions, and potentially preventable emergency room visits and readmissions." As part of this experiment Lutheran led one of the twenty-five Performing Provider Systems in New York State. Upon the merger NYU Langone assumed responsibility for this program.

Donoghue said, "We are leading the state in terms of the changes we have made for potentially preventable admissions and potentially preventable emergency room visits. The changes we have seen for the patient population dealing with this are extraordinary. The head of Medicaid often mentions NYU as more or less the poster child for those targeted activities." Previously, Lutheran was seldom seen as a poster child for anything.

"It's been fascinating to see how rapidly they improved," William Constantine said. Constantine, an NYU Langone trustee, said, "The changes took two years to take hold. During the transition, I watched the patient care reports focusing on untoward events. I saw an unacceptable number coming from Lutheran. I would ask the leadership team at Lutheran, 'When are we going to see a turnaround in the healthcare results?' Now Lutheran is matching and in some cases surpassing Tisch."

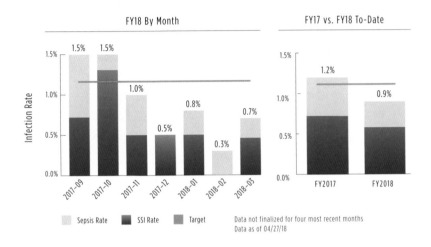

Reductions in surgical infection rates at NYU Langone Health–Brooklyn from 2017 to 2018

Manley-Cullen agreed that "many of the quality metrics in Brooklyn are just as good if not better than those in Manhattan."

Actually, in many respects, Rudy argued that "it's hard to say that one campus is doing better than another overall. We treat different patient populations. For example, post-operative blood clots are particularly high for orthopedic patients. Our orthopedic hospital will be most affected as they have the highest patient population with complex hip replacements and other similar surgeries."

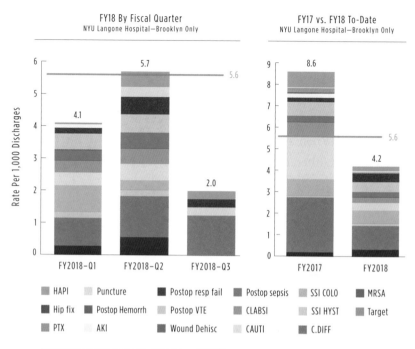

FY18 By Fiscal Quarter
NYU Langone Hospital—Brooklyn Only

FY17 vs. FY18 To-Date
NYU Langone Hospital—Brooklyn Only

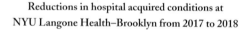

HAPI Puncture Postop resp fail Postop sepsis SSI COLO MRSA

Hip fix Postop Hemorrh Postop VTE CLABSI SSI HYST Target

PTX AKI Wound Dehisc CAUTI C.DIFF

Data not finalized for four most recent months; Data as of 04/27/18

**Reductions in hospital acquired conditions at
NYU Langone Health–Brooklyn from 2017 to 2018**

Anthony Welters, a trustee of NYU Langone and senior advisor in the office of the CEO of United Health Group, said it is not surprising that the Brooklyn hospital surpasses NYU Langone in some respects. "Social safety net hospitals are more efficient and effective in some areas because of some of their training and the nature of the population they serve," he said, adding, "They often provide excellent diagnostic services. They are great at triage. Typically, they have a closer relationship to the population they serve than do most other hospitals. They understand what it takes to get Sarah to take her medicine."

> "Social safety net hospitals are more efficient
> and effective in some areas because of some of their
> training and the nature of the population they serve. . . .
> They have a closer relationship to the population
> they serve than do most other hospitals."

In general, however, there seems to be increasing convergence in the results achieved in Manhattan and Brooklyn. Manley-Cullen said, "I would say it will probably be four or five years to completely transition to the point where I could not be able to tell the difference between Brooklyn and Manhattan."

FROM LOSS TO PROFIT

NYU Langone Hospital–Brooklyn is now generating surplus revenue. One reason is improved financial management. After installing the NYU Langone financial management systems, NYU Langone Hospital–Brooklyn began producing cost recoveries averaging $3 million per month. As was the case at NYU Langone, Epic billing systems allowed staff at NYU Langone Hospital–Brooklyn to identify gaps in billing and start charging for services performed.

The surplus is all the more surprising when viewed in the context of another change that occurred, the reduction in admission rates. As the former Chief Financial Officer, Michael Burke, noted, "We are now admitting thirty percent fewer patients. Because of our rate improvements, our revenues are not really down that much. We have shown that we can break even or do well in Brooklyn with admitting thirty percent fewer patients." Burke insisted these choices are being made on the basis of ambulatory care principles, not limiting access to patients who will require less and pay more. In fact, Burke said, "We are actually providing more charity care, $1.5 million to $2 million a month of additional charity care that they otherwise were not providing to the community."

Overall, Burke said, "In a relatively short period of time, the Lutheran acquisition will, quite literally, pay for our investment in it, and begin generating significant incremental revenue and surplus for NYU Langone."

CAN OTHERS FOLLOW THE NYU LANGONE PATH?

Can others follow the same path? Rudy said, "I think it will be very hard for a safety net hospital, given their financial restraints, to make the needed changes without support from another hospital system. Real time data are critical to effective transformation. When you are looking at data that are six months or a year old, you are already six months or a year behind seeing trends. You need real time, actionable data." Safety net hospitals may not be able to afford something like Epic on their own.

In a discussion of the importance of the Brooklyn experience for other safety net hospitals in the United States, Welters told me, "In terms of benefits to society, I am most excited about the lessons NYU Langone is learning from their experience in Brooklyn."

Prior to the acquisition, Welters said, the "philosophy" at NYU Langone was "We are good. We want to be great." But he added, "More recently we have broadened our goals to embrace what I believe is our social responsibility. NYU Langone, with its central location in the heart of Manhattan, probably has the best payer mix in New York City. It would be very easy for our leadership to focus only on this market and to stay within our comfort zone." Welters told me safety net hospitals have unique lessons they can offer to larger, more sophisticated and more affluent institutions. These hospitals can teach "what it takes to fully engage with high-risk populations. That is where the safety net hospitals are at their best."

Given this context, Welters said he thinks that the acquisition of a troubled safety net hospital in Brooklyn is "the most significant thing we as a board, and Bob as a chief executive officer, have done. Now we can answer the question, 'Can you bring the same level of discipline and accountability to a critical hospital serving an underserved population to raise both its performance and quality metrics? Can we achieve outcomes comparable to those of the NYU Langone hospital?'"

The acquisition of a troubled safety net hospital in Brooklyn is "the most significant thing we as a board, and Bob as a chief executive officer, have done."

In his view, "While the results are preliminary, they are positive. If we are successful there, the integrated delivery model I believe can be replicated throughout the country, in particular, in urban areas where these critical hospitals serve an underserved population that may initially lack the managerial leadership and the technology needed to thrive. If NYU Langone demonstrates success in Brooklyn, it will be a game changer." In my talks with Grossman, he made the same point.

From my perspective it is clear that safety net hospitals and others that serve Medicare, Medicaid, and uninsured populations can benefit enormously from the NYU management system. The question is, How can we as a country support the transition from what exists today to what can be, without the support of an NYU Langone? My answer is that we can't do it without additional and substantial supportive information systems and infrastructure. Developing such support is a central challenge to our nation as we come to rely increasingly on Medicare, Medicaid, and other forms of government insurance, if for no other reason than it being the result of the realities of our aging demographics.

WINTHROP HOSPITAL, LONG ISLAND

NYU Langone is now in the process of merging with a hospital very different from its acquisition in Brooklyn. This is the merger with Winthrop-University Hospital in Mineola, Long Island. The merger process began in September 2016. Winthrop operates almost six hundred beds in the center of Long Island. According to Richard Donoghue, "The structure of our relationship with Winthrop is almost identical to the structure at Lutheran."

The Research and Academic Center at Winthrop Hospital in Long Island

In the press release announcing the agreement, there were two key components, "NYU Langone will provide an initial capital investment and develop a long-term master plan which will serve as a framework for future changes and expansion of the campus for both inpatient and ambulatory activities, based upon projected needs. . . . Implementation and integration of the Epic electronic medical records system will be focused on Winthrop's ambulatory practices, to develop a system-wide, state-of-the art IT infrastructure and connectivity to support clinical integration and population health management initiatives and analytics."

Donoghue said of the Winthrop deal, "We did not buy them. We agreed to invest $100 million in their physical plant. They felt they were not big enough to survive on their own. They did not generate the kind of margins necessary to make the investments in their physical plant and to invest in the physician practices that they deemed appropriate. When Winthrop saw the investments we were making in physician practices on Long Island, they agreed to become controlled by NYU Langone Health."

"We did not buy them. We agreed to invest $100 million in their physical plant. They felt they were not big enough to survive on their own."

According to the terms of the agreement, the merger with NYU Langone will be completed in five years, and Winthrop would then become an integrated operating unit of NYU Langone. Donoghue added, "The merger has gone so well that I believe the full merger will be complete in about two-and-a-half years."

While Winthrop needed a partner with deeper pockets, Donoghue said, "Our motivations arise from a different source. Care has consistently been moving out of the hospital into less complex settings. Those

settings must be close to where people live and work." Moreover, Donoghue said, "when the ambulatory care networks in a geographic region
reach a certain density, there is a need to have a hospital in the area to
serve their needs." He called this "a local hub effect," and noted the
basic rationale for acquiring Winthrop is the same as that underlying
the amalgamation with Lutheran in Brooklyn.

Why go to Long Island in the first place? Donoghue said, "Surveys
show that at least one member of a family on Long Island commutes to
Manhattan for work. Many have had a longstanding relationship with
NYU Langone. We want to stay connected to that patient population."
The Winthrop patient population is very similar to the patient population at NYU Langone in Manhattan. About fifty percent of Winthrop's
patients are covered by commercial insurance, compared to forty-eight
percent in Manhattan. By contrast, most of the Brooklyn hospital's
patients are under Medicare or Medicaid.

After almost two years of affiliation, Donoghue said, "Things are
moving well. The Langone information systems are now installed in all
of the doctors' offices. The hospital will have the system in by September 2019. Many of the clinical chairmen in the Manhattan operation
have connected with their counterparts at Winthrop. The relationships
are very healthy."

As the hospital integration proceeds, Donoghue added, "We will be
opening up a new medical school on the Winthrop campus in September 2019." The idea is to create a small medical school that would focus
on training doctors for primary care fields and would adopt the NYU
Langone three-year degree model.

Although NYU Langone's initial commitment to Winthrop totaled
$100 million, Donoghue said, "We are planning to build a $300 million
ambulatory care center, and a $500–$600 million inpatient pavilion in
addition to the $100 million we committed initially."

I asked Donoghue to provide a framework to help me understand the NYU Langone acquisition strategy. In reply he said, "Hospital acquisitions are in service to the ambulatory care networks. Others acquired hospitals first. In my view, we have expanded in a thoughtful way. We were aware of how the care markets were evolving. Many who acquired hospitals now find themselves saddled with these expensive dinosaurs that either need enormous capital infusions or need to be closed."

In replying to a similar question, Bob Grossman said that the primary goal of future expansion is "to continue deepening the existing network of ambulatory care facilities."

In summary, NYU Langone has applied its unique management system to both an urban safety net hospital and one that serves an upscale suburban population, and the results seem to be positive.

CHAPTER 14

Looking Forward

Evolution is key to continued success in any organization. Adapting to change is especially critical for academic medical centers that are in the eye of the storm of changes in healthcare service and payments, as well as the rapid pace of biomedical research. As impressive as the transformation of NYU Langone Health has been so far, the institution has its eyes on the future.

"The world is relentless. We are relentless
in our pursuit of excellence."

The leadership of NYU Langone is not content to rest on its laurels. NYU Langone recognizes that quality is a journey, not a destination. The medical staff continually measure how well they are doing and how to do better. Dashboards highlight shortcomings and pinpoint areas in need of improvement. Paresh Shah, vice chairman of Surgery, Quality, and Innovation, summed up the attitude nicely for me when he said, "We look at where we stand on the Vizient rankings. We have been gratified to be number one three years in a row. We had the hat trick through to this year. And that was great. But, I tell my team all the time, number one does not mean that you are good, it just means you are better than the rest. There is a big difference. So number one does not mean we are good enough."

In Bob Grossman's words, "The world is relentless. We are relentless in our pursuit of excellence."

THE ROAD AHEAD

As he did for the first ten years, Bob Grossman has drafted a road map for the next ten years. Again, the plan for the future is condensed to a single handwritten page.

PATIENT FOCUSED

The words *patient centered* were central to the vision for the future in the first map, and here the words *patient focused* appear at the very heart of the plan. All elements of the plan for the future connect here.

Patient focused is supported by the words *high reliability organization.* In Grossman's words, "The central theme is high-quality patient care and building a highly reliable organization across everything we do." Those are the "key elements of the strategic plan for the next ten years. This is what will distinguish all that we do over the next ten years." The words *value* and *efficiency* reflect the commitment to providing the best service to the patient while ensuring the sustainability and growth of the institution.

Looking Forward

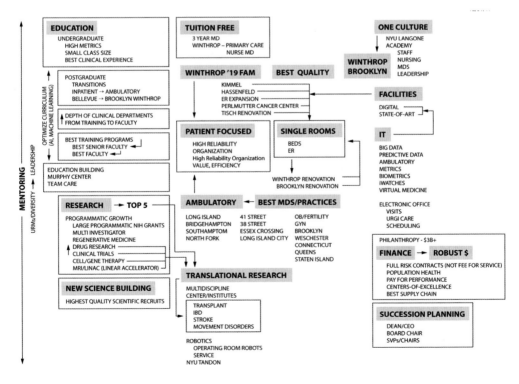

Grossman's handwritten road map for the next ten years

EDUCATION
UNDERGRADUATE
HIGH METRICS
SMALL CLASS SIZE
BEST CLINICAL EXPERIENCE

POSTGRADUATE
TRANSITIONS
INPATIENT → AMBULATORY
BELLEVUE → BROOKLYN WINTHROP

DEPTH OF CLINICAL DEPARTMENTS
FROM TRAINING TO FACULTY

BEST TRAINING PROGRAMS
BEST SENIOR FACULTY
BEST FACULTY

EDUCATION BUILDING
MURPHY CENTER
TEAM CARE

TUITION FREE
3 YEAR MD
WINTHROP – PRIMARY CARE
NURSE MD

WINTHROP '19 FAM | BEST QUALITY
KIMMEL
HASSENFELD
ER EXPANSION
PERLMUTTER CANCER CENTER
TISCH RENOVATION

PATIENT FOCUSED
HIGH RELIABILITY
ORGANIZATION
High Reliability Organization
VALUE, EFFICIENCY

SINGLE ROOMS
BEDS
ER

WINTHROP RENOVATION
BROOKLYN RENOVATION

ONE CULTURE
NYU LANGONE
ACADEMY
STAFF
NURSING
MDS
LEADERSHIP

WINTHROP BROOKLYN

FACILITIES
DIGITAL
STATE-OF-ART

IT
BIG DATA
PREDICTIVE DATA
AMBULATORY
METRICS
BIOMETRICS
iWATCHES
VIRTUAL MEDICINE

ELECTRONIC OFFICE
VISITS
URGI CARE
SCHEDULING

RESEARCH → TOP 5
PROGRAMMATIC GROWTH
LARGE PROGRAMMATIC NIH GRANTS
MULTI INVESTIGATOR
REGENERATIVE MEDICINE
DRUG RESEARCH
CLINICAL TRIALS
CELL/GENE THERAPY
MRI/LINAC (LINEAR ACCELERATOR)

AMBULATORY ← BEST MDS/PRACTICES
LONG ISLAND   41 STREET   OB/FERTILITY
BRIDGEHAMPTON   38 STREET   GYN
SOUTHAMPTOM   ESSEX CROSSING   BROOKLYN
NORTH FORK   LONG ISLAND CITY WESCHESTER
                                     CONNECTICUT
                                     QUEENS
                                     STATEN ISLAND

NEW SCIENCE BUILDING
HIGHEST QUALITY SCIENTIFIC RECRUITS

TRANSLATIONAL RESEARCH
MULTIDISCIPLINE
CENTER/INSTITUTES
TRANSPLANT
IBD
STROKE
MOVEMENT DISORDERS

ROBOTICS
OPERATING ROOM ROBOTS
SERVICE
NYU TANDON

PHILANTHROPY - $3B+

FINANCE → ROBUST $
FULL RISK CONTRACTS (NOT FEE FOR SERVICE)
POPULATION HEALTH
PAY FOR PERFORMANCE
CENTERS-OF-EXCELLENCE
BEST SUPPLY CHAIN

SUCCESSION PLANNING
DEAN/CEO
BOARD CHAIR
SVPs/CHAIRS

MENTORING
URMs/DIVERSITY ↑ LEADERSHIP
OPTIMIZE CURRICULUM
(AI, MACHINE LEARNING)

The three words in their own box at the top of the map, *Education, Tuition Free,* and *One Culture,* are goals of the more mature organization NYU Langone has become.

The three words in their own box at the top of the map, *Education, Tuition Free,* and *One Culture*, are goals of the more mature organization NYU Langone has become.

EDUCATION

The top left of the road map is devoted to educational goals. *Mentoring* of all students and junior staff is an overarching theme signified by the horizontal arrow at the extreme left. Similarly, there is an emphasis on leadership to drive excellence and *diversity*. It is clear that NYU Langone intends to maintain its leadership in medical education. Reforms in medical education will continue, as captured by the words *optimize curriculum*. The medical school will continue to adapt to changing realities of medical care. There will be an increased focus on the introduction of new educational techniques including *machine learning* and *artificial intelligence (AI)*.

The medical training will continue to evolve. Here the word *undergraduate* denotes students at the medical school pursuing an MD degree. Training will be personalized through *small class size*. The medical school will provide students in training with exposure to patients early on as captured by the words *best clinical experience*.

Postgraduate specialty education will also evolve. There will be a transition from an emphasis on inpatient care to one on ambulatory care, which, as we have seen, is increasingly important to how care will be delivered nationally. As a direct consequence, NYU will educate an increasing number of medical graduate students in their Brooklyn and Winthrop hospitals and fewer in Bellevue.

The part of the road map immediately below outlines an internal path to build the *best faculty* by increasing the overall *depth in each of the clinical departments* that in turn are able to create the *best training programs,* which will produce the *best junior faculty,* which will become the recruiting ground for the *best senior faculty.*

Here the map also emphasizes an important aspect of patient care. Today teams of physicians, nurse practitioners, nurses, and medical technicians work together to provide the best care available for each person. Medical schools must train everyone for the *team care* environment of the future. The future will include new buildings and facilities to support education, summarized in the map as *education building* and *Murphy Center.*

The words at the top center of the map, *Tuition Free,* were an aspirational goal that NYU Langone Health achieved in 2018, thanks to significant philanthropic support. Just under these words, we find *3 year MD.* Shortening the total period of undergraduate and graduate medical training and lowering the cost was an important objective for NYU Langone.

A NEW PRIMARY CARE MEDICAL SCHOOL

The words *Winthrop-Primary Care* that follow represent the commitment to create a new medical school based at Winthrop Hospital on Long Island, which was described in greater detail in chapter 13. The school will specialize in the education of *primary care* doctors. Nurses will be admitted at Winthrop to produce nurse-MD primary care doctors, what I believe is a new initiative in medical education.

Richard Donoghue, senior vice president for Strategy, Planning, and Business Development, explained further: "Bob Grossman came up with the idea of opening a new medical school on the Winthrop campus, and their board, their medical leadership, their executive leadership were all enthusiastic about the possibility."

CULTURAL CONTINUITY

The third boxed word at the top of the road map is *One Culture*. A culture of excellence is central to the transformation of NYU Langone Health. To ensure that the future reflects the accomplishments of the recent past, the road map emphasizes the importance of enhancing and perpetuating the culture they worked so hard to build. The words *NYU Langone Academy* reflect the plans to create an academy to provide leadership training for nurses, doctors, and other staff members. Transplanting the culture of midtown Manhattan to the newly acquired hospitals in *Brooklyn* and *Winthrop* is an important goal in building the new NYU Langone that will serve a much wider geography.

HOSPITAL RENOVATION AND EXPANSION

There will be a continued focus on the renovation of existing facilities and building new ones to enhance patient care, research, and teaching. New inpatient facilities include the Kimmel Pavilion and the Hassenfeld Children's Hospital. Expansion of the emergency care and Perlmutter Cancer Center are also planned. The existing Tisch, Brooklyn, and Winthrop facilities will be renovated. The plans already in the works call for an investment of more than $1.6 billion over the next few years. The great majority of the rooms in the new and renovated hospitals will be *single rooms.*

EXPANSION OF THE AMBULATORY CARE NETWORK

Ambulatory care deserves its own box in the center of the map. Grossman told me, "We recently acquired a 325,000-square-foot building for ambulatory care on 41st Street. We are adding additional space on 38th Street at the Center for Musculoskeletal Care which will include additional operating rooms. We have an ambulatory care center that recently opened in Essex Crossing in the Lower East Side." Overall, Grossman said, "In 2019, we will complete the full asset merger of Winthrop. That will bring us to about three hundred and fifty practice sites throughout the New York metropolitan area."

There are plans to expand the ambulatory care network in *Long Island* to *Bridgehampton, Southampton, Long Island City*, and the *North Fork*. Further expansion in *Brooklyn* is also planned. The ambulatory care network of NYU Langone may eventually extend to *Queens, Staten Island*, and even into nearby *Connecticut*. The expansion of the ambulatory network will be accompanied by an expansion of the type of outpatient services provided, including *obstetrics and gynecology* and *fertility services.*

NYU Langone has taken a small step beyond the New York City metropolitan area. It opened an ambulatory care unit in Palm Beach, Florida, at the end of 2017. The primary purpose is to provide continuing service to patients who live in Manhattan but spend the winter months in Florida. It will have between eight and fifteen doctors, Grossman said, but he said NYU Langone would not open a hospital in West Palm Beach because "I believe it will be hard for us to manage a hospital there. It is difficult to manage the quality we insist upon from a distance. My goal is to grow organically."

The growth in facilities is being accompanied by growth in the number of doctors on staff. As a member of the finance team put it, NYU Langone Health will "need at least five thousand doctors in the integrated network to be big enough so that all the payers have us in their network. Otherwise, we are considered out of network and excluded from patient referrals." In 2018, NYU Langone had just over three thousand seven hundred physicians on staff. The hope is that NYU Langone reaches five thousand within the next five years.

NYU Langone Medical Associates in West Palm Beach, Florida

RESEARCH AND DISCOVERY

Research and *discovery* continue to occupy important space on the map. The goal is now to become among the *top five* biomedical research centers in the country, both in terms of research support and the quality of science. There will be continued emphasis on multidisciplinary collaborative research grants, *program project grants*. They will strengthen research in the emerging fields of regenerative medicine and cell and gene therapy.

Research will be supported by *hiring the highest quality scientific recruits* and constructing a *new science building*. The planned interaction between NYU Langone and the *NYU Tandon* School of Engineering is of special interest. Both Chandrika Tandon, the chair of the Tandon School, who is also a trustee of NYU Langone, and Bob Grossman believe there is a bright future in applying the latest advances in engineering to medicine. A close collaboration between the two research efforts is planned. Such a collaboration may lead to significant advances in *robotic surgery* and nano devices.

Translational research, the interface between fundamental research and clinical medicine, is highlighted. The words deserve their own box situated between the description of the expanded research effort and clinical initiatives. The clinical initiatives include *multidisciplinary centers and institutes*, such as the Neurosciences Institute. New areas of clinical emphasis include *organ transplantation, inflammatory bowel disease, stroke*, and *movement disorders*.

INFORMATION TECHNOLOGY

Information technology (IT) occupies the lower right side of the map. Future efforts will build on past accomplishments. As NYU Langone builds out its current activities and moves in new directions, such as community medicine, there is a familiar theme that will be shaping its future: extending the technology that is so deeply embedded in everything that it currently does.

In describing the future of information technology at NYU Langone, Grossman said, "Our information system is the foundation of what we do now and will do in the future. Information is everything. Without solid real time information you are flying blind. You cannot improve the quality of care without the necessary data. You cannot understand what is happening in research without the data. You cannot manage your finances without all the data."

Medicine is entering an era of big data, wherein very large amounts of patient data can be analyzed to improve care. *Big data*, including a full range of what is called "omic data," including genomic, proteome, microbiomic, and metabolomic data, may well improve the capacity to predict and prevent disease, summarized here as *predictive data. Metrics, biometrics,* and *ambulatory care* will all contribute to big data that when analyzed may prevent and treat disease more effectively.

> "We know technology is not the entire solution.
> I would like to find ways to have our patients use
> analytic tools to understand and manage their
> medical issues so they can better manage their care."

Going forward, Nader Mherabi, NYU Langone's chief information officer, said, "We are now focused on what information systems can do to improve patient experience and what we can do to involve the patient in his or her own care. We believe that information technology, including *virtual health*, is part of the answer." He also said, "We are trying to engage patients with technology where it makes sense. We know technology is not the entire solution. I would like to find ways to have our patients use analytic tools to understand and manage their medical issues so they can better manage their care."

Marc Triola, NYU Langone's associate dean for Educational Informatics, also sees a growing role for information technology—but only if it's done right: "Some people portray both privacy and confidentiality as the main barriers, but I don't agree," he said. His concern is that most patients think current information systems are inefficient and burdensome. "I would give anything for them to be as convenient as using Netflix or my online banking services."

In addition to simplifying patient interaction with information technology, Triola would also like broader dissemination of medical data. He said, "Up until now, hospitals have operated as feudal systems. Each hospital, even each hospital that adopts Epic, has been given free range to make local decisions that affect how data can be shared. The data becomes increasingly differentiated and fragmented. Translation is required to make one dialect of healthcare data talk to another. That involves a huge amount of expense. What we need is a unified set of standards for clinical data representation that make that translation of data from one hospital to another as seamless as possible. At the end of the day, it is about aligning financial incentives and business practice. It is the right thing for the patient. It is the right thing for the healthcare system."

According to Triola, "We should switch to a streaming model of care. There needs to be a constant flow of information, data, education, and recommendations between the patient and the healthcare professional." In his view, "the healthcare professional needs a new infrastructure to support the patient. The infrastructure will include advanced computation capabilities, including artificial intelligence, healthcare educators, and systems that integrate patient information across the entire medical ecosystem. Applied to a problem like high blood pressure, both the patient and physician will receive a continuous feed of information about a person's blood pressure." This will be the *electronic office* highlighted in the road map.

If this is achieved, he said, the patient and physician working together "will be able to apply the right corrective measures, including medications, in the right amount, at the right time. The process will be similar to what diabetic patients do today. They check their own glucose blood levels and dose their own medicine. Right now I may see a patient three or four times a year tops. That is when I measure their blood pressure, leading to decisions that are going to affect the pills they take for the rest of their lives." He wants to replace that with a more interactive approach, "but not one that simply means the patient should go to the doctor more often."

Grossman foresees a role for devices similar to the Apple Watch: "People will be monitored in real time wearing iWatches or other devices. We will be able to have continuous feeds for blood sugar levels, blood pressure, heart rate, everything. I want us to be at the cutting edge of the electronic revolution in medicine."

"We will be able to have continuous feeds for blood sugar levels, blood pressure, heart rate, everything. I want us to be at the cutting edge of the electronic revolution in medicine."

Information technology seems destined to facilitate and encourage the continuing devolution and decentralization of medicine. The next step in medicine may well be an increased emphasis on community medicine and preventive healthcare, facilitated by electronic monitoring.

Doctors are unlikely to resume making house calls, but individuals will be increasingly able to have ailments examined and diagnosed at home via electronic monitoring, which will record and report their vital signs and their medical concerns.

NYU Langone is hardly alone in seeing technology transforming the delivery of medical services. In an article entitled "A Prescription for the Future," published in its April 8, 2017, edition, *The Economist* said that in the future, "rather than checking patients' vital signs only at intervals, or parking ICU-nurses next to beds, live data-streams from medical machines and wearable devices could flow straight to such command centers, where supercomputers could screen them for anything worth bringing to the attention of medical staff." The article quoted Toby Cosgrove, head of the Cleveland Clinic, who said, "When I think of the hospital of the future, I think of a bunch of people sitting in a room full of screens and phones." In this vision, *The Economist* said, "a hospital would resemble an air traffic control tower, from which medical teams would monitor patients near and far to a standard until recently possible only in an ICU. The institution itself would house only emergency cases and the priciest equipment." NYU Langone expects to be in the forefront of this new paradigm for delivering medical services while still honoring the critical importance of the doctor-patient relationship.

HOME AND COMMUNITY CARE

NYU Langone is deeply involved in several initiatives that will alter the structure of medical care. These changes continue the devolution of care from the hospital to the ambulatory care facility to, in many cases, the patient's home.

Many at NYU Langone express increasing interest in community medicine. This represents an extension of the outreach that began as NYU Langone decentralized its activities through ambulatory care. In a further move away from the centralized hospital system, NYU Langone, like a number of other medical centers, is moving in the direction of enhanced community outreach. It would seek greater involvement with people where they live by emphasizing "wellness" and preventive medicine.

The Lutheran Hospital acquisition is helping diffuse NYU Langone services into the community, William Constantine said. The Lutheran Hospital acquisition introduced NYU Langone to public school healthcare. Overnight it inherited oversight of the health programs at thirty-five schools spread over the five boroughs. These programs typically offer primary care delivery by a nurse practitioner and an assistant or two, and in many cases, a full-fledged dentist. "This is a proactive program," one staff member said. "It could take care of Johnny who came to school with a sore throat." The program, which is funded by the city, "is in a position to escalate care to the nearest clinic if need be," she added.

Constantine said, "At the beginning of the year, about ten percent of the parents do not want their children to participate. I asked 'Why? Is that religious?' The reply was, no, it's a lack of knowledge. Many are probably new people in this country who do not trust the system. By year end, participation is close to one hundred percent."

While Grossman believes "ambulatory care is the twenty-first century model," he is already looking beyond it. He argued that the next step is bringing medicine to the patient in his or her home, as opposed to having them come to the hospital or ambulatory care center. As he sees it, "home is really important, especially for the elderly. We are developing the strategy now. Home care will rely heavily on nurses and home care aides. Advances in remote monitoring and electronic home care make it much easier. We are not perfect at home care yet, but it is our intent to be. Excellence in ambulatory and home care is essential to supporting this strategy over the next ten years."

The postwar baby boom generation, those born between 1946 and 1964, were the largest population cohort in U.S. history, and they are moving into retirement and creating an enormous "older" or "elderly" population. This amplifies the potential impact of home care: Whatever mechanisms are developed to transfer medical diagnosis, treatment, and monitoring from a medical facility to a patient's home will have a massive impact because of the sheer number of aging, and aged, baby boomers who will be seeking and receiving this emerging kind of care.

FINANCE

NYU Langone received more than $2 billion in philanthropic support over the past ten years. The target of the next ten years is *three billion*.

There must be a continued effort to increase revenues through generating what is written on the page as *robust income*. Specific areas include participating in *full ask contracts*, whereby NYU will take on full responsibility for managing the health of populations *(population health)* and participate in pay for performance contracts with payers that include provisions that tie payments to patient outcomes. Becoming a recognized *center of excellence* can increase income. Building the *best supply chains* can reduce costs. All of these objectives are hard to achieve but necessary for financial success.

SUCCESSION PLANNING

Successful organizations plan carefully for succession. The road map includes a section on *succession planning* in the lower right corner. No trustee or CEO is there forever. Toward the end of our series of conversations I discussed succession planning with Bob Grossman. It is clear that he is thinking just as carefully about *who* comes next as he is about *what* comes next. Grossman and Ken Langone remain vigorous leaders. Grossman was seventy years old in 2017. Meanwhile, Langone turned eighty-two in September 2018. Many of NYU Langone's senior executives are in their sixties.

Grossman views himself and all members of the executive suite as stewards of the institution. He expects all leaders to be fully committed to NYU Langone's success and progress. As Grossman himself has said, discussions regarding leadership are too often focused on defining the qualities and behaviors associated with success. Too often, people neglect to discuss the need for criticism, real-time appraisals of lapses in performance, and, when necessary and in the most extreme cases, the dismissal of executives or chairs.

Grossman is willing to make the tough choices, when necessary. He is able to separate friendship from performance and can turn to longtime friends and colleagues and ask them to resign, if he feels it is necessary. When people who underperform are left in place, dissatisfaction festers. Grossman understands that such a situation is counterproductive to success and can undermine an entire organization. "How you deal with these dyspeptic situations will ultimately define your leadership," wrote Grossman in the Association of Academic Health Centers publication, *Leadership Perspectives*. "Letting someone go is never easy. Strong leaders have an obligation to push past the hesitation and make changes for the health of their organizations."

Grossman looks at his own role with the institution in the same way. In one of our discussions, Grossman told me, "I hope to continue doing what I am doing now for five to seven more years. I think Ken will remain chairman for four years." He added, "We have succession planning for him already." Langone is thought to favor an insider replacing Grossman when the time comes, because he believes it takes outsiders too long to become familiar with an institution before they can begin taking control of it.

When a successor is named for Grossman, he said, "that person should have their own team." But that transition may occur naturally because much of the NYU Langone senior executive team, including Abramson, Brotman, and several others, will all be aging out around the same time Grossman steps down, facilitating a harmonious changing of the guard. While succession issues remain just over the horizon for NYU Langone's senior management, Grossman has already installed a new and youthful executive team at NYU Langone Hospital–Brooklyn, and he said there is "already succession planning at Winthrop. I think it is very important that over the next five to seven years we put people in place so we do not miss a beat."

While preparing for new leadership, Grossman is also developing a mechanism for maintaining the changes that have taken place. He said, "We are becoming a huge health system. The question is how do you infuse the system with one culture?" NYU Langone currently sends up and comers to a leadership program in Boston, but longer term, Grossman said, "the answer is to create an academy where we teach the staff, the doctors, about our culture."

Successful organizations plan carefully for succession.

To do this, NYU Langone will develop a centralized leadership training program. There, participants can learn and absorb the culture—what it is, how it evolved, and why that knowledge is important. "An entire curriculum to maintain and enhance our culture will be created," Grossman said. Grossman saw this academy having an impact beyond top management. "We are constantly acquiring new physicians and physician practices. We will soon have a new hospital. We will continue to grow organically. We must devise systematic means to maintain and enhance our culture." While it is not clear whether the proposed "academy" is simply a training concept or a more formal institution, it is clear Grossman intends to inculcate the next generation of NYU Langone leaders with the principles and practices that he has regarded as critical to the institution.

NYU Langone has completed a remarkable journey over the past decade. There is no shortage of things it can do in the years ahead to bring further improvements in current activities and to broaden its plans to include new activities. Medical science continues to change rapidly, and so does medical economics. NYU Langone will have to deliver new services in new ways in new places. And at the same time, it will have to continue offering medical education in new ways to meet these needs. Biomedical research is, by definition, about the new and unknown, and NYU Langone will need to extend its leadership role in research. Early in its history NYU Langone was a leader, and then it fell by the wayside. It is once again a leader, and it must strive to sustain that role.

> Early in its history NYU Langone was a leader,
> and then it fell by the wayside. It is once again a
> leader, and it must strive to sustain that role.

The right path will not be obvious, but there is good reason to be confident that the astute leadership and intelligent strategy that guided NYU Langone over the past decade will serve it well as it moves into the next decade and beyond. The mission of the NYU Langone Academy is to transmit the NYU Langone culture from one generation to the next. So too is the process of selecting the next person to assume the role of both CEO of the hospitals and dean of the medical school.

CHAPTER 15

What Can Be Learned from the NYU Langone Transformation?

T he transformation of NYU Langone provides a valuable case study in organizational change. The medical center's rise from mediocre to world class in a decade was not preordained. It was not an accident; it was not a relative improvement based on the decline of others. Rather, it pulled itself up by its own bootstraps.

This successful transformation is the result of a complex process, and there are important ideas about organizational change that can be extracted from the NYU Langone story. While various observers may each see things in slightly different ways, it is clear that there are several ideas and themes other institutions should take away from the NYU Langone transformation.

LEADERSHIP

In organizational change the three most crucial variables are leadership, leadership, and leadership. NYU Langone was transformed because it had strong and wise leadership that established, pursued, and achieved impressive goals by executing well-crafted plans with great efficacy.

Few would dispute that Bob Grossman was the key figure in transforming NYU Langone. He established the goals, set the strategy, and directed the execution. He commanded, cajoled, coerced, and co-opted those who were instrumental in achieving institutional change. Grossman said, "We executed in three domains simultaneously: education, research, and clinical medicine. Is that replicable? To replicate what we did, you would have to find someone who is there for the marathon. It's about leadership."

The Grossman story is all the more intriguing given that *a priori* there were few signs that he would prove to be an impressive leader. Prior to becoming CEO of NYU Langone, Grossman was highly regarded as a radiologist and scientist, but he had no management experience beyond running a medical center department. He was not well known or well connected in the highest reaches of New York's medical and philanthropic world. Indeed, he had been living in Philadelphia for a number of years before joining NYU Langone's radiology department.

By all accounts, he had a poor initial job interview, and survived the process only because Kenneth Langone and a few other search committee members saw something in him that they found impressive, and Langone prevailed on his fellow board members to keep Grossman in the running. Grossman himself said he was an "unfiltered leader."

Yet he rose to the challenge. From his first days, when he essentially fired more than half of NYU Langone's top management, he was a decisive executive who knew what he wanted and how to get it. As soon as he took office, he enacted tough measures; he instilled concern and fear in many quarters. But he won and retained the respect and even affection of those in his organization. Perhaps the results achieved by NYU Langone could have been achieved with another leader, but the transformation of the institution seems inextricably bound up with Bob Grossman.

Chandrika Tandon, an NYU Langone trustee who has been a partner at McKinsey & Co., the management consulting firm, and has also been active in restructuring major corporations, said, "I have worked with a lot of leaders. I never met a man like Grossman. He operates at the highest level of abstraction. He also operates at the most micro level, which is extraordinary. You rarely meet leaders like that." Tandon has worked with a number of CEOs, and she said of Grossman, "I would place him in the top ten percent. The only reason he would not be the number one is because NYU Langone is a single big business. I think Bob, if he had been given more businesses, could probably do the same thing."

To be sure, he was not a one-man band. There have been a number of highly regarded managers in the Grossman regime. Indeed, one of Grossman's major accomplishments as a leader has been identifying, recruiting, and motivating an array of administrators and faculty members who proved to be strong leaders in their own right. He was not one to avoid hiring impressive underlings as a way to maintain his own position. Quite the contrary; he hired a group of forceful leaders to run various NYU Langone departments and units. They achieved a great deal, but it is fair to say that the paths they followed in improving their units were paths that Grossman had identified.

While he focused on sweeping change, Grossman understood the role of small gestures and optics. He fixed Tisch Hospital's beleaguered elevators to achieve what he and others called an "early win" that showed change was in the air. He built a new dormitory for medical students and improved the cafeteria because it was where many of NYU Langone's assorted constituents and stakeholders would find themselves spending time. He offered praise as well as reprimands. And he solicited the views of many even as he sometimes formulated his plans by himself. He admitted mistakes and took responsibility, a critical posture for a leader imposing new and extensive accountability on all those around him.

He offered praise as well as reprimands. And he solicited
the views of many even as he sometimes
formulated his plans by himself.

While his major accomplishments can be assessed in terms of organizational charts and ratings, bricks and mortar, and scores of ambulatory care centers around New York City, Grossman's principal accomplishment was to create and embed a new culture—a culture that emphasized accountability. Everyone had goals, and they had to achieve them. That accountability was placed in the service of creating a patient centered institution. Accomplishments were not ends in themselves; they were ways of creating a patient centered medical center. "We totally transformed the culture of this institution," he said, adding, "and it is more than a meritocracy. It has an aspirational culture."

The management structure at NYU Langone did not lend itself to classical organizational charts, with their descending tiers of boxes connected to one another via solid lines and dotted lines. Grossman often talked about "clouds." Various senior executives were like clouds that were separate but also overlapped at various points and various times. Grossman liked to recount the story of a senior management consultant who initially expressed dismay at the NYU Langone structure because it didn't fit into any established patterns or categories. On second thought, the consultant concluded, NYU Langone did resemble one organization: Apple. And that organization, Grossman would say, has not seemed to have done too badly.

HOPE IS NOT A STRATEGY

If you don't know where you're going, there are many ways to get there. Grossman knew where he was going. He developed a comprehensive strategy for organizational transformation, and he integrated that with a carefully honed plan to execute it.

Early in his tenure, Grossman sketched out a sweeping set of goals and tactics for NYU Langone. This single page, which has taken on an aura akin to the Dead Sea scrolls, specified precisely what he intended to do: He envisioned a "world class, patient centered, integrated academic medical center." What's remarkable is that not only could he spell it out all at once, but he went on to achieve virtually everything on his list.

At each step in the revitalization of NYU Langone, it was clear what was supposed to happen next. The precision of his early road map was remarkable, and so was its breadth: Grossman was simultaneously rebuilding (often literally) a hospital and its campus, redesigning and implementing an innovative medical school curriculum, and regenerating a research operation. He had plans for all three, and a decade later, it is clear the results were a direct outgrowth of the original plans.

INFORMATION TECHNOLOGY

"Bob and his dashboards!" Everyone from the president of NYU to a broad range of NYU Langone faculty and staff members agrees that Grossman's emphasis on information technology has been a hallmark of his regime. The crucial role of the dashboards may be a running joke among NYU Langone insiders, but it reflects an important development in organizational transformation: Large complex organizations require more than clear thinking about strategy and tactics. They require vast amounts of information. It's the only way to know what is being done, what needs to be done, and how well things are being done. Data are the new lingua franca of management. Grossman was emphasizing big data well before it became a buzzword at other organizations.

Grossman went to great effort—and great expense—to install a comprehensive management information system. He essentially tore out a system that had only recently been installed and replaced it with a more wide-ranging system at a cost of millions of dollars. He took a personal interest in designing and developing a dashboard as a way to monitor a vast array of processes and practices, expenditures, and income on a real time basis. And he kept, and keeps, his eyes peeled on the dashboard day in and day out.

As noted earlier, it is an adage of modern management that what gets measured gets managed. Because so many aspects of NYU Langone's operations were being measured, they would be managed. It became clear what was working and what was not, what needed attention and what was proceeding as planned.

Senior managements have always sought to keep an eye and a grip on the disparate parts of their organizations. But the way they do so has changed. *In Search of Excellence,* a runaway bestseller in 1982, was written by Tom Peters and Robert H. Waterman Jr., two management consultants from McKinsey & Co. In it, they lauded senior organizational executives for the practice of "managing by walking around." As Joyce Long noted, Grossman was, in fact, one of those who "managed by walking around. He is not just sitting looking at his dashboard all day, although he does look at it a lot." In addition, she said, "He arranges forums with all different levels of people. He receives a lot of suggestions. We always follow up on them. A lot of good ideas come from these."

There is much to be said about management walking around and having a firsthand look at all aspects of the organization. But much has happened in recent years to suggest there are also substantial benefits to be derived from a systematic and comprehensive oversight of the organization. The idea is not new; it is the capabilities that have changed.

In an era of big data, much more can be weighed and measured in an organization. And there are systems that can marshal and integrate the vast amounts of data that can be generated.

As a result, management by walking around is being supplemented by management by looking at a dashboard. There are always things going on in an organization that management cannot see by walking around but can monitor by having the digital equivalents of thermostats and sensors, dipsticks and yardsticks probing every corner of the organization. The constantly expanding capabilities of management information systems creates an opportunity for those who are in search of excellence.

Management by walking around is being supplemented by management by looking at a dashboard. There are always things going on in an organization that management cannot see by walking around but can monitor by having the digital equivalents of thermostats and sensors, dipsticks and yardsticks.

Bob Grossman not only drove the development of an elaborate management information system at NYU Langone, but also integrated it into every aspect of its operations and pushed it deep into the culture of NYU Langone. Everyone involved in managing the institution or leading its assorted activities came to be steeped in data. Existing staff members and faculty knew they had to rely on data, and they also knew they had to generate it. Prospective hires were told about the information culture, and if there were any doubts about them being willing and able to be a part of it, they were not hired. Because of the detailed management information system, the inner workings of the institution became highly transparent.

Because so much was measured, everyone could be held to account for his or her results. It was difficult to make unsubstantiated claims about achievements. It was not easy to make excuses. And no one could pass the buck: Here is what you committed to achieve, and here is what you have achieved. You can look it up. This was clearly threatening to laggards. Grossman said, "They love it when nobody knows what they are doing because they are not doing anything except costing you money."

NYU Langone's information technology delivered a fatal blow to any division of information and ideas into separate silos. Information was not power when everyone had information about everything. Integration was facilitated and even forced by virtue of the free flow of data. This result was not an accident or byproduct of the emphasis on information. "I totally blew up all the silos," Grossman said. Now, "there are no silos, no hiding. It is one vision, one database, one message all over." Of course, Grossman also uses more prosaic mechanisms to advance integration, such as having a luncheon meeting with the department chairs every Thursday as another way "to break down barriers and to communicate."

There is presumably some chance that the transformation of NYU Langone could have proceeded without this cornucopia of information and the culture of accountability that it facilitated, but it's abundantly clear that it proceeded much better precisely because of it. Grossman and his cohorts knew where to focus their attention, what needed work, and how people were faring at their assorted missions.

EXECUTION

There is no shortage of elaborate strategies and detailed plans at many organizations. There is also no shortage of best-laid plans failing to be implemented properly. NYU Langone executed its plans with great success. While Grossman initially sketched out his strategy on his own, he would go on to consult widely with the NYU Langone community. This consultation provided a two-way flow of information: Grossman explained what he was seeking to achieve, and he heard from the assorted managers and leaders regarding what they wanted to achieve as well as what they thought of his proposed plans and processes.

Grossman's approach was to formulate goals and ask those charged with achieving those goals what resources they needed to get there. Then, he would let them run their own show. He was an enthusiastic cheerleader and optimistic observer, but he was not second-guessing his line managers. Instead, he would objectively measure their results and hold them to account if the goals they had agreed to were not met.

Given Grossman's forceful personality and far-reaching measurement of every department's activities, his hands-off approach might seem a bit of a paradox. After all, Grossman developed an information system that seemingly let him know everything about everything. He knew how well things were working and what progress was being made. There were standards and benchmarks for everything. He knew what he wanted to happen. But instead of using his tools to micromanage each department and unit, he let these entities manage their processes. He used his dashboard to measure progress, not to run the processes. Everyone was accountable for the results achieved by his or her mission or activity. Those who didn't meet expectations could expect to be reprimanded, reassigned, or even removed from the organization.

While the Grossman approach was tough—the costs were high for those who didn't deliver—it was generally accepted for two reasons: First of all, the goals and the progress in achieving them were mutually agreed upon, transparent, and objectively measured. Secondly, once goals were set, Grossman provided substantial freedom to those running the various units in pursuing these goals. By and large, this was a highly motivating approach.

The former chief financial officer, Michael Burke, said, "Doctors in academic centers tend to be hypercompetitive. Give them a dashboard and a scorecard, and they will strive to be at the top, whether they are in the hospital or the medical school. The dashboard allows very detailed comparisons. For example, a doctor can compare his infection and readmission rates for a specific procedure to that of others who are performing the same surgeries. He can compare outcomes and the length of stay for his patients to that of other doctors. Knowing how you compare to others provides a powerful incentive to understand the reasons for the difference and to improve."

Managers were eager to meet and exceed objectives, to outperform others, to please Grossman, and perhaps most importantly, to please themselves by showing they could do the job. Grossman applied these principles to himself. He took responsibility and admitted mistakes. And he expected others to do the same.

> "Doctors in academic centers tend to be hypercompetitive. Give them a dashboard and a scorecard, and they will strive to be at the top, whether they are in the hospital or the medical school."

THE BOARD OF TRUSTEES

While the transformation of NYU Langone was driven by its executive management team, Grossman and his team derived great benefit from the board of trustees. They contributed advice and counsel, opened doors, raised funds, and lent their power and prestige to the institution. That, of course, is what boards of trustees are supposed to do. But the NYU Langone board and its leaders did it particularly well in important ways.

Oversight by a board of trustees that meets intermittently to oversee the work of an organization's senior management is a governance structure that has existed for decades; it is how almost every major business corporation, educational institution, and nonprofit is structured. But the role and value of boards can be arrayed along a spectrum whose endpoints are both disastrous: There is the board that does not take its duties to heart; it is a rubber stamp for management rather than a supervisor. It doesn't question or probe decisions, either through lack of interest or belief that its role is just to support management. As a result, it contributes nothing and fails to provide oversight of the organization's management. At the other end of the spectrum is the board that seeks to run the organization: It makes every decision, second-guesses management, and interferes in the smallest decision and the smallest detail.

NYU Langone has a board that is far from either extreme. It provides counsel without being overbearing; it takes initiative without usurping management; and it engages with the staff without creating fear or favor.

It was the New York University board that made several crucial decisions regarding NYU Langone dating back to the late 1990s: This board chose to undertake an ill-fated merger with Mount Sinai Hospital. But the NYU board also quickly chose to unwind that merger. And it made the decision to centralize executive management of the hospital and medical school in a single chief executive. That crucial and widely debated decision made it possible for NYU Langone to embark on its transformation. During that process, the board continued to be deeply engaged in monitoring, but not directing, the institution's turnaround.

Once freed from its merger, a reconstituted NYU Langone board also made several key decisions. The composition of the NYU Langone board was typical of major New York institutions: Its members were drawn from the city's elite roster of Wall Street titans, business executives, and philanthropists, plus a smattering of academics. These board members were not simply the same *kinds* of people who were on dozens of other boards of directors at prestigious New York City medical institutions, philanthropies, and businesses; many of the NYU Langone board members were the *same people* who also sat on these other boards as well. But there were several key figures who made the NYU Langone board particularly important and effective in the rebuilding of the institution.

The first was Kenneth Langone. Having done well on Wall Street and then made a fortune as a cofounder of Home Depot and other enterprises, he would go on to devote himself to nonprofit boards. Although he served as a director of several institutions, he took a particular interest in the NYU Medical Center. Ultimately he would give NYU Langone $200 million, and they would name the institution after him. He has been widely described as a force of nature at NYU Langone. He was one of the trustees who saw something in Grossman that led him to convince his fellow trustees to bring Grossman back for a second interview after what many said was a disastrous first interview. He clearly liked Grossman's success in obtaining equipment from Siemens. Perhaps Langone saw something of himself—the entrepreneur—in Grossman.

Once Grossman was installed, Langone made himself available for advice and counsel. And Grossman regularly sought his advice. At many points in time, he talked to Langone daily, even several times a day. Beyond that, Langone not only donated a vast sum, but encouraged his friends to be generous as well. As a sizable donor to Republican political candidates, he also interceded when NYU Langone needed federal assistance in the aftermath of Hurricane Sandy.

In contrast to many board leaders, instead of being a distant figure who was seldom seen beyond monthly or quarterly board meetings,

Langone was a highly visible figure in the halls of NYU Langone. He was there all the time. He regularly chatted up employees, gave pep talks, and asked everybody for their views and suggestions. He attends employee recognition ceremonies and eats in the cafeteria. He famously said that he loved to find a scrap of paper on the floor so he could bend down to pick it up—and illustrate that everyone at every level could help improve the place. Langone's approach was not necessarily a strategy but perhaps a genuine outgrowth of his gregarious nature. He is an astute observer and can turn an ordinary observation into a lesson for management or a suggestion for a new approach. In any case, it served NYU Langone well.

A second crucial figure was Martin Lipton. A name partner at a major law firm, he was a leading figure in mergers and acquisitions at the highest level of American business. He was also a devoted alumnus of NYU. Over the course of more than sixty years, he would be a student, an adjunct faculty member, a chair of the university's board, and an important figure on the NYU Langone board. He would help with fundraising, serve as a bridge between NYU Langone and the NYU administration, and do whatever else he could. Lipton was a trusted advisor to Grossman, and at the same time, he was close to NYU president John Sexton. There are no accounts of him bending down to pick up scraps of paper off the hospital floor, but metaphorically he was always doing so.

Ken Langone thought he could make a difference to an important New York institution by joining the board and making a gift. Lipton is the classic devoted alumnus: The university did much for him, and he wanted to give back.

Members of the Tisch family were a third important element of the board, and their motivation was also clear. Laurence Tisch was an NYU alumnus and, like Lipton, very active in helping his alma mater. The NYU hospital was named after his family, as was NYU's School of the

Arts. After Larry Tisch passed away, his widow would retain an abiding interest in Tisch Hospital. The Tisch family has continued to make sizable monetary gifts to NYU. In addition, Larry's son Tom and Tom's wife, Alice, are members of the NYU Langone board.

To be sure, these trustees were not the only board members who played an active role. They opened their checkbooks. They offered advice and counsel. They could be counted on to make the phone calls or provide the introductions or connection needed to get something done. But Langone and Lipton in particular went beyond the normal board role to be important figures in the transformation of NYU Langone. They gave Grossman good advice, and they helped him in whatever ways they could. They told him what they thought, but they didn't tell him what to do. Because they were so engaged and active, however, they greatly assisted Grossman to succeed in executing his plans and achieving vast improvements in so many aspects of NYU Langone's operations.

FINANCIAL SUSTAINABILITY

One reason NYU Langone was able to execute its plans is because it had the money to pay for them. In many of the initiatives it pursued, it was not beholden to others for the funding necessary to take action. The transformation in NYU Langone's financial picture from red ink to black was an important enabler of a variety of achievements. When Grossman arrived, NYU Langone's finances were in disarray. It was losing a substantial amount of money, and its financial management was unimpressive. Grossman transformed the institution's finances, filling its coffers with profits—or surplus as they say in the nonprofit world—to pay for his elaborate plans. The marked improvement in NYU Langone's finances were the result of Grossman's four step program: fixing the bill-collection system; increasing revenues from research; transforming to ambulatory care; and increasing fundraising.

RESILIENCE

As the boxer Mike Tyson famously said, everybody has a plan until they get punched in the mouth. NYU Langone got punched in the mouth in the fall of 2012. The transformation of NYU Langone was proceeding apace when Hurricane Sandy flooded major parts of the Medical Center complex and knocked out electrical power for six days. The campus was largely closed for two months. But NYU Langone was able to survive this superstorm and come roaring back. On the five-year anniversary of Sandy, New York newspapers chronicled a number of situations and institutions that were still suffering the effects of the hurricane. These included subway tunnels still awaiting repairs and housing in Far Rockaway that had not yet been rebuilt. But for NYU Langone, Hurricane Sandy is ancient history.

NYU Langone surmounted this crisis because of organizational resilience. Like all medical centers and other well-managed institutions, it had contingency plans and disaster recovery plans. But like others, it had no plans that dealt with a catastrophe on the scale of Sandy. So once it was closed down, Grossman and his colleagues had to fashion a plan. They acted quickly, decisively, and effectively. In short order, they arranged for staff doctors to see patients at NYU Langone ambulatory centers and other facilities. They relocated medical school classes to the NYU Washington Square campus and elsewhere. They held staff meetings in unheated, waterlogged facilities. And they made plans to reopen. There was, it should be emphasized, never any discussion of not reopening; it was, rather, when and how.

One particularly important decision was to continue paying all staff while the institution was effectively closed. For doctors it was much appreciated; for minimum-wage hospital staff members it was a crucial step that enabled them to pay their rent or mortgage. For all concerned, it not only made NYU Langone look good, but also kept the staff intact. Otherwise, they would have drifted off, and reopening would have been complicated by a need to recruit, train, and deploy large numbers of new employees.

Meanwhile, in large ways and small, Grossman took up Chicago mayor and former White House chief of staff Rahm Emanuel's celebrated dictum that one should never let a crisis go to waste. While all systems were down, they installed major changes in the management information system. While buildings were empty, they painted some rooms and removed asbestos from others. While rebuilding, they also did some reconfiguring.

While good management was crucial to reopening NYU Langone, money in the bank was critical as well. Having righted the institution's finances in the first few years of the Grossman regime, by the fall of 2012, NYU Langone had substantial amounts of cash on hand. It would have to wait for FEMA funds, and it would have to wait even longer for payments on its insurance claims. But it could act because it had its own resources to pay bills and expenses.

Thus, the resilient NYU Langone phoenix rose from the ashes, or more precisely, from the puddles and muck, and proceeded on its upward trajectory almost as if nothing had happened.

INSTITUTIONAL FRAMEWORK

NYU Langone was part of a larger organization, New York University. NYU did not have the Harvard tradition of every tub on its own bottom. In many ways, NYU Langone's position was akin to a wholly owned subsidiary of a corporation. The literature of management science is rife with stories of organizations whose plans were skewed if not thwarted by a parent company, for good reasons or bad. The NYU central administration had an abiding interest in the well-being of the Medical Center: It represented a significant portion of the university's revenues and expenditures. When it was faring poorly financially, there was concern that its financial problems could bring down the entire university. Part of the institutional memory at NYU was the experience in the 1970s when the university had faced a financial crisis that required it to sell its Bronx campus and hive off its engineering school in order to stay afloat.

The Medical Center's well-being also mattered to NYU's reputation. If it was not well-regarded, it reflected poorly on the reputation of the university. Conversely, if it fared well, it reflected well on the university. Having a good medical school does not mean a university therefore also has a good history department, but in a general sense at a university, the whole can be greater than the sum of the parts.

There are many demands on a university president. He or she has many constituencies to serve, many critics to mollify, and many conflicts to manage. What Grossman wanted above all from the university president was benign neglect and no second-guessing. He got both of those, and, again, one major reason was that NYU Langone did not need money from the Washington Square coffers. As a result, Sexton largely left Grossman alone. Sexton was certainly aware of Grossman's plans, and while he was presumably supportive of them, he was no doubt pleased that he could focus his attention—and his budget—elsewhere.

For an executive with Grossman's direction and drive, the ability to push forward without unnecessary interference was a welcome gift.

Because Sexton had confidence in Grossman, when faculty members were up in arms over Grossman's plans to require them to do more research and win more grants at the potential cost of jobs, the university president did not heed their complaints. No one could do an end run around Grossman by pleading their case to Sexton. In the case of both Sexton and his liaison with the Medical Center, Bob Berne, the quality that set their management style apart and led in large part to Grossman's success was the ability to step back and allow Grossman to do his work, stepping in with advice when needed and providing support when times became tough. For an executive with Grossman's direction and drive, the ability to push forward without unnecessary interference was a welcome gift.

SUMMARY

The lessons to be learned from the NYU Langone story are neither unique nor especially new—with perhaps one exception: The important role played by technology is, in fact, new and different. Beyond that, NYU Langone embodies some of the eternal verities of organizational development: Leadership, strategy, and execution are critical and need to be done right. Good boards and strong finances are needed to support the basics. Resilience is important because it is inevitable that something unexpected will occur and something will go wrong. In former secretary of defense Donald Rumsfeld's immortal typology, there will always be the known unknowns but also the unknown unknowns.

While the components of NYU Langone's transformation may seem obvious and even prosaic, in fact, each of these attributes is decidedly difficult to implement successfully. It is clear that organizations need good leadership; it is far less clear how they can be sure of getting it. The same is true of strategy—every organization should have one, but many are flawed. And even the best leaders can fail in executing strategies. At NYU Langone, one need only hark back to the end of the last century, when plans for merging with Mount Sinai Hospital and/or its medical school proved to be a disastrous strategy combined with a flawed execution.

Under Grossman's leadership, NYU Langone got it right. It was not an accident. Grossman said the key is "understanding the aspirations of the institution and aligning the strategy with those aspirations. It is very difficult. It does not happen overnight. It is a marathon." Bob Grossman and those who advised him and worked with him put together the pieces of a puzzle that enabled the institution to develop a sound strategy and successfully implement it. They thought carefully about what they wanted; they worked hard; they measured and managed, and they watched and listened. The result is that they were able to marshal the resources and the attributes needed to transform NYU Langone from mediocre to world class.

> In Grossman's view, "culture trumps vision;
> culture trumps strategy; culture trumps everything."

While there are a number of ingredients that contributed to the turnaround of NYU Langone, surely the most important was Bob Grossman's relentless pursuit of excellence and his enduring commitment to building a culture of accountability and excellence across NYU Langone. In Grossman's view, "culture trumps vision; culture trumps strategy; culture trumps everything." When Grossman joined NYU Langone, it had its own well-established culture, one that facilitated mediocrity. Grossman knew that he would never be successful in implementing his vision and transforming the organization without transforming the culture first. He was able to capitalize on the adversity facing NYU Langone in 2007 to help people understand that change was necessary. By building an aspirational culture of achievement, a culture that embraced a leadership committed to achievement, Grossman and those around him built a world class institution.

SETTING AN EXAMPLE

There are many examples of superb medical work being done around the world to improve access to high-quality care at an affordable cost, everything from eye care in India to dementia care in the Netherlands. I see this every day in my work with my foundation, ACCESS Health. In my previous book, *Affordable Excellence,* I described the impressive healthcare system in Singapore, an island nation that provides high-quality medical care at a fraction of the cost of any other developed nation.

Some may question whether this small island nation's approach to medical care is scalable. In *World Class,* however, we present an extraordinary example that took place in one of the world's largest and most complex urban environments—New York City—and in one of the most complicated, competitive, and expensive healthcare environments in the world—the United States of America. The NYU Langone Health story proves the U.S. can do much better in organizing and delivering medical care.

In our nation's continuing debate on how to pay for healthcare, we sometimes lose track of the true goal: delivering world class care at an affordable price. We should only buy excellence. If institutions are properly organized, excellence is not more expensive. Indeed, by doing the job better, excellence can save money rather than cost money. High-quality care prevents the need for additional medical care, and restores health more effectively. Inferior care leads to inferior results and costs far more over the long term than doing it right and doing it well the first time.

As Bob Grossman likes to say, "We believe that quality is cost effective." If we focus on creating world class healthcare, I am convinced we will create affordable healthcare as well. The NYU Langone Health experience points the way.

Acknowledgments

I am grateful to my friend Jeffrey Lehman, the vice chancellor of NYU Shanghai, for introducing me to the NYU Langone story and for suggesting that I speak with Robert Berne, an NYU professor and its executive vice president for health. Bob Berne's candor, generosity, and enthusiasm in our initial conversations regarding the transformation at NYU Langone aroused my interest in the NYU Langone story and spurred me to undertake this project.

This book would not have been possible without the support not only of Bob Berne but of the entire leadership team at NYU Langone. First and foremost, I am grateful to Dr. Robert Grossman, dean and CEO of NYU Langone Health, who gave endlessly of his time and energy while I was researching and writing this book, as did his wife, Elisabeth Cohen. Andrew Brotman, senior vice president and vice dean for clinical affairs and strategy, chief clinical officer of NYU Langone Health, was equally giving.

I am deeply appreciative of the assistance provided by Ken Langone and Martin Lipton, two trustees of NYU Langone Health who played a crucial role in its transformation. My interviews with both of them helped form the backbone of this book. I am also grateful to the other members of the NYU Langone board of trustees with whom I spoke.

World Class would not have been possible without the insights offered by John Sexton, now president emeritus of New York University. I am equally grateful to Steven Abramson, senior vice president and vice dean for education, faculty, and academic affairs; Dafna Bar-Sagi, senior vice president and vice dean for science, chief scientific officer; and Richard J. Donoghue, senior vice president for strategy, planning, and business development.

My conversation with Nader Mherabi, chief information officer, senior vice president, and vice dean, helped shape the parts of the book that discuss the use of data and information technology to improve the quality of care. I am also deeply appreciative of Michael Burke, formerly the senior vice president and vice dean, corporate chief financial officer; Joseph Lhota, senior vice president and vice dean, chief of staff; and Bret Rudy, chief medical officer, NYU Langone Hospital–Brooklyn, for the time they spent with me explaining the complex finances and intricate operations of NYU Langone. I am also thankful for the insights offered by Nancy Sanchez, senior vice president and vice dean, Human Resources and Organizational Development and Learning; Vicki Match Suna, senior vice president and vice dean for Real Estate Development and Facilities; Robert Press, formerly the senior vice president and vice dean, chief of Hospital Operations of NYU Langone Health; and Annette Johnson, senior vice president and vice dean, General Counsel.

I am also very grateful to the NYU Langone professors and staff members interviewed as part of my research: Dr. Martha Radford, a cardiologist and chief quality officer; Dr. Jan T. Vilcek, research professor, Department of Microbiology, professor emeritus of Microbiology, Department of Microbiology; Dr. Steven Galetta, professor and chair of Neurology at NYU Langone Health; Jonathan Weider, assistant dean for Advanced Applications and assistant professor of Educational Informatics; Dr. Marc Triola, associate dean for Educational Informatics, director, Institute for Innovations in Medical Education, associate professor, Department of Medicine; Richard Tsien, chair, Department of Neuroscience and Physiology, director, Neuroscience Institute, and Druckenmiller professor of Neuroscience; Richard Woodrow, clinical associate professor, NYU School of Medicine; Dr. Thomas S. Riles, Frank C. Spencer professor of Surgery and associate dean for Medical Education and Technology; Catherine Manley-Cullen, RN, vice president, Nursing and Patient Care Services, NYU Langone Hospital–Brooklyn; Sheilah Rosen, manager of the Office of the Dean and CEO, NYU Langone; manager, Special Projects; and Joyce M. Long, administrative director, AccessFirst Trustee Health and Wellness Program.

Lisa Greiner, senior director of Institutional Communications at NYU Langone Health was a central support throughout my research and while finalizing the manuscript. Tom Hayes and my brother Eric Haseltine provided valuable advice.

I would like to express my sincere appreciation to Harvey Shapiro for his editorial guidance and for his wise counsel and support throughout the writing of this book.

I am grateful for my wife Maria Eugenia Maury for her unfailing and loving support through the entire process of research, writing and publication of *World Class*.

Finally, I would like to thank my colleague Anna Dirksen, director of communications at ACCESS Health International, and the team at Greenleaf Book Group, including April Murphy, Tyler LeBleu, and Sam Alexander, for their assistance in moving the book toward publication.

Cast of Characters

There have been a number of people deeply involved in the transformation of NYU Langone.

MEMBERS OF THE NYU AND NYU LANGONE HEALTH BOARDS OF TRUSTEES

Kenneth Langone, Vice Chair, New York University Board of Trustees, Chair, NYU Langone Health Board of Trustees

Kenneth Langone is the founder and chairman of Invemed Associates, LLC. In addition to serving on the NYU and NYU Langone Health boards, he also serves on the boards of St. Patrick's Cathedral, Ronald McDonald House New York, the Center for Strategic and International Studies, the Horatio Alger Society Foundation, and the Harlem Children's Zone and its charter school, the Promise Academy.

Martin Lipton, Chair Emeritus, New York University Board of Trustees, Trustee, NYU Langone Health Board of Trustees

Martin Lipton, a founding partner of Wachtell, Lipton, Rosen & Katz, specializes in advising major corporations on mergers and acquisitions and matters affecting corporate policy and strategy.

Anthony Welters, Vice Chair, New York University Board of Trustees, Trustee, NYU Langone Health Board of Trustees

Chandrika Tandon, Vice Chair, New York University Board of Trustees, Trustee, NYU Langone Health Board of Trustees

Thomas S. Murphy Sr., Honorary Vice Chair, New York University Board of Trustees, Trustee, NYU Langone Health Board of Trustees

William J. Constantine, Trustee, NYU Langone Health

Alice M. Tisch, Trustee, NYU Langone Health

Thomas J. Tisch, Trustee, NYU Langone Health

NEW YORK UNIVERSITY

John Sexton, President Emeritus

John Sexton served as the fifteenth president of NYU, from 2002 to 2015. In January 2016, he was succeeded by Andrew Hamilton and became president emeritus.

During his presidency, NYU was noted for the single largest expansion of tenured and tenure-track arts and science faculty in its history; creating an unrivaled global academic network, including the opening of successful degree-granting campuses in Abu Dhabi and Shanghai; restoring engineering after a forty year absence; the advancement of NYU's Medical Center; record gains in student admission; record fundraising; the creation of important new academic programs; an unprecedented period of faculty and student honors; and key capital investments and long-range planning.

Robert Berne, Professor of Public Policy and Financial Management, Executive Vice President for Health

Robert Berne, executive vice president for Health and professor of Public Policy and Financial Management, specializes in public sector financial management and is a nationally recognized expert in educational policy research.

317

NYU LANGONE HEALTH

Robert I. Grossman, MD, Saul J. Farber Dean and Chief Executive Officer

Robert I. Grossman, MD, was named Saul J. Farber dean and chief executive officer of NYU Langone Health in July 2007. Dr. Grossman joined NYU Langone in 2001 as the Louis Marx professor of Radiology, chairman of the Department of Radiology, and professor of neurology, neurosurgery, and physiology and neuroscience. In his previous position at the Hospital of the University of Pennsylvania, he was a professor of radiology, neurosurgery, and neurology; chief of neuroradiology; and associate chairman of radiology.

Steven B. Abramson, MD, Senior Vice President and Vice Dean for Education, Faculty, and Academic Affairs

As vice dean, Dr. Abramson oversees faculty affairs, including appointments, promotions, and tenure issues. Additionally, his office oversees undergraduate, graduate, and postgraduate education, continuing medical education, precollege programs, the admissions process, and NYU School of Medicine's accreditation.

Dafna Bar-Sagi, PhD, Senior Vice President and Vice Dean for Science, Chief Scientific Officer

Dafna Bar-Sagi serves as the principal strategist to advance NYU Langone's research enterprise. Additionally, Dr. Bar-Sagi oversees all clinical, translational, and basic science operations, graduate education, and administration for the research enterprise through the Office of Science and Research.

Andrew W. Brotman, MD, Senior Vice President and Vice Dean for Clinical Affairs and Strategy, Chief Clinical Officer

Dr. Andrew W. Brotman is responsible for physician/hospital programmatic initiatives and ambulatory care. In these roles, he also leads the Faculty Group Practice, manages partnerships with affiliate hospitals, including those in the NYC Health + Hospitals, and manages the faculty office complex.

Richard J. Donoghue, Senior Vice President for Strategy, Planning, and Business Development

Richard J. Donoghue is responsible for the strategic initiatives of NYU Langone, which includes both NYU Langone Hospitals and NYU School of Medicine. He is also responsible for the medical malpractice program and managed care contracting at NYU Langone.

Joseph Lhota, Senior Vice President and Vice Dean, Chief of Staff

Joseph Lhota is responsible for helping to further align and integrate medical care, research, and education at NYU Langone Health. Mr. Lhota assists NYU Langone's dean and CEO in managing all activities associated with directing a complex academic medical center, and serves as an advisor on issues of management and policy related to the strategic direction of the organization.

Nader Mherabi, Senior Vice President and Vice Dean, Chief Information Officer

Nader Mherabi is responsible for all information technology (IT) activities for NYU Langone Health. He previously was vice president for IT product solutions and chief technology officer for NYU Langone, responsible for technology strategy, infrastructure engineering, networks, data centers, application architecture, systems deployment, and support across the institution.

Nancy Sanchez, Senior Vice President and Vice Dean, Human Resources and Organizational Development and Learning

Nancy Sanchez is responsible for strategic human resources initiatives, practices, and operations, supporting over seventeen thousand faculty and staff across NYU Langone Health. Since her arrival more than thirty years ago, she has held numerous leadership roles in the Department of Human Resources.

Michael T. Burke, former Senior Vice President and Vice Dean, Corporate Chief Financial Officer

Annette Johnson, Senior Vice President and Vice Dean, General Counsel, Adjunct Professor of Medical School Administration

Vicki Match Suna, AIA, Senior Vice President and Vice Dean, Real Estate Development and Facilities

Steven L. Galetta, MD, Philip K. Moskowitz, MD, Professor and Chair of Neurology at NYU Langone Health

Joyce M. Long, Administrative Director, AccessFirst Trustee Health and Wellness Program

Catherine Manley-Cullen, RN, Vice President, Nursing and Patient Care Services, NYU Langone Hospital–Brooklyn

Martha J. Radford, MD, Chief Quality Officer, Professor of Medicine and Population Health

Thomas S. Riles, MD, Associate Dean for Medical Education and Technology

Sheilah Rosen, Manager of the Office of the Dean and CEO

Bret J. Rudy, MD, Chief Medical Officer, NYU Langone Hospital –Brooklyn

Paresh Shah, MD, Professor of Surgery, Chief, Division of General Surgery, Vice Chair of Quality and Innovation

Marc M. Triola, MD, Associate Dean for Educational Informatics; Director, Institute for Innovations in Medical Education; Associate Professor, Department of Medicine

Richard Tsien, PhD, Chair, Department of Neuroscience and Physiology; Director, Neuroscience Institute; Druckenmiller Professor of Neuroscience, Department of Neuroscience and Physiology; Professor, Department of Neurology

Jan T. Vilcek, MD, PhD, Research Professor, Department of Microbiology; Professor Emeritus of Microbiology, Department of Microbiology

Richard Woodrow, Clinical Associate Professor, NYU School of Medicine and former Executive Director, Organizational Development and Learning

Robert I. Grossman
2007 Investiture Speech

C hairman Lipton, Chairman Langone, President Sexton, Senior Vice President Berne, faculty, staff, students, and friends—thank you very much for your support, faith, and hope. Over the past four months, I have done a great deal of listening to all of you about your concerns and aspirations. I have also read about the illustrious history of our Medical Center. One of the most striking aspects of my research is how few times the word "dean" is mentioned.

Clearly the message is that the dean is just an enabler for all the talented and extraordinary members of our Medical Center. And speaking of extraordinary—my first official activity was to welcome the new medical student class of 2011 into our profession. These spectacular 160 students were chosen from almost 8,000 applicants—80 of these 160 future doctors are men. This celebration is termed the "White Coat Ceremony." Our auditorium was filled to capacity—standing room only—with the new students, proud parents, friends, and family. It was an emotional event.

The featured speaker was Dan Roses, one of our outstanding faculty, who gave an illuminating talk on the history of Bellevue and NYU

Medical School. My own reaction was, in many ways, similar to that of the audience.

Awe—at the amazing individuals who were faculty or students at our institution.

Responsibility—for the students being given the stewardship of their future patients' lives—and for me being entrusted with the training of future physicians and the stewardship of the traditions, culture, and growth of this magnificent Medical Center.

I am privileged to be part of this 166-year legacy of excellence. We were founded by some of the greatest physicians in the mid-19th century. John Revere, the youngest son of Paul Revere, would become the first professor of medicine, and Valentine Mott, the greatest surgeon in the U.S., would lead the Department of Surgery.

S. D. Gross, Mott's pupil and later a professor of surgery, wrote that Mott's name was as indissolubly linked with the history of surgery as Wellington's with the Battle of Waterloo.

Gross himself, by the way, was the subject of what the *New York Times* has called "hands down, the finest 19th century American painting." It's a portrait called *The Gross Clinic*, by Thomas Eakins, and it's still making history: A while back, it stirred a major national controversy when it was sold by the Thomas Jefferson University—for $68 million!

Think about that: NYU surgical training captured in the greatest American painting of the 19th century—indeed that is influence!

Now, let me sketch our future on the incredibly rich and robust canvas bestowed by those NYU giants whose legacy we gratefully acknowledge and on whose shoulders we now stand.

The vision is to build on our history of greatness to become a world class academic Medical Center, competing successfully with the Hopkins, Harvards, and Penns. We have all the ingredients to ascend to this rarefied status:

We sit in the heart of the greatest city in the world;
We are part of a remarkable university;
Our excellent hospitals and School of Medicine have
areas of extraordinary strength;
There are—as we were reminded just a few weeks ago
at Dean's Honors Day—giants among us, who reinvent
our legacy of excellence every day;
And we have genuine devotion to a future of innovation
and collaboration.

So we have incredible assets to build on. But we also have a lot to do. What will it take? I see five underlying conditions for success.

First, we must remember that decisions have to be based on what is best for the Medical Center as a whole. The outside competition is fierce and we cannot have our constituencies at cross-purposes. That is why we have already taken many steps to bring the hospital and School of Medicine closer, with the aim of becoming a fully integrated academic medical center not just in name, but in fact.

We must use the strengths of each to enhance the other, and construct creative programs that take full advantage of all segments of our Medical Center and the wider university. A hospital without a School of Medicine is not a world class medical center. Clearly Cleveland Clinic and Mayo Clinic perceived this and have started medical schools. President Sexton and others have articulated and appreciate that it is extremely difficult to be a great university without a great medical school.

Second, we must get our financial house in order if we are to achieve world class status. We are a $2 billion enterprise with over 19,000 individuals. Our growth will be severely limited until the School of Medicine's finances are corrected. The faster we perform this task, the greater our endowment and the more we can invest in ourselves.

This means establishing benchmarks for productivity across the entire enterprise. Our research portfolio has to grow dramatically. Strategic investment and accountability go hand-in-hand.

Third, to enable many of our objectives requires rigorous pursuit of philanthropy. We must raise over $2 billion. I am committed to accomplishing this task. We have a magnificent and generous board, and we will work tirelessly to achieve this goal.

Fourth, we must be mindful, every day, that the most impressive attribute of this Medical Center is the people! All the individuals who work in our hospitals and school, performing their daily tasks enabling the smooth operation of our Medical Center, are to be respected, and their excellence and dedication should be acknowledged and celebrated.

My team seeks to create a working environment that encourages contributions and demonstrates that we are partners in excellence. Diversity is fundamental to our mission. It is not good enough to talk the talk. We must actively recruit and retain at all levels of our organization. We need appropriate role models and mentors. Our Medical Center should respect and reflect our communities.

And finally, for you as an individual—to be astonishingly successful requires that each and every one take responsibility. Winston Churchill said it best: "The price of greatness is responsibility!"

This characteristic must permeate the entire Medical Center. For example, if the clinical care is great, the food is splendid, and the room is immaculate, but someone caring for the patient is not considerate, all the other components of the hospital experience are tainted. Each of you plays an essential role. We are a team, and to achieve our potential necessitates that we continuously improve our performance and functionality.

If we fulfill those five prerequisites—working toward the full integration of our Medical Center, fixing our finances, raising funds, creating a culture of mutual respect, and taking individual responsibility for all of our actions—then we will have a very solid foundation on which to build a glorious future. I will not rest until we have fulfilled each and every one of these specific aims.

There remains, of course, one enormous piece to complete the picture. And that is—to become world class we must objectively excel in research, clinical medicine, and education. And we must promote and prioritize initiatives that facilitate and enhance our ascent. So let me turn now to our goals for each facet of our mission.

In research, we will create an environment that continues to respect great science and facilitates collaborative investigation. Our gifted faculty will be stakeholders in the process, helping design a strategy for future scientific investment, and designating benchmarks that monitor these ventures.

The goal is to grow our scientific portfolio, attract and keep the best scientists, and provide infrastructure that augers their success. We shall invest in—and create incentives that foster—interdisciplinary and multidisciplinary approaches to research and science. Team science is consistent with the NIH Roadmap and represents an increasing trend in successful investigations.

Our school is part of an exceptional university and we wish to be a great partner in this incredible enterprise.

Recently, I had the pleasure of visiting the laboratory of one of our wonderful scientists. He introduced me to a young man, an NYU undergraduate pursuing a research project in the lab. One could appreciate how special the experience was for the undergraduate, but there was also the feeling that the laboratory truly valued the student's contribution. This student was a Russian immigrant who had just been awarded a Rhodes Scholarship. Excellence attracts excellence, and that is contagious.

This vignette also illustrates a simple but significant collaboration with the university—together we broaden our appeal, increase our opportunities, and create synergies that realize dreams.

Now, let me turn to clinical medicine. Our institution did not get to where it is without exceptional nursing and clinical care. We are a magnet for both and we wish to continue this tradition and build upon it.

Our vision emphasizes strategic programs. These include musculoskeletal diseases, neuroscience, cancer, cardiovascular diseases, children's health, and broad initiatives in aging, metabolism, stem cell and regenerative medicine, and inflammation. We will search for other meaningful opportunities that leverage our assets and fit into our strategy.

We will also continue to embrace the mission of caring for the underserved—Bellevue is a core asset. And our work there, for the past 166 years, a most noble cause. Examples of our commitment to Bellevue are the Kaplan Breast Cancer Center, which provides access to the screening and diagnosis of breast cancer, and our program in the surgical treatment of obesity—both initiatives are vital to improving the prognosis and survival of the underserved.

Lastly, we will build a new clinical facility, and this will be accomplished in the next seven years. The vision of this "environmentally friendly" hospital will be ahead of the curve. We are already engaged in the process of designing our new inpatient facility, as well as envisioning what our campus should look like in the 21st century. Many of you have been and will be involved in the process. The new facility, which will include a new children's hospital, will be smaller than the existing Tisch Hospital, and we will continue to utilize segments of Tisch to optimize our bed number. The rest of Tisch will be repurposed for ambulatory care and inpatient rehabilitation.

Once the inpatient Rusk Institute has relocated to new quarters where it will continue to thrive, the building that houses it today will be torn down, leaving an opportunity for the construction of additional programmatic initiatives—such as our institutes for aging and metabolism.

And now, education. We envision a medical school curriculum for the 21st century, acknowledging that contemporary learning requires creative new approaches in curriculum design and teaching methodology.

Our students acquire knowledge differently than previous generations. The digital revolution has been a blessing and curse. Students are confronted with incredible time pressure. The quantity and complexity of material that needs to be learned is ferocious.

Just as an example—when I began radiology training, mammography, ultrasound, and CT had not been implemented, and MRI had not been invented. That speaks to the pace of scientific discovery and the explosion of knowledge.

The new construct will foster team learning, management of medical information, and the integration of basic science and clinical material. Our goal is to bring students and faculty closer together.

We wish to emphasize lifelong learning.
Our educational facilities must be modernized.
Classrooms and lecture halls must be state-of-the-art.
Medical students, nurses, and allied health professionals
should learn together—each from the other.

And YES, new housing is essential for students and faculty—this is an issue we must confront if we are to grow and thrive!

So that, ladies and gentlemen, is how I see our future. Now let's hear your voices.

Your aspirations are my goals. Each one of you is an important constituent in this integrated enterprise. The material accomplishments that we achieve will benefit our patients and those who work in this healthy new environment. That is our stewardship.

How will we know when we become world class? It will be obvious. Objective markers will show our productivity—NIH ranking, *U.S. News and World Report*, Hospital Scorecards, Medical School admission criteria, resident match statistics, etc., etc. Most of all we will feel it—NYU Medical Center WILL be the benchmark!

My expectations are elevated and my standards lofty. And though we start with great strengths to build on, what I call for requires extraordinary efforts. To become a world class academic medical center is our shared aspiration. Together we will celebrate our accomplishments in this journey.

You have my word and my unswerving dedication to the task at hand. Our tenure is the beginning of a glorious new era in the illustrious history of NYU Medical Center, and we are partners in this magnificent endeavor. I am honored and humbled to have the great good fortune to lead us in this pursuit of excellence. This is my purpose, and we shall succeed.

—Robert I. Grossman, MD
October 2007

Index

Image Credits

ABOUT THE AUTHOR

William A. Haseltine

W illiam A. Haseltine, PhD, is the chair and president of ACCESS Health International, a nonprofit organization he founded in 2007. ACCESS Health fosters innovative solutions to healthcare challenges in the United States and internationally. ACCESS Health works closely with public and private partners to improve access to high-quality and affordable healthcare by shifting health systems away from hospital centric care and toward integrated, distributed healthcare systems supported by real time, comprehensive, and transparent information systems.

Dr. Haseltine has an active career in both science and business. He was a professor at Harvard Medical School and Harvard School of Public Health from 1976 to 1993, where he was founder and the chair of two academic research departments, the Division of Biochemical Pharmacology and the Division of Human Retrovirology. He is the founder of Human Genome Sciences Inc., and served as the chairman and CEO of the company until 2004. He is also the founder of several other successful biotechnology companies. He is well known for his pioneering work on cancer, HIV/AIDS, and genomics.

Williiam A. Haseltine, PhD, has authored more than two hundred manuscripts in peer reviewed journals and is the author of several books, including: